ORIGINS OF THE GREAT PURGES

D0087242

SOVIET AND EAST EUROPEAN STUDIES
Editorial Board

JULIAN COOPER, MICHAEL KASER, ALISTAIR MCAULEY,
MARTIN MCCAULEY, FRED SINGLETON, RON HILL, PAUL LEWIS

ORIGINS OF THE GREAT PURGES

THE SOVIET COMMUNIST PARTY RECONSIDERED, 1933-1938

J. ARCH GETTY

UNIVERSITY OF CALIFORNIA, RIVERSIDE

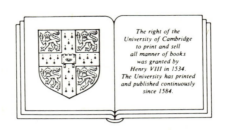

CAMBRIDGE UNIVERSITY PRESS

CAMBRIDGE

LONDON   NEW YORK   NEW ROCHELLE

MELBOURNE   SYDNEY

Published by the Press Syndicate of the University of Cambridge
The Pitt Building, Trumpington Street, Cambridge CB2 1RP
32 East 57th Street, New York, NY 10022, USA
10 Stamford Road, Oakleigh, Melbourne 3166, Australia

First published 1985
First paperback edition 1987

Printed in the United States of America

Library of Congress Cataloging in Publication Data
Getty, J. Arch (John Archibald), 1950–
Origins of the great purges.
(Soviet and East European studies)
Bibliography: p.
1. Kommunisticheskaia Partiia Sovetskogo Soiuza –
Purges – History. 2. Soviet Union – Politics and
government – 1917–1936. 3. Soviet Union – Politics
and government – 1936–1953. 4. Political purges –
Soviet Union – History. I. Title. II. Series.
JN6598.K7G43   1985   324.247′075′09   84-12718

ISBN 0 521 25921 5 hard covers
ISBN 0 521 33570 1 paperback

Contents

Tables

Preface

Until recently, political scientists and émigré journalists have done most of the work on Soviet political history. Some of their work has been very good, but it seemed to me that the subject could benefit from a historian's treatment. I therefore approached this study with a distrust of preconceived models and abstract constructs and with the goal of setting out exactly what happened in the Bolshevik Party in the thirties.

Avoiding the standard concentration on Stalin's personality, this work aims to rationalize our understanding of the period by evaluating structural, institutional, and ideological factors. I have tried to provide an interpretive framework that reflects the available documentary evidence and accounts for the often mysterious events of the thirties. I believe that it explains more and contradicts itself less than other reconstructions. Because of the nature of this field, no one can avoid speculations and guesswork about the origins and course of historical events. But in my view, interpretations based on critical use of the internal records of the participants are better grounded than those that rely on the literary memoirs of courageous but exogenous victims of the process.

Many of the people whose opinions I value were able to read and comment on all or parts of this study. I owe special thanks to my mentor and adviser Roberta Manning, whose energy, patience, and enthusiasm lasted through several drafts of the work. Her help and support were unflagging, and her generous suggestion that I include some of her own unpublished archival data in this work speaks for itself. I have also benefited from conversations with my colleague Gabor Rittersporn, whose research on politics in the thirties proceeded simultaneously with and independently of my own. Although we often reached different conclusions on the meanings of documents, we agreed on many of the broad outlines of Soviet political history in the thirties.

Even in those cases in which I disagreed with his interpretations, his unique, challenging, and sometimes brilliant insights stimulated constant reexamination of my own assumptions. Special thanks also go to my longtime friend Bill Chase for his sound advice and sense of humor. Other friends and colleagues who read all or parts of the manuscript and gave me the benefit of their suggestions include Kenneth Barkin, Paul Breines, Chester Dunning, Sheila Fitzpatrick, David Joravsky, Hiroaki Kuromiya, Mary McAuley, Robert H. McNeal, Paul Raymond, Sharon Salinger, Bob Supansic, Irwin Wall, and Charles Wetherell. Any errors or mistakes in what follows are, of course, mine alone.

I am also grateful for a Research Fellowship from the American Council of Learned Societies, a Senior Fellowship from the Russian Institute at Columbia University in 1981, and a fellowship from the Russian Research Center at Harvard University. I received generous financial and logistical support from the University of California, Riverside, Academic Senate Committee on Research and Laboratory for Historical Research.

Reference librarians at several institutions made my work less difficult. I am indebted to the reference staffs of the Butler and International Affairs libraries at Columbia; the Houghton, Widener, and Russian Research Center libraries at Harvard; the New York Public Library; the Lenin Library in Moscow; the Firestone Library at Princeton; and the libraries of the Hoover Institution on War, Revolution and Peace at Stanford University and the University of California, Riverside.

Finally, I thank *Slavic Review* for permission to quote from my "Party and Purge in Smolensk: 1933–1937" (vol. 42, no. 1, Spring 1983, 60–79). I am also grateful to the Houghton Library for permission to quote from the Trotsky Papers.

I would never have been able to complete this work without the emotional and material help of my wife, Nancy. Her fresh criticism, typing, and proofreading help – cheerfully given at a time when she was working and pursuing her own professional degrees – make her largely responsible for any contribution that this study may make, and it is to her that I dedicate the work.

J. ARCH GETTY
Riverside, California

Introduction: the Great Purges as history

Each says something about the nature of the world, and, though individually he adds little or nothing to our understanding of it, still from the combination of all something considerable is accomplished.

Aristotle

Until Khrushchev's time, Soviet citizens were taught that the Communist Party had uncovered a dangerous conspiracy in the mid-1930s. According to the official Stalinist view, it had gradually come to light in 1934–6 that many of the party's prominent personalities had been undercover "enemies" of the party who had worked to undermine the party and the Soviet regime from the earliest days of Soviet power. Led primarily by Leon Trotsky, this "gang" of "fiends" included other longtime Bolsheviks Grigorii Zinoviev, Nikolai Bukharin, Lev Kamenev, Aleksei Rykov, and others who had posed as Lenin's trusted comrades. These traitors had always been spies, saboteurs, and oppositionists who wanted to overthrow the socialist regime, split the party, and ultimately restore capitalism in the USSR. They plotted with the German Gestapo to overthrow the party leadership in a bloody coup that was timed to coincide with the invasion of the USSR by one or more fascist states. In a series of major public trials, these traitors were unmasked by the secret police and the party, whose vigilance had discovered the treason. The plotters admitted their guilt in open court, and the Soviet people were unanimous in their condemnation of the treason. The vigilant secret police justly uprooted the treason, followed proper judicial norms, punished only the guilty, and ultimately saved the Soviet government.[1]

Western specialists and Soviet dissidents have provided another explanation of these events that is more complicated but ultimately as Manichean as the Stalinist story.[2] According to this view, Stalin in the

1

early thirties demanded the arrest and execution of oppositionists and dissidents for treason. He seems to have been opposed by a combination of Politburo "moderates" consisting of S. M. Kirov (head of the Leningrad party organization) and Sergo Ordzhonikidze (commissar of heavy industry), who supposedly resisted the imposition of the death penalty upon party members and carried the day in the dispute.

Kirov's elevation to the central party leadership in 1934 represented both a political and personal alternative to Stalin's leadership. Stalin supposedly then decided to have Kirov assassinated. He was shot in his Leningrad office on December 1, 1934. The circumstances seemed to imply police complicity in the assassination. Within hours of the assassination, Stalin had rammed through emergency legislation speeding up summary trials of suspected "terrorists," mandating execution of the death penalty immediately after sentence, and suspending the right of appeal. The press linked the assassin (one Leonid Nikolaev) with the former Zinoviev–Kamenev oppositionists, and many of these were arrested in an escalating wave of police terror. In the period that followed, the Kirov assassination was used as proof of the continued existence of enemies and as justification for increasing arrests, trials, and terror. Nikolaev and dozens of others were executed by the Narodnyi Kommissariat Vnutrennykh Del (NKVD; people's commissariat of internal affairs, or secret police) in retaliation for Kirov's death.

According to the Western view, Stalin used the Kirov assassination as an excuse for a "mounting campaign" of terror. A "rising crescendo" of purges (the purge of 1933, the Verification of Party Documents of 1935, and the Exchange of Party Documents of 1936) escalated the "heresy hunt." In a series of public show trials, former oppositionists (Zinoviev and Kamenev in 1936, Piatakov and Radek in 1937, and Bukharin and Rykov in 1938) were vilified and then executed for treason and sabotage. In the "whirlwind" of 1937 and 1938, the party and state were decapitated. Prominent persons from all fields disappeared without trace. In June 1937, Marshal Tukhachevskii and most of the leaders of the Red Army were arrested and shot for treason and much of the military high command followed them to the execution cellars of the police. It seems that nearly all the regional leadership of the party was arrested and shot, as were nearly all the Old Bolsheviks. The Ezhovshchina (time of Ezhov) took its name from N. I. Ezhov, the head of the NKVD.

There are a number of speculations as to why Stalin carried out this bloody operation. Fainsod argued that he did it to rid himself of possible rivals for supreme leadership (Kirov, or perhaps Bukharin), thereby ensuring his continued personal power.[3] Similarly, Isaac Deutscher and others thought that Stalin foresaw the coming war and wanted to guarantee that there would be no fifth column behind the Soviet lines and that his orders would be carried out unquestionably by a totally loyal staff.[4] Some believe that Stalin had to terrorize the entire country to establish "totalitarianism," a theoretical system in which all independent sources of authority and even autonomy are crushed.[5] The atomization of society by wild and random terror is seen as a prerequisite for the creation of the new totalitarian state.[6] Brzezinski gave a twist to the totalitarian model when he argued that the Great Purges were carried out to demonstrate the power of an already established totalitarianism and not to create one.[7]

Other commentators have focused on pathological rather than political causes for the Great Purges. They argued that Stalin suffered from a variety of psychological disorders (paranoia, manic depression, schizophrenia, etc.); these caused him to distrust everyone around him and led him into an obsessive hatred of the Old Bolsheviks, who knew about his inadequacies and thus threatened his diseased psyche.[8]

Most Western and dissident Soviet accounts of the Great Purges share certain assumptions: The political events of 1933–9 constitute a unified phenomenon (the Great Purges), which can be studied as a process; the Great Purges were planned, prepared, and carried out by a single agency (Stalin); and the Old Bolsheviks of Lenin's (and Stalin's) generation were the purges' target. The present study tests these assumptions against the available primary evidence and finds them untenable.

Although the improbable Stalinist story is very different from the Western view, the two share another interpretive assumption about structure. Both versions assume that the party (and police) bureaucracies were efficient and obedient. Indeed, both Western and Stalinist writers have been interested in showing that the Soviet bureaucracy was grimly efficient: totalitarian to Western writers, monolithic or solidly united to Stalinists.[9] The near consensus on a monolithic apparatus has made it easy to overlook evidence (and personal experience) and to believe that an untrained and uneducated bureaucracy in a huge, developing peasant country somehow functioned and obeyed well enough to be termed totalitarian. In its investigation of the structure of the Bolshevik Party in the thirties, this study questions the applicability of the totalitarian model.

Rethinking Stalinism

A weak tradition of source criticism and a developing historiography on related problems both suggest the need to reevaluate the thirties. In their writings on the Great Purges, scholars and journalists have traditionally relied rather heavily on the memoirs of émigrés and defectors from the Soviet Union, as well as on the personal accounts of victims of terror.[10] These "first hand" accounts published in Western Europe, the United States, and even the Soviet Union were written by persons from a variety of backgrounds. Mensheviks, Trotskyists, factory managers, military officers, intelligence agents, diplomats, and ordinary victims all seem to have left their memoirs.

Personal accounts are valuable sources and provide vivid descriptions of the experiences and psychological impact of events of the persons who wrote them. Victor Kravchenko's experience as a young Soviet engineer in the 1930s, Solzhenitsyn's prison literature, and Eugenia Ginzburg's memoirs from the labor camps provide personal impressions and details available nowhere else. One can partially feel what it was like to be terrorized; one can understand, if not experience, exile to Siberia.

Yet historians have been justifiably skeptical of memoirs and autobiographies. Louis Gottschalk, the famous historian of the French Revolution, believed them to be untrustworthy sources written late in life for a mass audience by people whose intentions were dubious. Aside from the obvious critical problems with memoirs (authenticity, bias, selectivity, etc.), recent investigations into the genre have emphasized the novelistic elements in such works. Paul Fussell, in his celebrated study of World War I memoirs, has observed that "the memoir is a kind of fiction, differing from the 'first novel'... only by continuous implicit attestations of veracity or appeals to documented historical fact.... The further personal written materials move from the form of the daily diary, the closer they approach to the figurative and the fictional."[11]

Even if one should take a liberal attitude toward the use of memoirs in principle, it is not clear what the Great Purges memoirs can reveal about why the terror happened, or even about exactly what happened. In general, they provide more heat than light: They can tell us how their authors felt but not how Stalin felt. None of them were close enough to the seat of power (some were not close at all) to know inner-leadership disputes and alignments, much less Stalin's aim and methods. They were victims who saw the process from below, and their observations on high politics are merely guesses. Yet reliance on this class of evidence has been pervasive and of long standing. The inaccessibility of archival sources on the Great Purges has led to a willing suspension of disbelief and to something less than rigorous methodology.

For no other period or topic have historians been so eager to write and accept history-by-anecdote. Grand analytical generalizations have come from secondhand bits of overheard corridor gossip. Prison camp stories ("My friend met Bukharin's wife in a camp and she said . . . ") have become primary sources on central political decision making. The need to generalize from isolated and unverified particulars has transformed rumors into sources and has equated repetition of stories with confirmation. Indeed, the leading expert on the Great Purges has written that "truth can thus only percolate in the form of hearsay" and that "basically the best, though not infallible, source is rumor."[12] As long as the unexplored classes of sources include archival and press material, it is neither safe nor necessary to rely on rumor and anecdote.

Historical studies of other topics in Soviet history also suggest the need for a fresh approach. Indeed, despite a historiography dominated by totalitarian models, Great Man theories of history, and "revolution betrayed" polemics, certain specialists have for some time elaborated more complex interest-group and conflict approaches to Soviet political history. Some scholars have even argued that "institutional pluralism" is an apt characterization of Soviet politics.[13]

Recent specialized historical studies of the period after 1929 have shown that policymaking in the early Stalin years was sometimes unstructured and erratic. Formulation of social and educational policies, for example, was often uncertain, incremental, and tentative.[14] Similarly, the regime's agricultural and industrial policies during the late 1920s and early 1930s developed gradually from a series of conflicting initiatives, zigs and zags.[15] Both social and economic policies were posed, modified, and adopted in reaction to events. Recent studies of economic, intellectual, and political topics in the postwar Stalin years have also emphasized the fragmentation, indecision, and internal struggles within the leadership.[16] In general, researchers on the 1920s and 1940s have been struck by the ad hoc and voluntarist nature of Stalinist policy formation. It seems appropriate to take another look at the 1930s.

None of these works has suggested that Stalin was not the most powerful political actor, but some of them have implied that he was not necessarily the author of every initiative. He seems frequently to have exerted his authority by throwing his weight behind one or another faction or alternative.[17] In this view, Stalin's lieutenants had not only executive but also policymaking powers. Sometimes Stalin seemed to support both sides of a question and it was (and is) difficult to perceive his position. One should not, therefore, be surprised if Stalin, like Hitler, used an indirect and sometimes erratic "formula of rule" in the 1930s.[18]

This study examines the structure, organization, composition, and evolution of the Soviet Communist Party from 1933 to 1939. Although the analysis touches on such topics as membership policies and purges, party propaganda, political opposition, and economic disputes, the focus is the relationship between central and peripheral party organizations. This was what contemporary politicians meant by the "organizational question," and it was the main structural problem and conflict within the party apparatus during the decade.

This analysis lays bare a cross section of the party's structure from top to bottom, highlighting the channels of communication (and command), the loci of power, and the sources of political conflict. The findings suggest that the party in the 1930s was inefficient, fragmented, and split several ways by internal factional conflict. Although the sources are not good enough to permit many firm conclusions on the thirties, a critical use of the evidence suggests a technically weak and politically divided party whose organizational relationships seem more primitive than totalitarian.

In turn, this reinterpretation of the party's structure has implications for the events of the Great Purges. The events of 1933–9 were not all parts of the same planned crescendo of terror and did not constitute a single phenomenon or process. The membership purges of 1933–6 were not simply the predecessors of the police terror of 1937 and were related to it only obliquely. Indeed, all the political events of the thirties were not parts of the same phenomenon, and it is a basic assumption of the study that an analysis of the party's structure can help avoid such reductionist fallacies. Second, political decision making seems incremental, confused, and more contradictory than consistent. Although it is clear that Stalin made crucial decisions during the Great Purges, considerable circumstantial evidence suggests that he did so tentatively, belatedly, and, like most powerful politicians, by choosing or arbitrating among various options.

Unlike some approaches to the politics of the thirties, however, this analysis does not concentrate on Stalin's personality. Although he was certainly the most authoritative political actor of the period, speculations on his mental state, private attitudes, and prejudices are baseless, given the lack of primary evidence on these matters. The approach taken here is political (and sometimes institutional and ideological), never biographical. It is, of course, not possible to avoid guessing at Stalin's plans and intentions; in the account that follows, the difference between educated guesswork and supportable assertion should be clear.

This study is limited to the internal workings of the Communist Party apparatus during the 1930s, and there are a number of themes and events not discussed. The three major show trials are not analyzed in detail, for this has been done exhaustively by other researchers. No attempt is made to fix the total number of victims of the Great Purges. Because there are no convincing statistics, all calculations are quite subjective and appear to reflect the point of view of the person making the calculation.[19] There is also no attempt to describe the network of labor camps or to go into the details of who was arrested when, who was in what camp, and so forth. This ground, too, has been repeatedly trod. Space and the scope of this work do not permit thorough analysis of other issues relating to the history of the thirties (and perhaps to the Great Purges). Nationality issues, struggles over industrial management, the Stakhanov movement, the promotion of new cadres, and disputes over foreign policy deserve serious treatments in their own rights but are dealt with here only insofar as they relate to the struggles within the party apparatus proper.

Because of space and source limitations, this study focuses on the structure and politics of the period leading up to the height of the Ezhovshchina in late 1937. A lack of archival material and a less revealing press make it difficult to analyze the events of 1938 in any detail. This examination simply attempts to contribute to a clarification of certain political issues and struggles that formed the climate for the outbreak of political violence. Accordingly, the work is not an exhaustive history of the Great Purges, for only access to Soviet political archives will allow historians to write definitive works on the event. This study follows only one possible unexplored approach to the Great Purges: the structural and factional struggles within the party apparatus in the 1930s. In turn, though, such an exercise should have implications for an understanding of the causes of the Great Purges.

The work attempts to reconstruct political events in the Communist Party in the mid-thirties using only primary sources. The first category of sources consists of archival material from the Smolensk Archive, a collection of Communist Party records from the Western Region (*o-blast'*) from before the 1917 Revolution to about 1939.[20] These are the files of party organizations on all levels from regional to district to city to cell. They contain three types of records: membership files, minutes of meetings, and letters. The files also contain copies of letters, orders, and documents sent from Moscow to the regional and local party committees. Merle Fainsod used these records to write his famous *Smolensk Under Soviet Rule*, but, with few exceptions, the Archive has been largely ignored since that time.[21]

The second class of sources includes printed documents, published speeches, decisions, resolutions, and so forth. Historians have only recently begun to make critical and judicious use of the Soviet press. A careful reading of party decisions alone has shown interesting conflicts and even divergent points of view within the Stalinist leadership at the time of the Great Purges.[22] Such study involves no willing suspension of disbelief nor any blind acceptance of official cant, but only the common contemporary recognition that although Soviet documents are often devilishly selective and full of omissions, they are important indicators of what the leaders believed to be problems and of what they wanted done – considerations of no little importance in such a mystery story.[23]

No scholarly work has yet systematically fit the existing "cycles" of Soviet primary sources (national and local) into a coherent narrative.[24] Such a combination of local and central sources provides an inside view of how the center issued orders and how those orders were implemented locally, and it allows one to map the political terrain of early Stalinism.

Chapter 1 discusses the tensions and disputes in the central party leadership and gives a picture of disorganization in the provinces. The next two chapters explore the center–periphery problems by looking at Moscow's unsuccessful attempts to reform party membership practices in the early thirties. Chapter 4 outlines attempts by party radicals and ideologists to revive party organizations with populist agitation. Chapter 5 follows a more ominous parallel radical campaign to solve the party's problems by rooting out "enemies of the people." The 1937 escalations of radicalism, tension, violence, and chaos are the subjects of Chaper 6, and Chapter 7 discusses the Ezhovshchina.

In the period of this study, many thousands of innocent people were arrested, imprisoned, and sent to labor camps. Thousands were executed. Nothing in the following pages is meant to minimize, justify, or excuse the terror, notwithstanding the terminology and rhetoric that close reliance on contemporaneous texts forces one to use. Certainly, any attempt to excuse such violence would be pointless and morally bizarre. There is also no intention to exonerate Stalin of any guilt or responsibility for these horrors; regardless of the real nature and extent of his participation, his position as party leader forces upon him primary responsibility for the events that ensued under his leadership.

Although the moral questions seem clear, the historical ones do not. If it were enough to fix guilt or blame, there would be no reason for any historical research. To ever understand why something happened, it is first of all necessary to know what happened.

1

The Communist Party in the thirties

Organization is the form of mediation between theory and practice.

Georg Lukács

Politics cannot be separated mechanically from organization.

V. I. Lenin

Reflection on the Soviet Communist Party in the 1930s has often produced the image of a closed, monolithic, disciplined organization that functioned without dissent and with a high level of centralized control. With Stalin's assumption of supreme leadership, the era of the 1920s with its freewheeling disputes on culture, its heroic personal struggles, and its debates on society and economics seemed finished. Stalin's control appears to have frozen the party into a mold of obedience rather than discussion, centrally initiated terror rather than freedom, and petrification rather than evolution.

Yet it would be naive to be taken in by Stalin's cult of personality and to accept Stalinist protestations of unity. It would be unrealistic to assume that differences of opinion in the party simply disappeared after 1929. The discussions surrounding the rate and character of industrialization, the nature of centralized decision making, the peasant question, and the parameters of political dissent certainly were muted after 1929, but they did continue.

A good deal is now known about the internal party debates on the nature and extent of collectivization that took place in 1929–31.[1] One also knows something about the disagreements and uncertainties surrounding the treatment of "bourgeois specialists" and the changes in educational and social policy.[2] Even later in the 1930s, writers have long suspected the existence of debates on the nature and extent of the Great Purges.[3] Despite the efforts of the Stalinist leadership to avoid "going public" on these debates, the outlines of controversy spilled over into the press and can be studied by careful scholars. Interest groups in the bureaucracy usually could not oppose the established line, but in cases where there was no firmly fixed policy, debate, negotiation, and lobbying were possible even in the Stalin years.

The constant shifts in official policy on certain issues strongly suggest debate and disagreement. The Stalinist press was constantly affirming the correctness of the leadership's policies and never stopped trying to rally the country around the "General Line." But what was the "General Line"? Was it the "destruction of the kulaks as a class" of 1930 or the slower collectivization of the following year? Was it embodied in the fantastic rates prescribed for industrial growth in the First Five Year Plan or the more modest projections of the second? Was it the expulsion and degradation of the party opposition or the welcoming of former oppositionists at the Seventeenth Party Congress in 1934? Was it represented by tight central control over personnel appointments or the relative autonomy of local party leaders in the regions?

In fact, the relentless calls to heed the teachings of the "Great and Wise Teacher" Comrade Stalin, and the constant proofs adduced in the press to the effect that the country and party were solidly united around the leader, take on a tone of desperation to scholars who read them years later. Why was it necessary to attribute every initiative and policy to the Great Teacher? Why was it politically desirable for the bureaucracy to mask the real political process behind a puerile facade of revealed truth from the Master? Could there be a political use for Stalin's cult of personality over and above his supposed need for adulation? It may well be that where one finds the loudest affirmations of unity are the places where unity is most lacking.

To evaluate the cohesiveness and unity of the party, it is necessary to investigate the internal party situation from top to bottom. Accordingly, the analysis begins with a survey of some of the political issues confronting the upper ranks of the party and then turns to an evaluation of the structure of the party's middle and lower ranks.

Peering through the dark glass of official cant and obfuscation that characterize Stalin-era journalism, one can identify factions and interest groups that supported various policies. It is harder to do this for the 1930s than for the 1920s because of what seems to be an unwritten policy not to force or even allow public debate on sensitive issues. But partisans of various policies continued to speak out, albeit in muted and sometimes esoteric form, and frequently both sides of a debate would invoke Stalin's name in support of their diametrically opposed remedies.

Although there were many struggles, squabbles, and personal conflicts, three central issues preoccupied party leaders in the period and comprised the context for the Great Purges. These three problems were economic planning, the fate of the former opposition, and the control and rationalization of the territorial party apparatus. Of the three, the struggle within the party apparatus is the focus of most of this study, although each of them was a component of the Great Purges.

These disputes remained peaceful and even latent until the end of 1936 and the beginning of 1937. At that time, a number of political compromises broke down and conflicts based on these issues erupted. The rupture of the peace provided an atmosphere for the outbreak of the Great Purges as Stalin sanctioned the use of violence to settle political disputes. All three issues surfaced at the famous Seventeenth Party Congress that met in Moscow in early 1934, so it is fitting to begin there.

A divided leadership: the Seventeenth Party Congress

The Seventeenth Party Congress, which took place between January 26 and February 10, 1934, went down in party history as the "Congress of Victors" and met in an atmosphere of triumph. The optimistic atmosphere was inspired by the successful harvest of 1933. This event was generally regarded as the first concrete proof of the "correctness" of the General Line of the party: collectivization of agriculture accompanied by rapid industrial growth. Until then the General Line had in no way proved itself, and its permanence had not been ensured.

The apparent unanimity of the Congress of Victors was an illusion. It seems, for example, that a number of delegates to the congress discussed removing Stalin or reducing his power. Rumors suggest that this anti-Stalin bloc was led by dissident regional party secretaries, but it is not currently possible to document or even elaborate upon this shadowy incident.[4] The minutes of the congress do, however, reveal another conflict among the assembled party leaders. An unusual floor fight developed between premier V. M. Molotov and commissar of heavy industry G. K. Ordzhonikidze over the rate of economic planning.

The First Five Year Plan (1929–32) has been described as a period of "cultural revolution" during which radicals and activists within the Communist Party (and in society) criticized capitalism and "bourgeois values" in everything from art and education to economic planning.[5] The movement was diffuse and contained many aspects – radicals criticized conservative professors, proposed visionary utopian schemes, championed "proletarian culture," and criticized "bourgeois artists." Coinciding with the political defeat of Bukharin and the Right Opposition, the cultural-revolution period also saw radicals establish very high production targets in industry (the "maximum variant" of the First Five Year Plan). Based on the "revolutionary-heroic" tradition in the party, which held that Bolsheviks could "storm any fortresses," radicals believed that enthusiasm was necessary and sufficient for economic success.[6] For them, advocating the lowering of plan targets ("slowing the tempo") was tantamount to counterrevolution, and the violent and chaotic early stages of rural collectivization took place under radical control. Radicals also sought to annihilate the prerevolutionary technical specialists and replace them with newly promoted workers "from the bench." Radical strength was greatest in the Komsomol, among young technical students, and among the enthusiastic party activists who carried out collectivization and led the "class war" against the New Economic Policy (NEP) and all it stood for.[7]

The other point of view might be called moderate and included those leaders, officials, and economic planners who, although not joining Bukharin's Right Opposition, nevertheless made many of the same gradualist assumptions about economic growth and agricultural collectivization. The Stalinist, or pro-Stalin, moderates were opposed to the "adventurist," voluntarist approach of the radicals and argued for "realistic" or "rational" – meaning lower – planning targets. Moderates valued professionalism and expertise more than enthusiasm and sought to protect the "bourgeois specialists" from radical attack. Consisting of more traditionally trained graduate engineers, professional economists, and establishment planners, this group argued that the fantastically high industrial tempos of the radicals violated "technical norms," in that the machinery would not stand the abuse of speeded-up production at the hands of the enthusiasts. Moderates further pointed out that the emphasis on quantity and speed would certainly decrease the quality of goods produced.[8]

Both the radical and moderate point of view existed *within* a Stalinist bloc that contained elements inclined toward both extremes. The radical–moderate dichotomy simply reproduced the wider political spectrum of which the Left and Right oppositions had been only the extremes. The apparent defeats of these two officially recognized oppositional groups only ostracized the more strident partisans who had been willing to force the issues and who were branded leaders of "factions." Unlike the Left and Right oppositions, the Stalinist radicals and moderates both supported the General Line, although with differing emphases.

These two points of view emerged in the literature of the First Five Year Plan period. In Valentin Kataev's novel *Time Forward!*, the young construction-brigade leader Ishchenko was alarmed that another brigade had poured more cement than his and begged his superintendent:

You can strike me if you like. . . . Excuse me. . . . But – this is a fact! I'll give you three hundred and fifty, and if it should be even one mixture less. . . tear my hat off! The lads guarantee it! Give the order to the second shift, comrade, and you will see!

For the Ishchenkos, "the concept of enthusiasm was one of the elements of his understanding of technique."

Nalbandov (an Old Bolshevik engineer) was one of the moderates. His "first-rate technical education" told him,

This is a construction, not a stunt. . . . Laws were being revised altogether too boldly and too irreverently. They [the radicals] were invading the fields of mechanics too brutally. They were subjecting the affirmations of foreign authorities to doubt too impudently. They were shaking traditions. . . . Enthusiasm – that is very beautiful perhaps, but not very scientific.[9]

V. V. Kuibyshev, head of Gosudarstvennaia Planovaia Komissia (Gosplan; state planning commission), and V. M. Molotov, the prime minister, may have been radical spokesmen for fast tempos. Among the moderates, Gleb Krzhizhanovskii (one of the few Old Bolshevik engineers and a friend of Lenin) was important, although it is probably safe to assume that the vast majority of professional economists and planners were moderates.[10] G. K. (Sergo) Ordzhonikidze, commissar for heavy industry in the thirties, would also become a spokesman for moderation.

Stalin's position and support changed frequently. Before 1928, he supported the gradualist and moderate policies of the New Economic Policy. He then sided with the enemies of the NEP who favored destruction of capitalism in town and country and the repression of what remained of the prerevolutionary intelligentsia. By the spring of 1930, however, there were signs that he was again associating himself with criticism of radical excesses. His "Dizzy With Success" article and his

"Reply to Kolkhoz Comrades" statements, issued in March and April 1930, condemned violence against kulaks in the countryside and denounced enthusiasts who had been "carried away."[11] Agrarian radicals like Karl Bauman were demoted and removed in connection with rural excesses. Stalin's new shift toward moderate policies was evident in June 1931, when his "New conditions – new tasks" speech noted that the older intelligentsia was not uniformly evil and its members should be left in peace if they worked loyally.[12] Although Stalin continued to call for high industrial tempos in principle, he would soon sanction much lower targets for the Second Five Year Plan.[13]

The conflict between radicals and moderates surfaced in the struggle over production targets for the Second Five Year Plan (1933–37). Gosplan, under V. V. Kuibyshev, began to draft the plan in early 1931 and submitted a first version to the Sovnarkom (council of peoples' commissars) in the fall of that year. The government was so divided that it closed all public discussion of the Plan and even suspended publication of Gosplan's journal *Planovoe khoziaistvo* [Planned economy]. Discussion surfaced again after only four months when, in February 1932, Molotov and Kuibyshev presented a second variant of the Plan with targets considerably reduced from the first draft.[14]

Further work, negotiation, and dispute produced a third version of the Plan for consideration at the Central Committee plenum of January 1933. This variant contained the lowest targets to date, and its moderate approach was endorsed by Stalin. At the plenum, Stalin defended the first plan, saying that it had "whipped up the country and spurred it onward." He defended the previous high targets (against moderate or rightist critics) as being realistic for the simple reason that they had been realized. Yet he sided with moderation and announced lower overall annual targets of 13 to 14 percent for the next period, compared with 22 percent in the first Plan.[15]

He rationalized this decision in several ways, practically apologizing to the radicals for lowering the tempos. First, he said, it was possible to go slower in the second period because the first Plan had been such a smashing victory – it was thus time to *master* the machines that the first Plan had so successfully provided. Second, he defended lowering the tempo by noting that 13 to 14 percent of the 1932 level was actually more growth than 22 percent of the 1928 level had been, so it was impossible to regard the change as a retreat of any kind. Clearly, Stalin was trying to satisfy both points of view within the economic leadership of the party.[16]

Confirmation of the Second Five Year Plan was a top item on the agenda at the Seventeenth Party Congress, and Molotov, as head of the government, delivered the main report on the Plan. One might think that after Stalin's intervention in January 1933 the matter of industrial targets had been settled. It only remained for the Seventeenth Party Congress (January–February 1934) to confirm the Plan. But the advocates of high production tempos had not given up. Many of Molotov's listeners must have been stunned to hear him announce projected annual rates of industrial growth of nearly 19 percent for the second Plan.[17] Discussions and "debates" on the speeches at party congresses had by this time become routine and quite bland, so it was even more unusual and scandalous when Ordzhonikidze openly challenged the figures given in Molotov's speech as being inconsistent with previous party decisions. Ordzhonikidze proposed lower annual targets (16.5 %) which seem to have been a compromise between the 13 to 14 percent previously discussed and Molotov's 18.9 percent.[18]

Rather than face an open debate on the issue, the leadership decided to form an ad hoc commission to settle the matter behind closed doors. The commission included Stalin, Molotov, Ordzhonikidze, the other members of the Politburo, and certain other economic experts. The congress commission, in closed session, decided to accept Ordzhonikidze's reduction of Molotov's figures. Toward the close of the congress, Molotov made a "Statement" in which he announced the results of the commission's deliberations. His laconic remarks were intended to gloss over the dispute. "The proposals made at the Congress which indicated the necessity for exercising great caution in respect of the tasks of the Second Five-Year Plan, owing to the present situation in general, were adopted by the commission unanimously." And, after announcing the lower 16.5 percent annual rate for economic growth, he remarked, "As you can see, the amendments do not alter the fundamental tasks set by the Second Five-Year Plan."[19]

Molotov was right, of course. Even the reduced rate of growth was extremely high, and the reduction did not fundamentally change the direction of the Plan. But the reduction did modify and moderate Molotov's radical and utopian projections. For present purposes, it is most important to note what the incident reveals about division and dispute within the party.

It was unusual, even unique, for a speaker to challenge a main report at a party congress in the Stalin years, and Orzhonikidze's breach of etiquette suggests the depth of disagreement over tempos. It is surprising that the leadership had not reached a compromise or accommodation before a meeting that was meant to be a model of party unity, and one would certainly expect such a crucial issue to have been settled before the public ritual of a party congress. The personal conflict between Molotov and Ordzhonikidze (and the political one between radicals and moderates) would remain alive in the months and years that followed.

Other changes show that Stalin's support was shifting and that the influence of the radicals was waning. Rigid proletarian quotas for admission into the industrial academies were dropped, partially because of a shortage of qualified applicants among the workers and partially because the moderates complained that many of the worker-engineers (both degree engineers and *praktiki*) were incompetent.[20]

Stalin seems to have backed radicals in the First Five Year Plan and moderates in the second. The working assumption from the beginning of 1933 until mid-1936 was that the moderates would be allowed to run the Second Five Year Plan according to their own lights, whereas the radicals would be shunted into party pursuits such as agitation, propaganda, and political education.[21] All Stalin's public statements in the period suggest that he supported this compromise.[22]

Various aspects of the ''relaxation'' in society (which many authorities have erroneously believed was forced on Stalin by a Kirov-led opposition) were manifestations of this moderate climate. At the end of 1935 and in 1936, however, moderates were troubled by a new manifestation of radicalism in their own economic backyard, and one vehicle for the challenge was Stakhanovism.[23] The uneasy truce between Ordzhonikidze and Molotov and between radicals and moderates would break down. Molotov would defeat Ordzhonikidze and radicals would denounce moderates as traitors in a climate of growing political suspicion.

A second issue facing the party involved treatment of former oppositionists. The victory of the General Line at the Seventeenth Congress was demonstrated by the return of defeated oppositionists to party life, provided they publicly accepted the Stalin line. Many of them, including Zinoviev, Kamenev, Preobrazhenskii, Piatakov, and Bukharin, addressed the congress itself. Although several of them were greeted with catcalls and interruptions from the floor, the fact that they spoke at the congress at all indicated a relatively ''soft'' attitude on the part of the regime toward the oppositionists, at least in early 1934. To understand the vacillating relationship between the Stalinist group and the opposition, it may be useful to review the history of the struggle.

Between 1923 and 1932, a number of opposition movements were formed to resist the policies of the central apparatus. The Trotskyist Opposition (1923–26) criticized the undemocratic and hypercentralized practices of the party's secretarial apparatus, demanded freedom of criticism and election within the party, and insisted on a more revolutionary Comintern policy abroad. The Zinoviev–Kamenev Opposition of 1926 criticized the propeasant New Economic Policy defended by Bukharin (and Stalin) and proposed a more rapid development of industry. These two groups fused in 1927 to form the Left, or United, Opposition, which combined the critiques of Trotsky and Zinoviev and buried the differences that had separated them.[24]

The Bukharin-Stalin faction crushed these leftist challengers by accusing them of fomenting a split in the party for personal reasons. The leadership used the patronage power of the central personnel apparatus to demote, transfer, disperse, and ultimately expel members of the opposition by 1927.

When Stalin and his supporters began to lean to the left in 1928, proposing the rapid collectivization of agriculture and fast tempos of industrial growth, Bukharin and his followers defended the gradualism of the NEP. Stalin branded Bukharin, Rykov, and Tomskii as oppositionists (the "Right Deviation") despite the fact that it was Stalin who was opposing current policy. The Right Opposition called for gradual, more spontaneous collectivization and moderate rates of industrial growth; they predicted disaster in the countryside if Stalin's adventurous course were followed. Stalin's faction defeated this opposition with tried and true weapons. He cynically accused the rightists of disloyalty, of lack of party discipline, and of favoring the "restoration of capitalism in the USSR." Members of the Right Opposition were removed from their positions of control in the trade unions (Tomskii), the Moscow Committee (Uglanov and Riutin), *Pravda* (Bukharin), and other institutions, although, unlike the Trotskyists, they were not sent into exile.[25]

At the same time that rightists were being defeated, a number of left oppositionists were being readmitted to the party. With Stalin's shift to the left, Radek, Piatakov, I. Smirnov, and other Trotskyists recanted their "errors" of 1927 and announced their solidarity with the new policies of the Stalinist apparatus. In fact, until 1935, it was only necessary for an oppositionist to recant to be readmitted to the party. So, beginning in 1929, the former leftists returned from their exiles and rejoined the party. Trotsky, from his lonely exile in Turkey, reacted bitterly to what he considered desertion by his followers. Of the major figures of the United Opposition, only Trotsky and Rakovskii remained in opposition and continued to denounce the policies of the apparatus.[26]

While Bukharin, Rykov, and Tomskii had abandoned opposition and publicly (if unenthusiastically) associated themselves with the Stalin policies, other rightist oppositions surfaced between 1929 and 1932. The group headed by A. P. Smirnov, the Syrtsov–Lominadze Group, the Eismont–Tolmachev Group, and the circle promoting the Riutin Platform all put forward similar proposals. Slowing or halting of collectivization, reducing the speed of industrial expansion, and reconciliation with the former opposition groups were common points. The Riutin Platform of 1932 apparently went furthest of all in calling for the removal of the Stalinist leadership.[27]

Stalinist repression of these new dissidents was immediate but uneven. Some were expelled from the party, but others were merely censured publicly. Thus A. P. Smirnov was expelled from the Central Committee but not from the party. Lominadze was expelled from the party for a short time, but soon was readmitted and appointed the party secretary in charge of the important Magnitogorsk construction project. Although Bukharin and Rykov were criticized for inspiring and knowing of these opposition platforms, they remained members of the Central Committee.[28]

Rumors suggest that the leadership was divided on how to deal with the opposition. It is said that Stalin favored harsh treatment of Riutin while others in the Politburo argued for leniency. Other rumors have it that there were two factions – hard and soft – that were in conflict about how to treat the dissidents. According to these stories, Stalin remained neutral while the two groups sought to influence him.[29] Rumors are not evidence, and there is not much one can say about Stalin's attitude with any certainty.

It is clear that treatment of the opposition was variable. Zinoviev and Kamenev were in bad odor from 1927 to 1929 but were reinstated during the First Five Year Plan. They were arrested and exiled, however, at the end of 1932 (or beginning of 1933). At the beginning of 1934 (the time of the Seventeenth Congress) they were welcomed back. They addressed the congress and their articles appeared in *Pravda* throughout 1934. Stalin proclaimed at the congress that opposition in the party had been "utterly demoralized and smashed...there is nothing to prove and, it seems, no one to fight."[30] They were rearrested and imprisoned in early 1935 in connection with the assassination of Kirov, but were not charged with capital crimes until 1936. It seems, therefore, that the

regime was not following any single consistent policy regarding the opposition. It seems safe to assume that the appearance of oppositionists
at the Seventeenth Congress represented the ascendancy of the soft
line, whereas the jeers they received showed that all were not satisfied
with the arrangement.

The lives and fortunes of former Bolshevik notables like Zinoviev,
Kamenev, and Bukharin have fascinated Western specialists. Yet it is
unclear what impact the fates of the defeated oppositionists had on the
current party membership or its apparatus in the 1930s. Most members
had joined the party since 1929 – after the oppositionists had been demoted and disgraced – and many of them certainly regarded these politicians as has-beens or even "former people." Former oppositionists
had been socially and politically ostracized by members of the party apparatus, and the repression or rehabilitation of hapless, unemployed
Trotskyists or Bukharinists may not have been particularly relevant to
the concerns or careers of current officials. Any swing of the political
pendulum toward repression of the opposition certainly threatened the
relatively few oppositionists, those associated with them (even in the
past), and known political dissidents. But the arrest of old Trotskyists
did not imply the repression of members of the apparatus. On the contrary, a crackdown on the former opposition may, in certain circumstances, have been welcomed by some strata in the party.

Unlike economic planning or control of the party apparatus, the fate
of the opposition was not necessarily a crucial matter for party officials
in the thirties. Rather, the Trotskyism issue would serve as a meta-
phorical vehicle that political actors used to pursue other controversies.
Thus Molotov would attack the popular Ordzhonikidze without an
open and direct confrontation by accusing Ordzhonikidze's subordinates of Trotskyism. Similarly, central party leaders could attack provincial cliques by denouncing regional Trotskyism without opening a
public debate on the organizational nature of the regime. The arrest of
Trotskyists was not new to the party leadership and did not itself disrupt or threaten the chain of command. But the free use of the accusation "Trotskyist" was and did.

The third, and for present purposes most important, problem facing
the party was the functioning of the party apparatus across the country.
During the First Five Year Plan, regional party committees had taken
on expanded functions in economic administration. They had become
responsible for the organization of collectivization and the fulfillment of
economic plans in their territories. They issued economic and agricul-

tural directives on planting, harvesting, labor, industrial production, and other economic and administrative matters.[31] As party secretaries became industrial and agricultural executives, they necessarily neglected other more traditional party functions: agitation and propaganda, political education of new cadres, and maintenance of party files and records.

At the same time, regional party committees lost track of and control over party membership. In the 1929–31 period, party membership more than doubled as masses of workers and peasants were admitted to the party in an attempt to carry out collectivization and industrialization, as well as to inflate local membership figures. Many of the 1.8 million new members had no idea of the party's history or program and were regarded as politically illiterate. Events would show that some party members did not even know the names of the leaders of the party or government, much less the details of the political platform. Party committees had been too busy to pay much attention to training new members.

The massive influx of new members overwhelmed the party's record-keeping abilities. Many of the speakers at the 1934 Congress bemoaned organizational and membership problems, which included a low level of ideological sophistication among party members, the poor state of party records, and a serious inability of party organizations to ensure "fulfillment of decisions."

Central Committee secretary L. M. Kaganovich's speech to the Seventeenth Congress ("Organizational Problems of Party and Soviet Construction") touched on these themes. Briefly discussing the problems caused by indiscriminate mass admissions to the party between 1929 and 1932, he declared that "we must honestly admit" that the party has not been able to "test, train and consolidate" these masses.[32] His speech also suggested two proposed solutions to remedy a situation in which large numbers of party members were untrained, uneducated, and incompetent: purging the party and stepping up efforts to increase "political education" in the ranks.

The first prong of the party's efforts to improve an unwieldy membership involved a traditional party purge, the *chistka* (sweeping, cleaning, "purge") of 1933. Begun the previous year, the *chistka* was accompanied by a temporary halt to new admissions to the party and was designed to prune the ranks. Discussed in Chapter 2 in some detail, the *chistka* represented an attempt to increase the efficiency of party organizations by reducing their size. The implementation of the 1933 *chistka* and its successors (the Verification of Party Documents of 1935 and the Exchange of Party Cards of 1936) revealed further divisions within the leadership.

The second facet of the campaign to reform party organizations was the education of party members who remained. Kaganovich said that correct admissions policy and practices were only half the matter. The other half was to provide members with proper "ideological equipment" so that they might become politically "hardened." This would be done through a combination of party schools and practical political work "in the field." Pointing out that the party had already taken steps in this direction, Kaganovich said that between 1930 and 1933 the number of party schools had increased from 52,000 to over 200,000 and the number of students from 1 million to 4.5 million. The party had five times as many propagandists in 1933 as in 1928, 51 percent of whom were workers (compared to 8 percent workers in 1928).[33]

Ian Rudzutak, chairman of the Central Control Commission, noted in his speech to the congress that, depending on the organization surveyed, between 32 and 60 percent of party members did not even read the party press! Rudzutak and Kaganovich blamed the local party secretaries for neglecting the organization of educational "party work" to raise the political level. Because of this failure many local party secretaries were being expelled in the *chistka*; in some areas, the proportion of secretaries expelled approached that for rank and file members – as high as 42 percent.[34] Kaganovich enjoined local party secretaries to include propaganda work in addition to their regular organizational and economic duties. However, in 1933 half the secretaries of shop or factory party organizations had joined the party since 1929. And they themselves often needed "assistance in their Bolshevik training and particularly in their leadership of our...organizations."[35]

Kaganovich's speech outlined two solutions to the problems facing the apparatus, and nothing in his speech suggested any contradiction between the two. Purging the party of undesirables and improving the political literacy of the membership were activities that could be complementary. Events would show, however, that in the next few years battle lines would be drawn over the issue of exactly how to improve the work of the apparatus.

S. M. Kirov, the head of the Leningrad Organization and soon-to-be-elected secretary of the Central Committee, also discussed party problems in his speech to the Seventeenth Congress. He gave particular emphasis to the political retraining of the membership and asserted that the qualitative weakness of party members could be remedied through intensified programs of indoctrination and "political education." In fact, Kirov claimed that the *main task* of the party at the present moment was the broad and comprehensive propagation of Marxism-Leninism. His speech (which prompted a long ovation from the delegates) stressed that most, if not all, the problems facing the party could be solved or at least simplified by improved political education of party members.[36]

In his speech to the congress, Stalin traced the problem back to historical conditions and emphasized political education. Discussing the progress in industry and agriculture, Stalin noted that the capitalist elements in the industrial and rural economies had been eliminated since 1929 and that capitalism as an economic and social system was rapidly disappearing in the Soviet Union. The only remaining problem was "confusion on a number of questions of Leninism."

Stalin warned that "successes sometimes have their seamy side.... Of course, the First Five-Year Plan has been successfully carried out. That is true. But the matter does not, nor can it, end there, comrades." Accordingly, one of the "fundamental political tasks" facing the party was "to overcome the survivals of capitalism in economic life and in the minds of people." Because of the rapidity of economic success, "the development of peoples' minds lags behind their economic position." Given the "not very high theoretical level of the majority of the members of the party, the inadequate ideological work of the party organs, and the fact that our party workers are over burdened with purely practical work," the party must begin to intensify political education.[37]

Economic victory had entailed mass recruitment of potential supporters and the concentration of the party's attention on economic construction: Both these exigencies had led to successes on the economic front but to a less-than-satisfactory situation regarding political literacy and the education of party members. Reform was now necessary.

Kirov and Stalin were suggesting that party organizations should turn their attention away from direct supervision of the economic apparatus ("purely practical work") and toward political indoctrination, education, and "preparation of cadres." Indeed, there was a new emphasis in party circles on political and pedagogical work and a deemphasis on direct economic supervision. The educational and propagandistic functions of the party were repeatedly stressed. Slogans about the "seamy side of economic success" (which had dulled party activists to necessary political work), about more political work and less economic work for party members, and about how "cadres," rather than "technique," decided everything for the party were reflections of this change in emphasis.[38] Stalin, Kirov, and A. A. Zhdanov would be associated with the turn from economics to political education.[39] According to Stalin and the others, the elimination of capitalist elements in town and country and the "strengthening" of the staffs of soviet and ministerial economic agencies made it possible for the party to withdraw from direct economic administration.

Another aspect of this reorientation was an organizational effort to "put the party house in order." The leadership was concerned about the party chain of command. At the 1934 Congress, Rudzutak, Kaganovich, and Stalin complained bitterly about the "non-fulfillment of decisions" by local authorities in a number of fields ranging from the economy to "party work."[40]

In fact, Stalin's speech to the Seventeenth Congress was an attack on the work and conduct of regional party chiefs. In a section of his speech entitled "Problems of Organizational Leadership," Stalin listed several organizational "difficulties" that plagued the party. Officials did not carry out the decisions of the party in spirit but rather "pigeonholed" them, doing only what was necessary to avoid censure while covering themselves with loud protestations and positive reports. Such persons hid their organizational incompetence behind "idle chatter about leadership 'in general' " and were in Stalin's view "incorrigible." He noted, for example, that officials in the agricultural administration did their best to hide the real situation in the countryside from their Moscow superiors. Some of these leaders had been removed, but the problem still loomed large, mainly because it was so difficult to expose such persons.[41]

Incorrigible bureaucrats remained in the party because of the fear of "self-criticism"(*samokritika*) and their refusal to permit criticism by their subordinates. Stalin listed self-criticism as the first way to eliminate difficulties in organizational work, and it would become one of the most important themes in the next few years. Criticism was always cited as the prime weapon in the struggle against bureaucratism and was invariably mentioned in connection with it.

Stalin divided bad administrators or executives into three categories. First came the "incorrigible bureaucrats and red-tapists" who refused to organize important party tasks and were beyond reclamation. Second came those who, because of their past services to the party and their glorious records, felt themselves immune from censure and at liberty to ignore directives that, in their view, "were not written for them, but for fools." Third came the "honest windbags" who were honest and loyal to the Soviet power; unfortunately, they were incompetent, "incapable of organizing anything," and "capable of drowning any living cause in a flood of talk." All three of them hindered the work of the party and should be transferred from leading work to lower positions.

Stalin considered the choice of personnel to be the main way to redress organizational problems, although it was necessary in the meantime to organize a systematic "check on the fulfillment of decisions" as the "key to fighting bureaucratism and office-routine." "We can say with certainty that nine-tenths of our defects and failures are due to the lack of a properly organized system to check up on the fulfillment of decisions."[42]

Stalin's outburst against the regional party secretaries was the opening shot in a center–periphery struggle that would preoccupy the party leadership for the next three and one half years. Attempts by central Moscow party authorities to bring the regional organizations into line would be resisted by local machines who were anxious to preserve their autonomy. This central–regional struggle is as old as politics itself and is not peculiar to Soviet history. What is perhaps unusual to the Soviet case is the extreme violence of the outcome.

The struggles over economic planning, treatment of the opposition, and the balance of power within the territorial party apparatuses were separate problems in the early 1930s. Political leaders argued over the rate of economic growth, the status of the opposition, and how to reform the regional party networks. Additionally, there was an ongoing tug of war between the center and the provinces over patronage and fulfillment of decisions. It was not until the middle of 1936 that these debates began to converge and create a critical mass that led to an explosion of political violence. For now, though, it is necessary to look lower in the party and to examine the chaotic state of local party organizations by using the Western Region (Smolensk) as a case study.

A disordered organization: how Smolensk was really ruled

On paper, the organization of the party apparatus seemed rigid and hierarchical. The Tsentral'nyi Komitet (TsK; central committee) included about seventy full members in the thirties and was responsible for implementing party policy on a continuous basis. It elected three smaller executive bodies. The Politburo was responsible for deciding all questions of general policy; the Orgburo took care of organizing the implementation of measures decided by the Politburo (distributing orders, forms, reports, etc.); and the Secretariat took charge of the day-to-day administrative functions of the Central Committee. In the absence of a meeting (plenum) of the Central Committee, the Secretariat was legally empowered to act in the name of the whole committee.

On a regional basis, a hierarchical system of committees was the rule.[43] Below the All-Union Central Committee, there was a series of national parties, each led by its central committee: the Communist Party of the Ukraine, of Belorussia, and so forth. Within each national party, there was a series of territorial (*krai*) and regional (*oblast'*) party organizations, each led by its committee (i.e., *kraikom*, *obkom*), which was in turn led by a *buro*. Below the territorial and regional levels, the organization was repeated on the city-committee (*gorkom*) and district-committee (*raikom*) levels. In territories, regions, cities, and districts, the committee elected a *buro* composed of the committee's secretaries, the heads of its departments, and important local officials of the party.[44]

Below the district level, there were party cells based on place of employment (primary party organizations; PPO), each led by one or more secretaries theoretically elected by the PPO membership. At every level in the entire committee structure of the party, from PPO to Central Committee, secretaries were appointed to carry out the day-to-day details of operation. Because they were empowered, within certain limits, to speak in the name of the whole organization, the power of a secretary was considerable.[45] In fact, at any level, the first secretary was the effective head of government in that area.[46] Because of their power and importance, party rules dictated that election of secretaries must be confirmed by the next-highest party body; a newly elected *raikom* secretary must be confirmed by the *gorkom* or *obkom*.

At the territorial, regional, city, district, and cell levels, the party membership was divided into other groups that will be very important to the present study. The paid, full-time party staff, or *apparat*, consisted of secretaries, "responsible officials," or "responsible leaders." Below them were the activists, or *aktiv*, of the organization who participated fully in the party and who in their own right did "responsible work." The *aktiv* were those who spoke at party meetings and as propagandists or representatives ("instructors") devoted much of their time to party work. The leadership relied on them for implementation of decisions. Finally there was the party rank and file or "party masses."

Their participation was sought and encouraged with varying degrees of enthusiasm and success. One cannot understand subsequent purges and other political events without recognizing the interplay among the various levels of the party.

According to most Western views, power was transmitted from the top to the bottom, from the center to the localities. Commands originated in the Central Committee (or its Secretariat) and were passed down through the national parties, territories, regions, and districts to the cells. The structure was designed to ensure that control from the top was maintained through direct command and the use of *nomenklatura*, the power of personnel confirmation. Theoretically, every committee was completely subordinate to the one above it, and individual members had no power or control at all.

The political reality was much different. In fact, the chain of command collapsed more often than it functioned. The Communist Party, far from having penetrated every corner of Russian life, was more an undisciplined and disorganized force with little influence outside the cities. Soviet Russia in the thirties resembled a backward, traditional society far more than it did the sophisticated order of totalitarianism.

Smolensk was the capital of the Western Region (*Oblast'*), one of the administrative units of the Russian Soviet Federated Socialist Republic (RSFSR). Between 1929 and 1937, the region had a population of about 6.5 million and comprised the old Smolensk, Briansk, Kaluga, and parts of Velikiye Luki provinces. It was a kidney-shaped area of about 600 by 240 kilometers (at the widest point): an area almost as large as Czechoslovakia and Hungary combined. It bordered the Leningrad and Moscow regions on the north and east, and the Ukraine and Belorussia on the south and west. In the northwest and southeast, the Western Region shared short borders with Latvia and the Central Black-Earth Region. The medieval fortress city of Smolensk is about 420 kilometers southwest of Moscow.[47]

During the thirties, the Western Region was predominantly an agricultural area, although there were a few important and growing industrial concentrations. In 1931, only 12 percent of the population of the region was urban (up from 8 percent in 1925), but by 1939 the figure had climbed to 17 percent. The population of the city of Smolensk doubled. The most important economic product was flax, which was grown, spun, and processed in the region. Secondarily, fodder, peat, and stock breeding were important. Most of the population lived far from the cities on one of the 14,000 collective farms.[48]

The four most important factories were the Iartsevo Works (a textile factory dating from the nineteenth century), Factory Number 35 (producing airplane parts), the Rumiantsev Factory, and the Red Profintern Plant. Each of these undertakings had party organizations numbering in the hundreds and was a center of party activity. Additionally, various economic, social, and political agencies (as well as construction projects) had significant party organizations.

The Western Region consisted of 110 districts (*raions*), 91 of which were territorial. The remaining 19 were in the railroads, army, and other extraterritorial organizations. The party was represented in each of these by a district committee and numerous party cells. The total party membership in the Western Oblast' in the thirties varied from 66,895 in 1932 to 42,000 in 1936.[49]

The regional party leadership was the Western Regional Committee, or Zapobkom, and its *obkom buro*. The *obkom buro* met about twice per week and discussed a great number of issues from agriculture to personnel to planning for holidays. Frequently, these meetings included an ad hoc assortment of specialists, *raion* secretaries, and reporters on various topics. Throughout much of the period to be discussed, the Zapobkom Buro (and attached staff) had a fairly stable membership of about a dozen.[50]

The most powerful person in the region was first secretary of the Western Regional Party Committee Ivan Petrovich Rumiantsev. Rumiantsev was an "Old Bolshevik," having joined the party in 1905. He had been first secretary in Smolensk since 1929 when he and his people were sent there by Stalin to take charge in the wake of the famous 1928 Smolensk Scandal. By 1934, Rumiantsev was a well-entrenched, 58-year-old member of the Central Committee. He was truly a local notable in the area; factories, enterprises, and one *raion* (Rumiantsevskii) were named for him.[51]

Rumiantsev's people, to use the contemporary phrase, included second secretaries A. L. Shil'man (Rumiantsev's second in command and deputy) and G. P. Rakitov, who headed the government apparatus (Obispolkom).[52] Rumiantsev had brought Shil'man and Rakitov with him to Smolensk in 1929, and the three of them ran the Western Region. Kulakov, Rumiantsev's personal secretary, was head of the regional committee's special department[53] and carried the title assistant secretary of the Obkom.

Also important were Paparde, who represented the Komissia Partiinogo Kontrolia (KPK; Party Control Commission)[54], and V. I. Makarov, who ran the *obkom*'s Otdel Rukovodiashchikh Partiinykh

Organov (ORPO; department of leading party organs) and supervised personnel assignments.[55] I. M. Blat headed the regional office of the NKVD, and V. G. Arkhipov was first secretary of the Smolensk city party committee (Smolgoraikom). Finally, General I. P. Uborevich, chief of the Western Military District, sat on the regional party *buro*.[56]

How typical was Smolensk? Because it was a rural region, its party organization and level of political control were obviously much different and much weaker than in the urbanized party strongholds of Moscow, Leningrad, Ivanovo, or the Donbas. Although the Western Region was an underdeveloped area far from Moscow, so were most of the regions and territories of the USSR. Even where urban or industrial concentrations existed, they resembled islands of development in a backward, agricultural countryside. Most regions of the USSR resembled Smolensk more than they did Moscow. Until systematic work is done on other regions of the USSR, we will never know how typical or atypical the Western Region was. At present, though, there seem few compelling reasons to regard the region as strikingly different from dozens of others in its party saturation, political system, and level of development.[57]

The party's most grievous weakness in the thirties was its lack of influence in the countryside. In the Western Region, about 78 percent of the agricultural population lived on collective or state farms, and 40 percent of the arable land was still cultivated by individual private farmers as late as 1935. The collectivization of the rural population was 90 percent complete only by the end of the 1930s.[58]

Belyi District in the Western Region was a rural *raion* with a total population of slightly more than 91,000. Ninety-three percent (85,000) were classified as rural in the 1930s; the rest lived in the town of Belyi. In 1935, only 355 party members and candidates lived in the entire district – about 0.33 percent of the population. Of these members, only 144 lived on collective farms. But with about 260 collective farms in the district, party saturation amounted to only about 1 member for every other farm. In the entire district, there were only 7 party cells among the collective farm (*kolkhoz*) population; by the middle of 1936, the number had dropped to 4. In July 1936, there were only 21 party cells in the entire district: 4 cells in the country and 17 in the town of Belyi. The "urban" population, accounting for only 7 percent of the population, comprised 80 percent of the party cells.[59]

The situation was no better elsewhere. In Elnaia District of the Western Region, the 75 collective farms contained only 1 party and 2 small candidate cells with a total of 36 members and candidates – again an average of half a member per *kolhoz*. In Kozielsk District, one of the most important in the region, not a single *kolkhoz* party cell existed in 1937, although a year later 5 had been organized. On June 1, 1938, no party cells whatsoever existed in 12 of the 110 districts in the Western Region (each of which had an average population of 40,000–80,000). At that time, only 122 of the region's approximately 10,000 collective farms had party cells, a little more than 1 percent. Throughout the thirties, most collective farms contained no communists, especially among the actual work brigades. In 1935, only 1 in 4 collective farm chairmen were party members; only 4 percent of the heads of trade organizations were members. (By 1937, only 17.5 percent of the collective farm chairmen were communists.) Village soviet chairmen were not even part of the regional party *nomenklatura*.[60]

The party's saturation of other organizations was also slight. In 1937, no more than 3 of the 388 teachers, students, and staff at the Bielsk Technicum for Mechanized Rural Economy were party members: the director, one of the teachers, and one of the staff. Among the organizations of the Smolensk City Police Department in 1937 (the militia, not the NKVD), an average of only 21 percent of the officers were party members or candidates. In Stalinsk District of the city of Smolensk, only 7 of 14 department heads, acting department heads, and inspectors of the NKVD were party members.

Nationally, 67 percent of the population lived in the countryside and only 0.3 percent of the rural population belonged to the party. Of the population of the Western Region in the 1930s, only between 1 and 2 percent were party members.[61]

The party leadership of Belyi District was young, uneducated, and of recent party membership. Eighty percent of the members in 1937 were under forty years of age. Only 7.1 percent (17 people) had completed more than three to four years of primary education, and not one had any higher education. Nearly 70 percent of the district's party members had joined the Bolsheviks since 1928. Their age, inexperience, and lack of education must have made it difficult for them to win the respect of the population, much less govern it.[62]

Such a thin organization was unable to exercise total control or even to guarantee law and order in the period. Into the mid-thirties, armed, mounted bandits continued to roam the countryside, ambushing communists (and others) and setting fire to collective farm property. In one district, bandits operated with impunity, often stopping in to drink with the local soviet chairman and his friends. Particularly brutal murders of communists or Komsomols took place regularly.[63] Party leaders complained about the prevalence of prerevolutionary rural elites in local government. Some collective farms were headed by kulaks (well-to-do peasants supposedly "liquidated" by Stalin's policy of collectivization).[64]

Communications along the chain of party command were often weak and uncertain. In Kazakhstan, 120 districts (*raions*) had no telephone link with their regional centers, much less with the republic capital or Moscow. Orders from Moscow were generally telegraphed to Smolensk, although the telephone was sometimes used. Especially sensitive documents had to be sent by NKVD courier to ensure secure delivery. Connections to district centers were made by telephone, so it must have been troublesome indeed when the telephones of the Belyi District party committee stopped working for two months in 1937. (Although the repair office was "ten steps" down the hall from the first secretary's office, the latter was unable to effect repairs.)[65] Travel in the districts was often by horse. The progressive officials of the Belyi Land Administration visited the countryside by bicycle, although weather made travel difficult or impossible for much of the year.[66]

The weakness of party administration was not only quantitative, but qualitative as well. Of those persons dropped from the rolls in party membership screenings, most were described as "clutter" or "ballast": criminals, dissolute careerists, and thieves. Former White Army officers, active kulaks, and those previously excluded from the party for criminal activity found it easy to put themselves on the party rolls and to receive (often blank) party membership cards. Anyone with talent quickly rose in the party ranks because of the crying need for skillful organizers and administrators. As a result, even leadership positions in the thirties were frequently filled with drunks, embezzlers, petty thieves, womanizers, and the like, who freely abused their position. Lower offices were often filled by petty officials who spent the day drunk. Small family circles of friends and relatives existed to exploit the patronage and financial rewards of leadership.

A 1935 investigation showed some typical examples. One person in Voronezh had been a director of a *sovkhoz*, a *raion* instructor, and finally a party secretary. Expelled from the party three times for financial corruption and mismanagement, he had simply moved to a different, but nearby, organization and rejoined the party each time. There was little communication between party committees, and it was thus fairly easy in the fast-moving conditions of the 1930s to move from place to place, entering and leaving the party at will. In the Far East Territory, Comrade A. P. Iakovlev, deputy director of a political department, had been expelled from the party in 1933 but had moved to Leningrad and rejoined. In the Western Region, Comrade Shvernik had used his position to steal blank party cards and alter party records. In Odessa, a criminal had used false party cards to rob the State Bank, and in Smolensk one Nevroev had mailed batches of blank party cards to friends in Poland.

The 1935 check also showed that more than one-fifth of those expelled from the party were criminals wanted by law-enforcement agencies, military deserters, or people suspected of moral turpitude. In Belyi that year, of 24 persons expelled from the party, one-third were habitual drunks, and another one-third were wanted by the police on criminal charges. T. Grinev had not been to a party meeting in Belyi since 1929, and poor Pavel Magon was cited as having been "systematically drunk."[67] Physical and sexual abuse by intoxicated officials was a very common complaint among collective farm workers. Passersby could look through the windows into the offices of the Matrennikovskii rural soviet and watch the chairman and his friends drinking and carousing.[68]

In addition to these "degenerates," whom everyone agreed did not belong in a disciplined, Leninist party, there were also large numbers of party members who were "politically uneducated." This did not mean that they were politically deviant (in the sense of being ignorant of Stalin's line). Rather, this category of people did not know what Marxism was, had never read any of Lenin's works, and did not have the slightest idea what communism meant or what were the main planks of the party platform. Such persons, often described as "passive," included those who did not really care about *any* political beliefs, as well as those who were simply too busy with party and economic tasks to find the time to study political theory or party history. An investigation in the 1930s found party members who did not know who President Kalinin was.[69]

The problems relating to this "clutter" were compounded by extensive chaos in the party's files. The rapid influx of new members in the years of collectivization and industrialization had overwhelmed the party's record-keeping system. The condition of the party's written records was so bad in 1935 that neither the local party organizations nor the national Secretariat knew who was a member and who was not. For example, the Vitebsk party committee noted in 1933 that about 13 percent of the members on the rolls "had gone nobody knows where without being taken off the records." At the beginning of 1934, national party leaders would complain that there were more than 50,000 "dead souls," who were listed on the records but who either were dead, had disappeared, or were fictitious. By 1935, that number would be revised upward significantly.

Nearly half the party membership cards checked in Leningrad in 1935 were either invalid or false. They contained the wrong name, false dates of membership or birth, or no stamp signifying that they had been lawfully issued. Half the Leningrad file records in the supposedly powerful and omnipotent Secretariat were either inaccurate or missing.[70] The verification of 2,669 party cards in Leningrad Region revealed that 1,070 of them (40 percent) were invalid or false and 1,277 of the corresponding registration file cards (48 percent) were defective. Of the 1,070 invalid party cards, 700 had the wrong family or first name, 111 had erasures or other alterations, 78 had false dates of party membership, 77 had false dates of birth, and 58 had no stamp or official signature. In Gorkii, 5,000 persons had been admitted to the party in violation of procedural rules, and 3,500 others were carrying duplicate party cards because they had supposedly lost the originals. In one Leningrad district, 110 of 142 party cards were false or "defective."[71]

A party membership card was a very valuable commodity indeed. It entitled the bearer to special privileges, entrance to party buildings, and special rations of food and clothing; before the mid-thirties, it made the party member immune from arrest by civil authorities. The party card was the ticket to a good job and a high standing in society at large, and it identified the bearer as a trusted comrade. It would not be surprising, then, to discover that the cards themselves commanded a high price, especially from those such as kulaks, former Tsarist officials, and others for whom real party membership was impossible. The loose control over the disbursement of party cards was a matter of grave concern for party leaders in the early thirties. Leonid Nikolaev was a former Leningrad communist who had been expelled from the party but whose party card had not been confiscated. In December 1934, he was able to present his card at the gate to Leningrad party headquarters, secure free entrance to the building, walk upstairs, and shoot Politburo member Serge Kirov to death in his office.

It was common practice to pass along the valuable party card of a dead relative, and people routinely carried the card of a father, uncle, or brother. A large number of cards were stolen because the secretaries often kept blank cards on desk tops in unlocked offices. Some of these were systematically sent abroad for nefarious use by others. Some party secretaries, eager to impress others with their recruiting zeal, passed out blank party cards freely to anyone who wanted one.

With vast numbers of people moving around in the early 1930s as a result of industrialization, party organizations were unable to keep track of "real" party members. Quite often, a person would simply produce a party membership card, claim to have moved to the area recently, and ask for a position (or party rations or access to other party privileges). Especially if the person seemed skilled and useful, the local party officials did not bother to check references. Nobody really cared about the *partiinost'* (party membership) of an applicant when skilled (even literate) personnel were in short supply.

An article by Shil'man (second secretary of the Western Region) in the national party journal suggested some of the causes of the problem. Each year, he said, a hundred thousand people go out from the Western Region to all corners of the USSR to work in industry and construction – especially to Moscow, Leningrad, and the Donbas. Many former kulaks went to these urban areas and to Smolensk itself, looking for work and styling themselves as "workers." Perhaps after working in production or construction for a time, they were able to join the party (because of the favorable regulations concerning worker membership) and without any necessary recommendations from longtime communists. After a while they returned home or moved to another location where they were able to pass themselves off as workers and trusted communists and, if they had any education, to rise to leadership posts.

The attendant confusion made it difficult to enforce the rules about membership qualifications or even keep track of party members. Anyone with sufficient guile could easily become a party member. Subsequent revelations would show that this happened often. Thus, four-fifths of those subsequently expelled from the Smolensk city party organizations had joined the party elsewhere.[72]

In such a situation, party membership was easy to come by, and it was easy to pose as a party member. It was impossible for the central party authorities to keep track of personnel assignments or to use them effectively. Although party leaders had admitted as early as 1933 that the party's records were in a shambles, it was not until 1935 that serious work began to remedy this. In that year, the party leadership ordered a final ordering of the party records to correct a situation in which twenty party cells containing more than four hundred members existed in an Omsk *raion* without the knowledge of any superior party committee and without being listed on the party's records at any level.[73]

When the party's leadership became serious about ordering and correcting party records, local leaders were forced to find out exactly who was in the party and who was not. The Smolensk Archive is filled with preprinted forms like the following:

From: _____ Raion, Western Oblast', to _____ Raion Committee, _____ Oblast'. Do you have any information or knowledge about Comrade _____, who claims to have been a member (or worked in) your organization, from _____ to _____? Please respond as soon as possible.

These were used to check on the party status of thousands, perhaps hundreds of thousands, of persons who held party membership cards and claimed to be members. Many of these requests went unanswered by overworked local party officials. Those who did reply usually sent a short *kharakteristika* or biographical sketch of the person or merely replied that the person concerned was unknown in the place where they had supposedly worked.[74]

It is usually thought that by the late twenties Stalin's Secretariat in the Central Committee had compiled massive files on each party member and used these dossiers to manipulate personnel assignments and track down political deviants.[75] The Smolensk Archive indicates, on the other hand, that in many cases below the national level leading personnel were assigned by local committees. The Central Committee's role appears to have been limited to exercising a veto over a proposed candidate.[76] Local personnel assignments from Moscow were unheard of in this period except in the rare cases when important regional leaders (regional party secretaries, for example) were being chosen. In fact, as late as 1935, the Central Committee did not know much about party membership in the provinces. As the Secretariat noted:

It is necessary to say that in the apparat of the Central Committee we are presently beginning only now to find out [*uznavat'*] the composition of the leading party workers in the regions and *raions*.

Secretary VKP(b)–Ezhov
Deputy Director ORPO–Malenkov
August 8, 1935[77]

On a more impressionistic basis, the texture of the Smolensk party files is revealing about the level of sophistication (or lack of it) in the Communist Party, its members, and officials. The physical contents of the Archive reflect the confusion, inefficiency, and clutter of the organization.

Many important records and minutes of meetings are handwritten, and although typed records became more common in the late thirties, a large proportion of the material is scrawled or typed by persons not familiar with typewriters. Even the maintenance of regular records of meetings was not common practice until a Central Committee campaign in the mid-thirties ordered local party organizations to keep records of their deliberations.[78]

Some records were kept on dubious odds and ends of nonrectangular and torn paper that contained important lists or even the sole existing notes of meetings. A shortage of paper in the 1930s meant that memoranda, letters, minutes of meetings, and other documents were often written or typed on squared or columnar paper.[79] Although the central Moscow agencies and the Western Regional party organizations had their own stationery, it was rare for anyone below the regional level to have anything more than a notarial-type seal with its imprint.

The filing system of the various party committees defies rational comprehension. Even allowing for the intermittent and possible random nature of file selection by the Germans in Smolensk in 1941, it is clear that there were often few criteria for selecting what to put in which file. Some files were limited to a specific operation (like the verification of party documents in 1935); others to all the records of a certain, small organization. Many, however, seem to include notes and records of a wholly unrelated nature, not connected by time, location, or subject matter.[80]

The party was weak in the 1930s in another area that was related to the records – accounting confusion. Important Central Committee instructions – "the fulfillment of decisions" – were simply not carried out in the provinces. Castigating party officials who were paper pushers and "incorrigible red-tapists," Stalin and the central leadership had to threaten local officials with party expulsion to get them to act on basic "party tasks." Major campaigns always started behind schedule, three-month operations took more than a year to complete, and local leaders were frequently denounced and expelled by the central leadership for bungling or ignoring important party business. A whole series of "control commissions" were established and discarded in a generally vain attempt to check corruption, inertia, and incompetence in the chain of command.

The chain of command often broke down altogether. Bored, lazy, or overworked leaders would shunt important matters to subordinates "to get out of doing it," and as a result little or nothing was being accomplished in such important areas as education, record keeping, and youth work. But the central leadership was not the only group complaining about the stagnation and breakdown of the bureaucracy. Grass-roots members, the party rank and file, also took up the attack on the bureaucracy, partly at the instigation of the center. They hated "waiting around all day in the hallways" to see local satraps who were "harder to see than Kalinin." The growing unpopularity of the bureaucracy (and its corruption and bungling) is a major theme of the following analysis.

The party in the thirties was neither monolithic nor disciplined. its upper ranks were divided, and its lower organizations were disorganized, chaotic, and undisciplined. Moscow leaders were divided on policy issues, and central leaders were at odds with territorial secretaries whose organizations suffered from internal disorder and conflict. A bloated party membership containing political illiterates and apolitical opportunists plus a lazy and unresponsive regional leadership was hardly the formula for a Leninist party. Such a clumsy and unwieldy organization could not have been an efficient or satisfying instrument for Moscow's purposes.

The speeches to the Seventeenth Congress in 1934 showed that central party leaders agreed on the need for reform. They decided on a two-pronged strategy: to reduce the size of the party (the *chistka*) while stepping up efforts at political education. The following chapters will investigate these campaigns in some detail. The attempts at reform would reveal the chaotic and deplorable condition of local party committees and would show how little control Moscow had in the provinces. Problems and central–regional tensions became clear during the membership screenings of 1933–5, and it is to them that we now turn.

2

What was a purge?

In this area we can make very big mistakes.

E. M. Iaroslavskii, 1929

Western students have applied the word "purge" to everything from political trials to police terror to nonpolitical expulsions from the party. The label "Great Purges," which encompasses practically all party activities between 1933 and 1939, is an example of such broad usage. Yet the Communist Party defined and used the word quite specifically. The term "purge" (*chistka*–a sweeping or cleaning) only applied to the periodic membership screenings of the ranks of the party. These membership operations were designed to weed the party of hangers-on, nonparticipants, drunken officials, and people with false identification papers, as well as ideological "enemies" or "aliens." In the majority of purges, *political* crimes or deviations pertained to a *minority* of those expelled.

No Soviet source or usage ever referred to the Ezhovshchina (the height of police arrests and terror in 1937) as a purge, and party leaders discussed that event and purges in entirely separate contexts. No political or nonpolitical trial was ever called a purge, and under no circumstances were operations, arrests, or terror involving nonparty citizens referred to as purges. A party member at the time would have been mystified by such a label.

To understand the political events of the thirties in the Communist Party and in the USSR, it is necessary briefly to review various elements of the party's history and tradition: definitions of membership, principles of organization, and the theory and practice of purging the party. The following discussion reviews these norms and traditions as they developed in the late 1920s, using the party purges of 1929 and 1933 as examples of the accumulated experience of the period. Purges are central to an understanding of the 1930s because they were arenas of conflict for various factions and interests within the party.

The membership principles of the Communist Party of the Soviet Union are well known and go back to the earliest days of the party's existence. Lenin's ideas and conceptions of a disciplined and professional cadre of revolutionaries, first expounded in 1902 in his *What Is to Be Done?*, have continued to provide a perhaps unreachable organizational goal for the party throughout its history. In fact, questions of participation and discipline of party members provided the original source of dispute between Bolsheviks and Mensheviks at the Second Congress of the Russian Social Democratic Labor Party in 1903. According to Lenin's formulation, a party member was distinguished by "regular participation in one of the party organizations." Martov and the Mensheviks held that acceptance of the program, financial support of the party, and rendering it "personal assistance" were sufficient to constitute membership.[1]

Such apparently minor questions of membership definition were really matters of principle with far-reaching implications. Martov envisioned a mass party with a comparatively loose or open membership on the model of the German Social Democrats. Lenin, on the other hand, favored a small, disciplined, "hardened" core of professionals operating largely underground with secret links to workers' organizations. Implicit in Lenin's conception from the beginning was the right and power of the party to be selective in controlling admissions to and continued membership in its organizations. Most political parties of the day practiced expulsion of dissident factions and "hangers-on" at various times.

The question of large-scale regulation of the *composition* of the membership did not arise in practice before 1917 because of the party's small size and underground existence. Certainly before 1917 there were splits, defections, splinterings, and expulsions within Russian Social Democracy, but these often took the character of dissolved alliances or platforms rather than of a purge of a dissident faction from a large, permanent party. According to one Soviet scholar, the party was "self-purging" before 1917.[2]

Only after it came to power and attracted a mass membership did the Bolshevik Party find it necessary to prune its ranks. Between 1917 and 1921, the party increased its membership twenty-seven fold, to 576,000.[3] Before the Revolution, the party was more concerned with survival than with having too many members. After the Revolution, and especially after its victory in the Civil War, however, the party was confronted with the problems of building a socialist society in an under-developed peasant country. Such new tasks required even more discipline, organization, and dependability from a membership swollen by almost a half-million untested, unknown, and potentially unreliable persons who had entered the party since the Revolution.

As early as October 1918, *Pravda* was warning against "over-filling of the party," the danger being that "careerist" elements would enter the party's ranks. A careerist was defined as one who "uses a sojourn in the party for personal ends." These were persons who, sensing that the Bolshevik Party would be the victor, entered the party to take personal advantage of the power, position, and possibly wealth that would accrue to a member of the winning fraction.[4]

The Eighth Party Congress in March 1919 discussed such membership problems. Although some of the delegates wanted to institute a screening of party members, others recognized that it would be suicidal to do anything to make it difficult for workers to join or remain in the party. This conflict of opinion over purges would continue for twenty years. It was decided in 1919 to open admissions to the party for workers and peasants while being very selective in recruiting from other groups. At the same time, the party was to conduct a "reregistration" of all members to weed out unsuitable persons who had recently joined.[5]

The 1919 registration (which apparently continued in 1920) was the first of several operations officially called purges in subsequent party history. They include the 1921 party purge, a 1924 purge of nonproductive cells, a 1925 verification of village cells, selective "screenings" of various organizations in 1928, and a major party purge in 1929. All these membership operations were conducted for similar reasons and in similar ways.

It is to these operations and not to trials, arrests, or prosecutions, that the Soviet usage of the term "purge" applies. The 1919 operation was called *pereregistratsiia*, "reregistration." The 1921 purge, and each subsequent purge, was called *proverka* (verification) or *chistka* (a cleaning, cleaning out, combing out, or sweeping).[6] For consistency and accuracy, the term "purge" will be applied below only to a membership-accounting operation. The relationship between such purges and other events, such as trials or terror, will be a focus of the following chapters.

In general, a membership purge was initiated in response to a specific situation. The 1919 reregistration was made necessary by the influx of unknown new members during the Civil War. In most instances, a purge seems to have been the culmination of a period of large-scale admissions into the party, and, as such, became a regular feature and standard practice in the twenties. A resolution of the Communist International on July 30, 1920, called for parties to conduct *periodic* purges and reregistrations to clean the party of alien or petit bourgeois elements that "inevitably adhere to it."[7] One Soviet work notes that purges were combined with admission policies as a means to "regulate the composition" of the party.[8]

E. M. Iaroslavskii, Old Bolshevik historian and one of the heads of the Tsentral'naia Kontrol'naia Komissia (TsKK; Central Control Commission), was the author of books, articles, and speeches on the theoretical and practical reasons for purging the party. In *How to Conduct a Purge of the Party,* he noted that one of the functions of a purge was to rid the party of bourgeois and petit bourgeois elements and thereby strengthen it and increase its unity. Opposite notions also existed: that purging the party by getting rid of potentially useful people and exposing the party and its members to investigation and criticism were dangerous.[9]

The reasons for which one could be expelled in a purge varied throughout the twenties, but there were some constant themes. One category consistently marked for expulsion was that of "class-alien," "counterrevolutionary," or "hostile" elements. This group of offenders included former officers (but not always soldiers) of the White Armies, "regenerate bourgeois elements," kulaks, and other elements of the prerevolutionary power stricture. There was no official stricture against persons of bourgeois or kulak origin entering the party, as long as such origins were not kept secret. *Hiding* one's origins, however, was always grounds for expulsion.

Another category for expulsion was that encompassing official misconduct or corruption. This might be phrased "acts unworthy of a party member," "violations of party discipline," or "self-seeking careerism" in cases of continued violations. This "abuse of position" category often included theft, embezzlement, and the like.

A third group of offenses providing grounds for expulsion centered on nonparticipation or "passivity." This group always accounted for a large percentage of those expelled in a purge, as did a fourth group – the morally corrupt. Offenses such as drunkenness, sexual crimes, and financial corruption were taken as signs of "personal corruption" (*razlozhennie*).

There were also criteria that reflected more temporary problems in the party membership. Desertion figured importantly in the 1919 re-registration. In the 1929 purge, there was a category for those who had been unable to carry out the party line and "came out against decisions of the party," referring to the forced grain procurements of 1929 when many party members recoiled from the violence of the situation.

The official instructions for the 1929 party purge, as enunciated by Iaroslavskii, provide a good example of "purge criteria." Referred to both as *chistka* (sweeping, cleaning) and *proverka* (verification), this operation was to rid the party of the following groups: "social-alien," "bureaucratic," and "corrupt" elements; persons "sojourning in the ruling party for self-seeking and careerist aims"; bourgeois elements and kulaks opposing the carrying out of the party line; and shirkers, "weaklings," and others coming out against the decisions of the party. Iaroslavskii held that the party would be far stronger without such persons in its ranks.[10]

Listing of purge categories, whether in 1929, 1933, 1935, or 1936, showed considerable ambiguity in relation to various sections of the party. Charges of "bureaucratism," corruption, and "self-seeking careerism" would most likely be leveled against full-time officials. Other categories, such as "social-alien element," "shirkers," and "passive elements," were more applicable to lower-level rank-and-file members. The targets were therefore not clear and the strata that bore the brunt of a purge would depend on who controlled the purge proceedings.

With the exception of the 1919 purge, all the screenings before 1933 were conducted by the TsKK. This body was to be independent of the Central Committee and was elected by the party congress. Its original function was to prevent bureaucratization and official malfeasance among party officials, but its duties naturally came to include the expulsion of anyone not considered to be a mainstream communist – members of the various opposition groups as well as corrupt officials fell into this category. One of the reasons for the formation of the TsKK outside the Central Committee was to ensure its independence and, presumably, to decrease the possibility that the TsKK might hesitate to investigate an important official with control over the investigating agency. It was understood that purges were to be carried out "irrespective of person," that is, regardless of the rank of the member. Notwithstanding the intentions of the central party authorities, the targets of purges – whether conducted by the TsKK (1929), ad hoc purge commissions (1933), or party secretaries themselves (1935, 1936) – were most often relatively defenseless rank-and-file members.

Purge procedure varied widely according to the specific time and geographical location. In general, the procedure was officially announced in the press and at meetings, and a time and place was specified for each member to present himself or herself before the appropriate local or institutional control commission. The commission itself consisted of perhaps three senior party members, at least one of whom represented the TsKK. Another was usually the member's immediate "party leader" – perhaps a member of the *raion buro* or the secretary of the member's cell – who was theoretically in a position to know the member personally. The session may or may not have taken place before a larger meeting of members who could offer information on the member's work and thereby participate in the proceedings. After asking various questions of the member (about such things as party history, the party's position on various issues, and his/her specific work), the commission decided whether or not the member passed the purge and could remain in the party.[11]

If a member were expelled in such a purge, he/she still had recourse. An elaborate appeals procedure extended throughout various levels of control commissions, ending with the presidium of the TsKK in Moscow, to which any expellee could finally appeal. Members of the presidium spent much of their time hearing and acting upon such appeals, many of which led to reversal of the local decision and restoration to full membership.[12] Alternatively, at any level of the process, an expulsion could be commuted to a "censure," "reprimand," or a "reprimand with notation in member's dossier," the ultimate discipline short of expulsion. Control Commission officials in Moscow commonly reversed the expulsions of masses of rank-and-file members who had been wrongfully expelled.

The question of who could attend and participate in purge meetings was a political issue that was handled in various ways at various times. Because most Moscow party authorities were interested in using the purges to uncover local corruption, bureaucratism, and malfeasance, they encouraged lower-level mass input as a check against entrenched local party machines.

Thus, the November 1928 and April 1929 joint meetings of the Central Committee and the TsKK, which announced the 1929 purge, called for participation by nonparty workers and peasants and encouraged party organizations to "attract them to this work."[13] There are signs, though, that other party authorities disagreed. Apparently, local party machines had their supporters in the central leadership and even within the TsKK. Iaroslavskii's speech to the April 1929 joint plenum was interrupted by a questioner who asked if nonparty persons could attend purge meetings. Iaroslavskii replied that they could not on the grounds that "class enemies" might use the event as a forum for "demogogic speeches." A. Sol'ts, another prominent member of the TsKK, in an article called "Toward the Purge," noted that the "purge of the party does not, of course, carry a mass character."[14] Control Commission member A. Mitrofanov revealed that some provincial "and even Moscow" party papers had interpreted this to mean consultative participation by nonparty persons on purge commissions. One Moscow paper, he said, had put forward the slogan *"Klass chistit partiiu"* (the class purges the party). Mitrofanov expressed horror at such "liquidationist confusion" and "Trotskyist opportunism," which he regarded as attempts to revise and distort the party line and turn nonparty persons against the party. The party, he said, would only be a "passive object" in such an operation and could fall victim to demogogic enemies who would publicly try to discredit the party as the Trotskyists had done. Mitrofanov proposed alternative forms of mass participation: speeches at nonparty meetings, letters in the press voicing complaints, and criticism of party and government through meetings of social organizations. Nonparty persons could even participate in various open party meetings not dealing with the purge itself.[15] Such sentiments show that the leadership stratum was afraid of open criticism. They also suggest disagreement within the party leadership.

There was similar contradiction and confusion within the leadership about how far the purge should pry into the affairs of local officials. Iaroslavskii noted that at the November 1928 plenum of the Central Committee no distinction had been made between class enemies and those who were merely dissolute in their personal lives. This had led, he said, to the erroneous belief among some Moscow party activists that the party was ignoring those who were "rotten" in their personal lives. This was not true, said Iaroslavskii; such offenses would not be overlooked. At the same time, however, the purge would not allow "petty, captious digging" and "nagging" about the personal lives of communists. Questions like "With whom do you live?," "How large is your apartment?," and "How many tables and chairs do you have?" should not be allowed.[16] The implication was that rank-and-file enthusiasts might get carried away with the purge.

Similarly, Iaroslavskii warned against an "undifferentiated" approach toward party members' pasts. While noting that former White

Guard commanders should not be in the party, he cautioned against expelling people simply because of their social origin, especially if they had been working honestly for "the Soviet power": "That is why I would like to say here that it is impossible to proceed... *only from the point of view of biographical past and only from the point of view of social position.* In this area we can make very big mistakes"[17] (emphasis in original). He pointed out that although the party was struggling with the Right Opposition, this did not mean that "those who stand with us in our work" should be expelled. "That would be incorrect."[18]

The TsKK also warned against the use of "control figures," or projected purge quotas, which could lead to activist "competition between organizations." Local party organizations were enjoined to "clean" themselves according to individual circumstances.[19]

The signals from Moscow on the targets, conduct, level of popular participation, and intensity of the 1929 purge were ambiguous. On the one hand, the Central Committee had called for a purge "irrespective of person" and with maximum rank-and-file criticism of bureaucratism and corruption. On the other, most subsequent clarifications by the TsKK had sought to limit the possibility of populist participation in the purge. These contradictions might be explained simply as results of high-level confusion and indecision on the purge. Indeed, there was substantial chaos in central decision making. Another explanation, which is not inconsistent with the first, involves conflict at the center. The documents suggest that some in the leadership seemed to favor an open, populist purge that could have an impact on the local party machines. Others seem to have preferred to limit the purge in ways that would tend to protect local officials. Such a conflict at the center might well be mistaken for confusion or indecision.

The incidence, as well as the severity, of purges in the twenties is indicated in Table 2.1. The largest of these operations was the 1921 purge following the Civil War, which expelled one in four party members. At no time in the twenties did an all-union purge embrace even one-half that rate of expulsion. If one could speak of an average incidence of purges or screenings in the first decade and a half of Soviet power (except for 1921), the figure would be between 10 and 15 percent for an official purge and 5 percent or less for an average year of TsKK activities. Despite Iaroslavskii's public strictures against control quotas, there appears to have been a fair degree of consistency in practice.

The 1929 party purge is the only one for which detailed information

Table 2.1. *Incidence of purges in the 1920s*

Operation	% expelled [a]
1919 reregistration	10–15
1921 purge	25
1924[b]	3
1925[b]	4
1926[b]	3
1928 "screening" (7 regions only)	13
1929 purge	11
1930[b]	5
1931[b]	5

[a] This represents the percentage expelled of those undergoing the operation, which are not always the entire membership.
[b] Not years of official party purge.
Sources: Izvestiia Tsentral'nogo Komiteta [Proceedings of the central committee], no. 8, December 2, 1919; E. M. Iaroslavskii, *Za bol'shevistkuiu proverku i chistku riadov partii* [For Bolshevik verification and purge of the ranks of the party], Moscow, 1933, 47, 65; Merle Fainsod, *Smolensk Under Soviet Rule,* Cambridge, Mass., 1958, 44; T. H. Rigby, *Communist Party Membership in the USSR, 1917–1967,* Princeton, N.J., 1968, 97, 177–8; N. R. Andrukhov, *Partiinoe stroitel'stvo v period bor'by za pobedu sotsializma* v SSSR [Party construction in the period of struggle for the victory of socialism in the USSR], Moscow, 1977, 131.

is available on the reasons for expulsion. Iaroslavskii gave a list of reasons for expulsion according to incomplete data as of July 1930, and it is reproduced in Table 2.2.

Of those expelled for violations of party discipline, 10 percent were guilty of "fractional" or oppositional activity. Hence, only 1 percent of the expulsions (10 percent of 10 percent) in the 1929 purge were explicitly related to inner-party fractional struggles.[20] It is, of course, possible that oppositionists were expelled under one or more of the other (non-ideological) criteria, especially if they expressed open disagreement with party policy on grain procurement or other issues.

The Smolensk files help clarify the impact of the 1929 purge and amplify Iaroslavskii's figures. "Defects in personal conduct" (as opposed to ideological or class hostility) figure most prominently – 37 percent of all those expelled had drunkenness listed as one of their offenses, and in one factory 30 percent of the communists were said to be continually drunk. Careerism and passivity were frequent charges made against some 20 and 40 percent of the expellees, respectively.[21]

Table 2.2. *Reasons for expulsion: 1929 purge (in percent)*

Defects in personal conduct	22
Alien elements or connection thereto	17
Passivity	17
Criminal offenses	12
Violations of party discipline	10
Other	22

Source: XVI s''ezd Vsesoiuznoi Kommunisticheskoi Partii (b), [Sixteenth congress of the all-union Communist Party (b)], Moscow and Leningrad, 1930, 340.

If 1929 is typical of a 1920s-era purge in its causes and criteria for expulsion, then membership operations seem to have been implemented to rid the party of corrupt, inactive, undisciplined, class-alien, or criminal persons. The idea was to "clean" the party of those who were not full-time, dedicated, honest party members according to Lenin's strict code. It was not done, at least explicitly, to rid the party of all ideological dissenters or suspected oppositionists, although such persons may have seemed to a purge commission to be outside the aforementioned personal code. For example, a partisan of one of the oppositions who was a member of the intelligentsia, with its different lifestyle, values, and even appearance, might be regarded by proletarian party members as an "alien element" and be expelled on that basis, rather than explicitly because of oppositional membership.

There seems to have been a great deal of difficulty in 1929 in defining, limiting, and executing the operation. Iaroslavskii's detailed and careful explications and modifications of the original purge order reflected a fear in the leadership that the purge would be badly carried out, bungled, or even sabotaged. The fears of the leadership were justified.

Nationally, 1,530,000 members went through the purge. Of these, 170,000 (or 11 percent) were expelled. Subsequently, however, 37,000 of these expellees (22 percent of them) were reinstated into the party on appeal. In Smolensk, the figure was 43 percent restored to membership and in Voronezh 33 percent.[22] These readmissions eventually reduced the impact of the 1929 purge from 11 to 8 percent nationally and comprised the greatest number of reversals for a purge to date. Subsequent clarifications show that the vast majority of those reinstated to membership had been expelled for "passivity" (nonparticipation) and that most of these were rank-and-file members of working-class origin.

At this point, the 1929 purge situation reveals only the important actors in future events. At the "top" were the apparently divided leaders of the center. Next came the local leaders – representing both the party and the Control Commission – who were charged with carrying out the operation. Finally, there were the rank-and-file activists and members. The level and effect of their participation was both encouraged and discouraged; they were sometimes both expelled and restored. At any rate, the organizational structure of the Communist Party is important to an understanding of the political events of this period. In the future, debates over the conduct, purpose, and efficacy of purges would continue to divide the Moscow leadership. Purges would also highlight a double polarization between Moscow and provincial secretaries and between these regional leaders and the *aktiv*.

The *chistka* of 1933

Since 1931, when admission to the party had been opened wide in an attempt to deal with collectivization and industrialization, the party's membership had grown by 1.4 million. As a result of indiscriminate mass admissions by local organizations, large numbers of what party leaders called "alien," "parasitic," "unreliable," and "unsteadfast" persons had entered the party. These mass admissions were part of the attempt to attract all possible allies to the party in the struggle for the countryside. They had taken place "without proper verification" of the new members by local officials. According to the leadership, these new members were often "insufficiently stable" and "politically almost illiterate."[23] These descriptions referred to persons who were unwilling to carry out collectivization, those who did not understand the policies of the party, and those nonpolitical persons who simply joined the party for the patronage, position, or power associated with membership.

Accordingly, the Moscow leadership decided in January 1933 to conduct a party purge. The official reasons for and conduct of the *chistka* were amplified in an article in *Pravda* at the end of April 1933. The January plenum had only approved the purge in principle, leaving its organization to the Politburo and the presidium of the TsKK. The article, issued in the name of the Central Committee, noted that the reasons for the purge were to strengthen the party, raise the ideological level of its membership, and increase the authority of the party among the masses by purging itself before them.[24]

Accordingly, the party was to purge itself of the following categories:

1. Class-alien, hostile elements who try to deceitfully demoralize the party
2. Double dealers, who deceitfully undermine party policy
3. Violators of discipline who fail to carry out party decisions and who are pessimistic about the "impractibility" of party measures
4. Degenerates who merged with and do not struggle against kulaks, loafers, thieves, etc.
5. Careerists and self-seekers who are isolated from the masses and disregard the needs of people
6. Moral degenerates whose unseemly behavior discredits the party

These categories were slightly more ideological than those for the 1929 purge. There was more emphasis on "double dealers," "underminers," and "violators of discipline" who refused to "struggle against the kulak," but the main focus of the 1933 *chistka* was on weeding out undesirables who had flooded the party since 1929 and not on persecuting members of the opposition, many of whose leaders remained in the party. The official explanations of the *chistka* did not mention the possibility of purging persons because of their membership in the Right Opposition.

It is easy to see confusion and ambiguity, if not outright contradiction, in the stated reasons for the 1933 *chistka*. On the one hand, the operation was supposed to prune the swollen ranks of the party after the huge influx of 1929–32. On the other hand, purge categories such as "degenerates," "careerists," "double dealers," and those "isolated from the masses" seemed to target full-time officials as much as the newly recruited proletarian *aktiv*. Theoretically, of course, both lower- and upper-level party members could have been targeted at the same time; there is nothing inherently contradictory in specifying two separate target groups.

But in practice, Moscow must have known that, depending on how the purge was organized and conducted, one group or the other would have felt the brunt of the purge. If the operation were carried out by local party secretaries (or local purge officials associated with them or under their influence), the major force of the purge would probably be turned against rank-and-file members outside the local machines. If the purge were to take a more populist character, maximizing mass input and criticism, members of the local leadership machines would have more cause for worry. In the future, central authorities would change the administration of the purge to take this situation into account.

As in 1929, elements within the leadership seem to have been worried about leftist "excesses" directed against the bureaucracy. The *chistka* was to take place in a "comradely atmosphere," was to tolerate no "petty and captious digging into the personal lives of people" (almost a quote from Iaroslavskii's exhortation in 1929), and was not to be used to settle personal accounts.[25]

On the other hand, there were strictures from Moscow in favor of rank-and-file criticism of the local bureaucracies. Like the 1929 purge, the 1933 *chistka* was to be conducted "irrespective of person" or position. In fact, the official announcement called for "open and honest self-criticism of party members" and a verification of the work of each party cell, suggesting at least obliquely that the work of party leaders would be scrutinized.

Local purge officials were warned not to expel large numbers of rank-and-file members on such flimsy pretexts as "passivity" or simple political illiteracy. The 1933 announcement enjoined those conducting the purge to take into account the "overall development" of the member – not to try to trick him or her with technical questions on the intricacies of the party program and not to expel loyal workers and collective farmers just because they had not had time to improve their level of ideological education. Moreover, a member found to lack sufficient political knowledge (or discipline) was to be reduced from a member to a candidate, or from a candidate member to a sympathizer, reflecting an attempt to prevent some of the abuses encountered in 1929 relating to unjustified expulsions.[26] Events would show, however, that such appeals on behalf of the rank and file were in vain.

Hence, the 1933 *chistka* was in the tradition of the regular 1920s-era party purges. In fact, the official announcement stressed this point by summing up the history of purges in the 1920s, referring to the 1920 Comintern resolution and listing the 1933 *chistka* along with the 1920 reregistration and the 1921, 1924, 1925, and 1929 membership operations.[27] Like previous operations, the *chistka* followed a period of mass influx into the party and was aimed at correcting the ills attendant thereto.

But the organization of the 1933 *chistka* differed from that used previously and reflected the leadership's fear that rank-and-file members would continue to be expelled en masse. Most significantly, the conduct of the *chistka* was taken out of the hands of the Central Control Commission, and entrusted to a specially formed Central Purge Commission, which was to head a hierarchy of ad hoc purge commissions down to the *raion* level of the party.[28] Unlike previous operations, the 1933 *chistka* was not to be carried out by the TsKK. No explanations were ever given for this rearrangement, although the mass rank-and-file expulsions and blunders of 1929 may have been blamed on the TsKK and its regional apparatus.

The Central Purge Commission consisted of Ian Rudzutak,[29] L. M. Kaganovich,[30] S. M. Kirov,[31] N. I. Ezhov,[32] E. M. Iaroslavskii, M. Shkiriatov,[33] and a few other minor figures. The chairman and half the members of the commission represented the TsKK. But also included were two full members of the Politburo (Kaganovich and Kirov) and two important members of the Secretariat (Kaganovich and Ezhov). Hence, half the Central Purge Commission had no TsKK experience or connections.

It might seem that Stalin had lost confidence in the political reliability of the TsKK leaders, and perhaps no longer trusted them to weed out oppositionists. The supplanting of the TsKK apparatus by the regular party apparatus might seem to be a sign that Stalin wanted "his people" in charge of the purge. This seems unlikely given the composition of the new Central Purge Commission. Of the four old guard members of the TsKK three survived the Great Purges (Iaroslavskii, Shkiriatov, Stasova) in good order. In fact, of the nine members of the collegium of the TsKK whose biographies can be traced, all but one (Ordzhonikidze, a suicide) survived the Great Purges.[34] Thus political loyalty probably had nothing to do with the change in operational procedure in 1933, and the displacement of the TsKK probably had more to do with incompetence than politics.

The 1933 *chistka* was to be carried out under public scrutiny and with maximum party and nonparty participation. In a speech explaining the 1933 *chistka,* Kaganovich told Moscow party activists that the party needed the cooperation of large numbers of Soviet citizens in the purge and that active participation was to be encouraged.[35] Iaroslavskii suggested that the local nonparty press should explain to the public the principles of and reasons for the "cleaning." "Particularly great will be the part played by the 'lower' press–district papers, factory newspapers, wall newspapers, *kolkhoz* newspapers."[36] According to the resolution on the *chistka,* the operation was to take place at open cell meetings in the presence of nonparty persons to whom the aims and functions of the purge had been explained beforehand.[37]

The Central Committee ordered that local purge commissions be composed of "staunch" communists who had been in the party at least ten years, had never been in the opposition or in other parties, and enjoyed "authority" among the party members.[38] The names of members were to be published in advance and challenges were to be allowed. The Smolensk Archive contains precious little information on the 1933 *chistka,* but the files of the Kozielsk Raion Committee contain a list of the six members of the *raion* purge commission. A Deputy Chief of a Machine Tractor Station's Political Department (*politotdel*), a people's judge, an employee from the fuel industry, a sanitorium worker, a grain-purchasing representative of the Council of People's Commissars, and a senior mechanic in a local factory sat on the Kozielsk purge committee.[39] As far as is known, none of these was ever affiliated with the TsKK or the regular party apparatus or came from the ranks of the regular party membership.

The 1933 *chistka* had a stronger antibureaucratic emphasis than its predecessors. It would be much harder for local leadership cliques to protect their members by deflecting the heat to lower levels. It should not be surprising, then, to discover that local party secretaries did all they could to obstruct implementation of the 1933 operation. What is surprising is their continuing ability to protect their machines and demonstrate their "vigilance" with mass expulsions.

As of January 1, 1934 (i.e., after seven months of operation), the *chistka* had covered only ten regional organizations. According to Ian Rudzutak, 1,149,000 members had undergone the *chistka* by that time – only one-third of the party.[40] The original instructions and announcements on the *chistka* had ordered it to run from June 1, 1933, to November 1, 1933. In fact, the *chistka* was not officially dissolved (and its commission disbanded) until December 26, 1935. Even then, it was noted that the *chistka* had not yet begun in some areas and had been completed only in the "principal" ones.[41]

Why was the progress of the *chistka* so slow? Rudzutak delicately but clearly blamed local party officials. Many party leaders, he said, "had not helped" with the organization and implementation of the *chistka.* They had withheld necessary facilities and personnel because they did not take the operation very seriously. More than that, some of these leaders had actually obstructed the successful conduct of the purge. The Western Siberian Party Organization was singled out as an example – officials there had handled the operation badly. In some places, there was actually administrative "opposition" to the *chistka* in that local leaders simply refused to organize it; Vinnitsa Region was given as an example of this outrageous practice. And, where the *chistka* somehow managed to get off the ground, its conduct was all too often *formalno*– doing only enough to satisfy the bare requirements and going through the motions.[42] It seems that the *chistka* fell victim to desultory conduct, apathy, or even sabotage at the hands of local secretaries.

At the Seventeenth Congress, Rudzutak said that as of the end of 1933, 17 percent of the 1,149,000 members eventually examined were expelled.[43] Figures given years later would show that 18 percent of the party was expelled.[44] Up to July 1, 1933 (that is, after only one month of official *chistka*), the expulsion rate was over one-third, but by the end of the year had been cut in half. In the city of Smolensk, the rate was only about 2 percent.[45]

Table 2.3 gives a breakdown of purge criteria for the 1933 chistka. If the totals in Table 2.3 are compared to the 1929 data given in Table 2.2, it is clear that the *chistka* was typical of a traditional 1920s purge in this aspect as well. Figures from Leningrad show analogous results.[46]

In their speeches to the Seventeenth Party Congress in 1934, Rudzutak and Iaroslavskii gave contradictory information on the social origins of those expelled during the *chistka*. Rudzutak, speaking for the TsKK, said that 23 percent of those expelled were peasants and 14.6 percent were employees. Although giving no figure for workers, he noted that in some areas where mass admissions had been most flagrant, large numbers of workers were expelled.[47] It seems reasonable, in fact, to surmise that around 62 percent of the expellees were workers. However, Iaroslavskii, also speaking for the TsKK in a supplementary speech to Rudzutak's, noted that after the *chistka*, the proportion of workers in the party increased 2–4 percent, depending on the organization, and in the ten regions for which data were available, the proportion of workers increased from 67.7 to 69.4 percent.[48] Unless they were based on different data, these reports together suggest that a large number of workers were expelled (more than half the total expulsions), but that their percentage in the party actually increased because of attrition to other, less numerous groups. Rudzutak further noted that most of those expelled during the *chistka* had joined the party during the previous three to four years[49] – other figures given at the congress show that two-thirds of those expelled had joined the party since 1928,[50] and one-half since 1929.[51] It therefore seems unlikely that the 1933 *chistka* was directed against members of the old opposition or the latest "right deviation." It is doubtful that persons joining the party in 1929, who were the majority of those expelled, were members of the

Table 2.3. *Reasons for expulsions: 1933* chistka

Reason for expulsion	Percent of expulsions
Moral corruption, careerist, bureaucrat	17.5
Alien elements/hiding alien past	16.5
Violation of party discipline	20.9
Passivity	23.2
Other	17.9

Source: P. N. Pospelov et al., *Istoriia Kommunisticheskoi Partii Sovetskogo Soiuza* [History of the Communist Party of the Soviet Union], vol. 4, part 2, Moscow, 1971, 283.

opposition, especially if they joined in the enthusiasm of collectivization or the Five Year Plan.

Despite specific warnings, more than seventy thousand members, including "many workers and peasants," were "excluded for so-called 'passivity,' although in reality a majority of them were staunch party people." The expelled "passives" accounted for one in four of those ejected from the party in the purge.[52] Indeed, passives comprised the largest single group of those expelled, despite the fact that they had not even been listed as a target group in the original *chistka* instructions. The wishes of the Moscow authorities had been thwarted by foot dragging and by mass expulsions of rank-and-file members. One can hardly blame local party secretaries for being reluctant to purge more highly placed officials. The imperatives of plan fulfillment forced local party leaders to hoard and protect any skilled administrators they had.

In the course of summing up the *chistka,* party leaders discovered another bureaucratic problem that would loom large in the next three years: chaos in the party's records and bookkeeping. The Western Region's Iartsevo District Party Organization counted on its rolls 1,682 members and candidates before the *chistka*. As of July 1, 1933, after only part of the purge was completed, the organization numbered 1,543 – a loss of 139 members. Of the 139, only 85 had been expelled (5.1 percent). The remaining 54 members no longer in the party included 25 who had transferred to other organizations and whose names were never removed from the Iartsevo rolls and 29 who had simply disappeared and whose names remained on the rolls.[53] In Briansk Raion, the purge rate was 1.3 percent, with an equal number having disappeared since the last reckoning.[54]

During 1933–34, the party "lost" almost as many members as it expelled. While 17–18 percent of the party was expelled, the party decreased in size by one-third. The extra 15 percent (or approximately half a million persons) apparently withdrew from the party voluntarily or "disappeared" without the knowledge of local authorities.[55]

A month before the above information was compiled in Iartsevo and Briansk, an article appeared in the *Handbook for Party Workers* noting that 75 of the 623 members of a Vitebsk committee listed on the rolls "had gone no one knows where, without being taken off the records."[56] As the *chistka* progressed, more and more of these discrepancies and confusions arose. On October 11, 1933, a Central Committee order enjoined local secretaries to keep better records of their members, especially regarding payment of dues.[57]

The files of the Kozielsk Raion Committee refer to a secret unpublished decision of the Central Committee taken on November 13, 1933.[58] The decision ordered local party organizations to keep better track of party membership cards and records. Cards belonging to those who had died or withdrawn from the party were to be returned to the *obkom* immediately and thence forwarded to the Central Committee. As noted in Chapter 1, it was not common practice to return the card of a dead person, and party cards continued to be used by relatives of the deceased.

In his speech to the Seventeenth Party Congress in early 1934, Rudzutak referred to the problem of party *uchet* (accounting, registration). In the ten regions covered by the *chistka* as of January 1, 1934, officials discovered 56,500 "dead souls" – persons listed on the rolls but nowhere to be found. In the Donets Region alone, there were 15,000 such "disappeared" persons; Belorussia and Western Siberia counted over 3,000 each.[59] Rudzutak and others speaking at the congress were scandalized at this confusion, pointing out that neither the local nor national leadership of the party knew who was in the party and who was not. The chaos existing in town and country during the preceding period was blamed for this intolerable situation in "party management" (*khoziaistvo*). The problem was discovered but not solved in 1933 and would continue to plague the party until World War II. It was a central theme of the early events of the period under review and constitutes a major theme of the following discussion.

The party had perennial problems organizing and carrying out purges, and its careful attempts to explain the operations beforehand were often in vain. The 1933 *chistka* was entrusted to special commissions to ensure that it would proceed more smoothly, but it fared no better than its forerunners. In its raison d'être, in the instructions promulgated about it, in the (nonideological) categories marked for exclusion by it, and in its stated parameters, the *chistka* was an example of a regular and traditional membership screening (or purge), as it had evolved since the Civil War.[60] It was also typical of such a membership operation in that it involved a series of bureaucratic confusions, mistakes, and distortions. In fact, the organization and administration of the *chistka* represented one in a continuing series of organizational variants that were tried in a vain attempt to make these membership screenings run smoothly.

The incidence of the *chistka* (18.5 percent expelled) places it within the limits for purges in the 1920s. Like them, the *chistka* involved large numbers of readmissions after the fact. By the end of 1934, procedures for readmission of those demoted to candidates and sympathizers were finalized and published in the party's organizational journal.[61]

The crises of industrialization and collectivization had led to an influx of new party members to cope with these mammoth tasks. In turn, this strategy had produced an organization that was large and correspondingly unwieldly. Disorganization, disarray, and confusion caused by the swollen ranks of the party had led to the purge. Paradoxically, however, the *chistka* revealed more problems than it solved. Future events would show that it solved nothing at all.

Announced in January 1933, the *chistka* was not described until the end of April, when instructions were finally given. Although it was supposed to start June 1, it apparently began at once. Its conduct was marred by uncooperative officials whose attitudes caused the operation to founder for nearly two years. On balance, local party leaders were reluctant to conduct or assist purges. Purge operations required troublesome allocations of time and personnel. Local leaders were not interested in pruning the ranks and were careful that such prunings not involve "their people."

Finally, the 1933 purge revealed a truly chaotic situation in the party's records and membership-accounting procedures that would have disturbed *any* organization with a selective membership. The *chistka* solved few problems, if any, and, except for revealing the true nature of the chaos in the party and country, it must have been counted a dismal failure.

The following chapter traces the futile and divisive 1935 attempts to reform the party's records. Chaos in the files had been uncovered in

1933 during the *chistka,* and several unsuccessful attempts were made to correct it. As they had done consistently since 1929, the local leaders bungled or obstructed such operations. The need to restore order in the party records combined with continued failures to do so were further signs of the breakdown of party controls in this period.

3

The Verification of Party Documents of 1935: a case study in bureaucratic ineptitude

Party organizations must not transform the work of verifying party documents into a campaign of unmasking.

Smolensk City Party Committee,
1935

After a year and a half of confusion in party accounting (*uchet*), the leadership decided in October 1934 to conduct a general registration of membership that would eventually be known as the Verification of Party Documents, or *proverka*, of 1935. The *proverka* illustrates many of the problems in the party apparatus: the chaos in the records, delays, hesitant starts, bureaucratism, bungling, and the inability of the Central Committee to compel obedience in the localities. In response to poor implementation, the Moscow leadership would "go public" on the collapsed *proverka* and attack regional party leaders for bureaucratism and "opportunist complacency."

The files and first hesitant steps

The decision to conduct a general verification of party records had been taken more than a year after the first revelations of disorder, and several weeks before the assassination of Kirov.[1] The admission of new members into the party had been suspended since the beginning of the *chistka* in early 1933 so that such admissions would not interfere with the conduct of the purge, but the interminable process of the *chistka* and the disturbing situation in party records convinced the leadership not to allow any new admissions. The membership of the party was "frozen" from January 1933 until November 1936.

The first issue of the party's organizational journal for 1935 carried an article entitled "Again on the Irresponsible Attitude Toward Party Documents." It referred to a Central Committee order of December 13, 1934, on improving the record system and ordering regional committees to report the results to the center. But according to Kaganovich, only eleven *obkoms* in the entire country bothered even to respond to this order. Smolensk was one of the slow ones, while Gorkii and Leningrad (Zhdanov's former and present strongholds) were among the first.[2]

Ultimate responsibility for order in party records in the Stalinist patronage machine rested with Stalin himself, or more precisely with the Central Committee Secretariat and Department of Leading Party Organs (ORPO), which made key party personnel assignments. In the thirties, this department was headed by N. I. Ezhov.[3] From early in 1935, Ezhov was in charge of a special investigation into this matter, working from the ORPO, the Orgburo, the Secretariat, and the KPK.[4] Attempts to deal with this problem would be characterized by a good deal of improvisation, little planning, and mixed success.

In January 1935, the Central Committee sent representatives to various party committees to investigate the procedures used for safekeeping party records, blank membership cards, and files.[5] The emissary to the Smolensk City Committee (Gorraikom) was Comrade Ostrovskii, whose "verification" prompted the city committee buro to pass the following measures: (1) to appoint a chief of accounting, Comrade Vladimirov, whose job it would be to find and secure an office with a safe or locked box for the party records; (2) to stop giving out temporary or replacement cards without verification; (3) to start a new accounting book from January 1 for membership matters; (4) to communicate this information to all subordinate party committees for their emulation.[6] Previously, there had been no single list or book of the Gorraikom's membership.

Three months later, on April 8, 1935, Vladimirov and his assistant Vasilevskaia were only able to report that they had organized personnel and procedures for *investigating* the current safekeeping and recording practices of the city party cells, but they had taken no action. At that time, the buro ordered such investigation to be completed by the end of the month and released party cadres from other duties to help.

At the end of the month, the city committee buro met again to hear Vasilevskaia report how "in the process of investigation of party documents, were revealed a series of massive deficiencies, demanding an especially careful working out and verification." Either the verification was so poor, or the situation in the records so bad, that the *buro* was obliged to extend the term of the investigation for another month, to June 1, 1935. Further, the *buro* ordered the mobilization of an additional twenty-five responsible party members from various organizations to help "introduce order into party accounting." More communications were sent out to subordinate organizations. It is not known whether this May 1935 verification was ever completed.[7] A recent party history notes that "many party organizations were not able to fulfill the directives of the Central Committee."[8] On May 13, 1935, the Central Committee gave up and ordered a coordinated national verification of party documents, which eclipsed the city committee's feeble attempts.

The May 13 letter and the *proverka*

Since January, when the Central Committee representatives had traveled to the localities, the party press had highlighted the *uchet* theme. January issues of *Party Building* were followed in February by articles such as "The Disordered Situation in the Disbursement and Safekeeping of Party Documents" and "Give More Serious Attention to Party Cards." They described the situation in party records as "completely insufficient," noting that many cards were given out blank, unsigned, and unstamped to anyone who wanted them. Such new "members" were never registered or processed into the party. The unaccounted party cards were numerous – in the Donets organization there were 14,584; in Central Asia, 13,000; and in the city of Gorkii there were 1,000 bona fide party members not recorded anywhere in the files.[9] Beginning in April 1935, *Pravda* carried semiregular columns entitled "Party Life," and later "Party Accounting," which contained reports of disorders and corrective measures from around the country.[10]

It was not until the middle of May, however, that the central authorities were able to organize the national verification of party documents. At that time the Central Committee issued its "Closed Letter" of May 13, 1935, entitled "On Disorders in the Registration, Distribution, and Safekeeping of Party Cards and on Measures for Regulating this Affair."[11] The letter called for the verification of the membership card (*partbilet*) and registration file card (*uchetnaia kartochka*) of each party member. The letter, addressed "to all party organizations" and marked "secret," began by informing local committees that a "special investigation" had discovered great "arbitrariness" and a "completely intolerable chaos in the registration of communists." It went on to describe a series of examples in which opponents, enemies, and even foreign agents "enjoyed access to party membership cards" and used them as a cover.[12]

Contributing to this chaos, according to the letter, was the disorganized registration of members in the *raion* committees of the party. *Raikoms* were not keeping track of transfers, deaths, and changes in the educational and skill levels of their members and, as a result, it was impossible to assign members to work that fit their abilities.

The problem existed not only in the *raikoms,* but in all party organizations. In an unusual bit of self-criticism, the letter said that "even in the *apparat* of the Central Committee itself, the verification work of the accounting sector...revealed manifestations of disorder, irresponsibility, and lack of control over the business of giving out blank party cards." Regarding registration and record keeping as mere "office" or "clerical" tasks, party leaders at various levels had entrusted these matters to subordinate, purely "technical" workers. "Party workers forgot the Bolshevik tradition whereby the best organizers in the party personally occupied themselves with laborious organizational work, learning the composition of the organization, verifying the disbursement of party documents, and fulfilling all the details of 'party technique.'"

Noting that in the past several years party organizations had issued over 200,000 duplicate cards (to replace those lost or stolen), the letter said that more than 1,000 blank cards had been stolen. Party organizations were unable to account for over 47,000 cards because "they do not know to whom these cards were given."

Under such conditions, it would be easy for opponents, enemies, and foreign agents to pose as members and even rise to positions of responsibility. Because each lost or stolen party card could be the cover for one spy or "alien element," the letter advised party members that it was time "to introduce Bolshevik order in our own party house." This was to be done in "the next 2–3 months," and until such time as order could be restored in party accounting, no new admissions were to be processed. The May 13 letter ordered a verification that was to be completed no later than the end of the summer and that was under the direction of the ORPO of the Central Committee (headed by Ezhov and his assistant Malenkov).[13]

The letter then listed thirteen numbered "measures" that described the verification. The fine detail provided in the letter shows that the Central Committee was not particularly sanguine about the prospects of successful execution. The very first of the thirteen points demanded reports on the progress of the *proverka* every two weeks from even primary party organizations (cells) and clearly fixed a chain of personal responsibility for the fulfillment of the directive.[14] Operational and practical leadership of the *proverka* was to be in the hands of the regional second secretary and the ORPO (cadres) department head. (In Smolensk, these were Shil'man and Kiselev, respectively.) These two officials would "personally answer before the Central Committee of the *VKP (b)* for the conduct of the verification." City and district party secretaries were in turn personally responsible to the above two for the *proverka* in their areas.[15]

The *proverka* itself was to be handled by *raion* secretaries (with the help of one or more *raion buro* members, depending on the size of the *raion*.) They were to verify each communist individually and in person. The secretary was to ask questions on the member's life, history, work, qualifications, and education, and was to update the file information (*uchetnaia kartochka*) according to the answers.[16] If the secretary felt that there was anything suspicious about the member's documents (erasures, alterations), the card was to be held for investigation. Similarly, if the membership of any person was questionable, it had to be supported by statements from other party members who knew him or her. Otherwise, the person was to be expelled de facto by the confiscation of his or her card.

All this information was covered in the first three points of the letter. The remaining ten measures dealt exclusively with the handling of the cards and records themselves. Simple procedures such as the disposition of the party cards belonging to dead persons were spelled out in great detail. Blank cards were to be kept in special safes to which only the *raion* secretary had the key. No temporary cards were to be issued, and those in circulation were to be destroyed – their conversion to permanent cards could only take place with the express permission of the *raikom buro* or higher body. Information on lost or stolen party cards (complete with serial numbers and other information) was to be collected and reported to the ORPO in Moscow. The verification was not complete until a final report (*akt*) had been submitted and accepted. This report was to account for *all* numbered party cards known to have been issued to the organization, and it would thus explain the 47,000 unknowns. The report was to be submitted on prescribed forms, which were subsequently circulated by the Orgburo.[17]

The last part of the letter contained a plea and a threat. "The Central Committee hopes that party organizations understand the importance and the seriousness attached to this matter...and will unconditionally carry it into life." However, in the event that this was not to be the case, "the Central Committee warns leaders of party organizations from primary to region, that if they do not provide...leadership for this important task...and immediately restore order in this important business, then the Central committee *VKP (b)* will take measures of strict party penalty up to and including the question of expelling them from the party." Events would show that this was no empty threat.

Thus, the *proverka* was planned as a membership-accounting operation made necessary by a deep-running chaos in record keeping. No political categories were marked for expulsion, as had always been the case in purges of the past: Those with valid credentials would remain in the party, and those without them might not.[18] The operation was not intended as part of a mounting post-Kirov wave of terror – his name was never mentioned in the May 13 letter, although the assassin's party membership was already common knowledge. Verification officials were not ordered to inquire into the member's political-ideological beliefs or past activities. The emphasis was clerical and not ideological. It is possible, of course, that the ease with which the assassin had gained access to Kirov's office using his party card may have impressed party leaders with the depth of the *uchet* problem: How was it that someone like Nikolaev remained in the party? But the fact that a verification had been approved before Kirov's death, coupled with the six-month delay between the assassination and the *proverka*, suggest that the *proverka* was not a planned escalation of terror hard on the heels of the Kirov murder, or even the direct result of it.

The *proverka*, unlike the *chistka* of 1933 or its predecessors, was to be carried out by local party secretaries. Neither the Control Commission nor any ad hoc panel was involved. Regional secretaries were to verify and prune their own ranks. They could deflect the purge in any direction and expel whomever they chose. This organizational scheme increased the power of local secretaries, but practically guaranteed a repetition of the local "mistakes" that had accompanied previous purges.

Ezhov would later claim that the best thing about the *proverka* was that local secretaries had carried it out, whereas Zhdanov (an opponent of the screenings) called such administration "repressive" of the rank and file.[19] Both Ezhov and Zhdanov would publicly state, however, that the *proverka* was personally initiated by Stalin.[20] It seems, therefore, that in the organization of the *proverka*, Stalin displayed a liberal and lenient attitude toward the regional secretaries. He was giving them a free hand to clean up their own machines, despite the inevitable "mistakes" that would result.[21] This carrot-and-stick approach to the local secretaries would last for two years.

The verification bungled

The day after the release of the May 13 letter, *Pravda* concentrated on the *uchet* issue. In a new column entitled "Party-Organizational Questions," chaos in Ivanov Region was used as an example of the need for order in "party management" (*khoziaistvo*). May 16 saw a feature on the situation in the North Caucasus, and May 26 carried a front-page editorial on the subject. In the following days, various regional organizations passed resolutions calling for order in party management and record keeping.[22]

The *proverka* began immediately after the May 13 letter, although there is little information on these beginnings. Subsequent information shows that the second secretary of the Western Obkom, A. L. Shil'man, and the *obkom* chief of the ORPO, Kiselev, oversaw the early *proverka* in Smolensk. They submitted a routine report to Ezhov and Malenkov on the progress of the verification on June 20, 1935. All regional and territorial committees reported between June 11 and June 21, so Smolensk was one of the last.[23]

Only a week later, the Central Committee blasted the Western Region for its conduct of the *proverka* in a special published decision. The Central Committee expelled a *raion* secretary from the party outright, gave strong reprimands to Shil'man and Kiselev (not even referring to them as "comrades"), and threatened to expel them as well.[24] The decision ordered the Western Obkom to begin the *proverka* all over again, because the first one had been "clearly unsatisfactory."

Why was the Central Committee so displeased? The terse decision published in the party journal decried the "formalistic-bureaucratic" and "irresponsible" methods of work that had predictably included trusting the *proverka* to secondary-level party workers, who in turn gave it only cursory attention. There was no mention that any party organizations had expelled too few members or had proceeded too slowly.[25] In fact, the one concrete example of "defective work" involved a *raion* that had verified 80 members in one day and had thus been unable to give each communist an individual hearing. The secretary of this *raikom*, Stepanov, was the one expelled from the party by order of the Central Committee for going too fast, rather than for any lack of ardor. The decision castigated Shil'man and Kiselev for allowing such procedures, formally reprimanded them, and threatened to expel them if they continued "purely formal attention."[26]

Why had local officials disobeyed explicit instructions? There would seem to be two possible explanations. On the one hand, the secretaries simply minimized the importance of the operation and, busy with other duties, gave it a low priority. Eager to finish as quickly as possible and move on to more pressing tasks, they rushed the process. On the other hand, it is also probable that local officials were not anxious to scrutinize the actual membership status of their subordinates. Given the shortage of trained personnel, it was certainly not in the interests of party secretaries to expel valuable and experienced cadres simply because their documents were not in order.

An in-depth analysis of the progress of the *proverka* was made two weeks later. Under a cover letter signed by Stalin as secretary of the Central Committee, a secret summary report was sent to all party secretaries down to *raikom* level on July 10, 1935.[27] The report noted that, in the first month, 430,000 members, or one-third of the party, had passed through the *proverka*. Thus, if the *proverka* was to last two to three months, it was still on schedule. The first section of the report acknowledged that, in the first month of the *proverka* all organizations had reported to the Central Committee that the May 13 letter had been "considered and implemented." "*Regardless of this, in the first month the work of verification of party documents is . . . clearly unsatisfactory*" (emphasis in original). Echoing the complaint made against Smolensk, the report attacked local leaders who violated the orders of the Central Committee by entrusting the *proverka* to "an expanded circle of people" such as *raikom* second secretaries. Local leaders had relegated the business to their juniors "*to get out of doing it.*"[28]

Many organizations had handled the operation with such cursory attention that some communists received fewer than five minutes each "according to the plan of work." One *raion* in the Urals verified over 1,500 members in less than six days. Comrade Stepanov in Smolensk was expelled for a one-in-five-minutes rate of work and was cited in the national report as a negative example. Many regional party organizations were also attacked for going too fast. After only one month, the Black Sea party organizations had processed 87 percent of their membership, Kursk had done 67 percent, and Saratov 62 percent. Such rates of work precluded the requisite attention and individual approach, according to the report. Because of such poor and cursory implementation of the *proverka*, several organizations were ordered to repeat the operation from the beginning. Ultimately eighteen or nineteen regions would be ordered to begin again.[29]

Other organizations apparently were more careful in following the instructions. Leningrad, Moscow, and the Donets were favorably noted; they ranged from 15 to 37 percent completion by June 25.

It is clear that the Central Committee did not criticize Smolensk for purging too few of those checked. From later published material, it is known that in this first month of the *proverka* the Western Obkom had held back (expelled) some 150 party cards of the approximately 4,000 checked–a purge rate of about 4 percent.[30] Yet the July 10 Central Committee report cited the national average as 3.6 percent, so Smolensk was actually purging *more* than average. Moreover, many organizations (including some of the "too rapid verifiers") had purge rates below the average, but none was criticized for this. The Central Committee was not unhappy with the numbers or the rate of expulsions in Smolensk, but rather with the bureaucratic *way* in which the operation was being handled by the local leadership.

The final sections of the July 10 national report dealt with the "First Results of the Proverka" and listed a number of disorders revealed in the first month. Leaders did not know their members; glaring discrepancies existed between records and real membership; party cards had been given out wholesale; genuine members did not have cards at all; and expelled persons had kept their membership cards. Of the 47,000 cards to be accounted for in the operation, only 8,400 had been explained. Party cards of dead persons were being used by relatives, spies, White Guards, Trotskyists, and various alien elements. In fact, a supplement to the report gave a "Summary of important facts of uncovered enemies who had made their way into the party."[31] Based on reports from local committees, the supplement gave examples of "aliens, spies (and suspected spies), White Guards, and kulaks" who were using the party *apparat* to obtain and circulate blank or altered cards. The report concluded with another appeal for party organizations to take the *proverka* seriously and to observe party discipline in its execution.

Like its forerunners, the *proverka* was failing because of poor "fulfill-

ment of decisions" on the local level. This time, the center had intervened and attacked poor administrators by name, expelling them in
severe cases. The May 13 letter had been an attempt to remedy a real
problem, but it fell victim to bureaucratic inertia.

The second verification of party documents: local meetings

The Smolensk archive contains a wealth of information on the conduct
of the second *proverka* in 1935. The meticulous documentation of this
operation by local authorities was a measure of their apprehension in
the face of the Central Committee rebuke of June 27. This time, Smolensk party leaders were anxious to prove their "serious attention."

Reactions to the June 27 Central Committee rebuke in Smolensk
were immediate.[32] On June 29, a meeting of the entire regional and
city party *aktiv* considered the matter. This meeting was followed by an
extraordinary plenum of the regional committee on or around July 1.
Similarly, lower party committees held *proverka* discussion meetings
around the region between July 5 and 11 to consider the Central Committee decision.[33] This round of meetings in July demonstrates not only
the nature of purges in 1935, but also the conflict inherent between and
among the various strata of the provincial party apparatus.

The party leadership of the Western Region had good reason to be
apprehensive. The Moscow Secretariat had publicly censured them
and ordered a series of meetings to bring the *proverka* under public scrutiny. In doing so, Moscow encouraged *kritika/samokritika* (criticism and
self-criticism of and by leaders) with the regional and district secretaries
as the targets. The danger for Smolensk leaders was that the rank and
file would widen the purge beyond desirable limits and use the opportunity to denounce the regional leadership. Accordingly, local bosses
took steps to limit the scope of the purge while protecting their own
cadres.

In the first place, the regional leadership directed subordinate party
organizations *not* to turn the second *proverka* into a witchhunt. The
Smolensk City Party Committee warned that

The City Committee and the party activists must conduct themselves according to the instructions of the Regional Committee, "That *secretaries of the raion
committees and leaders of party organizations must not transform the work of verifying party*

documents into a campaign of unmasking, but rather must ensure, by conducting the
necessary organizational measures and by improving methods of party work, a
constant increase of party awareness, a raising of integrity in the struggle to
strengthen the ranks of party organizations, sweeping them of all alien and corrupt elements [and] opposing the formal-bureaucratic attitude toward fulfilling
the directive of the Central Committee.''[34]

Local party committees were enjoined against wholesale denunciations
and were advised to stress the party-work aspect of the operation.

At the meetings themselves, several topics were discussed in connection with the *proverka*. Although not actually violating the injunction
against turning the *proverka* into a "campaign of unmasking," a small
part of each meeting was unavoidably given over to personal accusations and denunciations. Such accusations often included having kulak
or merchant-family connections, hiding one's social origins or previous
misdeeds, or having at some time opposed party policy. Persons were
accused of having been Trotskyists, Tsarist policemen, or kulaks.

Most of these accusations, of *fakti,* concerned social origins. Usually,
it was the kulak, trader, religious, or White Army status of one's parents that provided the subject for criticism, although others were denounced for losing their party cards, violating party discipline in some
way, drunkenness, or anti-Semitism in the course of the meetings.
Thus at one meeting P. C. Gershkovich was denounced for hiding the
fact that his parents, as kulaks, had been deprived of electoral rights; I.
N. Kazakov was attacked for being passive in his party attitude and
"refusing to work on himself." M. V. Evstafev was criticized for losing
his party card in 1933 and not paying his dues since.[35] Rumors, suspi-
cions, and grudges no doubt played a large part in the meetings, and
denunciations were made without any supporting evidence. Members
who were simply unpopular received more than their share of barbs.

Communists were encouraged to bring up any suspicious information on members with whom they had contact, and such rank-and-file
participation in the *proverka* resulted in statements of many kinds. All
these, without apparent exception, were taken down on paper (or included as part of the protocol of the meeting) and investigated. In the
meetings of the Smolensk City Committee in July, 616 *fakti* arose from
the membership. Table 3.1 shows the targets of the denunciations.
More than a third of the denunciations were for connections with kulak
or nepman elements, and another third were for various kinds of personal, financial, or moral misconduct. The number of actual political
oppositionists uncovered was very small. But at least one in six of the

Table 3.1. *Targets of* proverka *denunciations, city of Smolensk, July 1935*

Kulaks, traders, families	226
Degenerates, drunks, womanizers, violators of discipline	143
Official malfeasance, theft, embezzlement	106
Lost or dubious party card	62
Trotskyists, Mensheviks, etc.	28
White Army officers, Tsarist police	41
Anti-Semites	10
Total	616

Source: Smolensk Archive file WKP 384, pp. 71–73.

denunciations (and possibly many more) was directed against official crimes or leading cadres. These general ratios would be confirmed in the final reports on the *proverka*.

Anxious to appear hardworking and fearful of *fakti* that might implicate their own cadres, local leaders investigated each *fakt* personally. The records of such meetings show that each statement was assigned to a party secretary (*raion buro* member) through marginal notation. Then, the protocol was cut into strips – each strip contained one *fakt* plus the name of the responsible official who would investigate its validity. Later, after investigation, the protocols were reassembled for the files.[36]

Each statement was checked and categorized as "supported" or "unsupported." Investigation often took the form of inquiry about the member in his local organization. Because a number of the *fakti* concerned persons no longer living in the Western Region, many of these inquiries had to be conducted by mail.[37] The reply was either a short *kharakteristika* (character reference) or a note informing Smolensk that they had never heard of the member in question.[38] Of the 616 *fakti* on Smolensk members mentioned above in the city committee, 108 were given in the meetings of party organizations in other regions.[39]

The disposition of these denunciations suggests the motivation and atmosphere of the campaign. Preliminary investigation of the *fakti* in the city committee during the summer of 1935 showed that about four-fifths of them were supported and one-fifth unsupported. Later results in the city committee and in a number of other *raions* around the Western Region were close to this ratio.[40] But even a supported denunciation did not usually lead to punishment.

Detailed information on the results of the investigations of *fakti* in the

Table 3.2. *Results of* proverka *denunciations, city of Smolensk, summer 1935*

Of 712 statements:	492 were checked by the end of summer
	166 were sent to other regions
Of 492 checked:	323 were supported
	98 were unsupported
Of 323 supported:	134 were expelled from the party
	48 received reprimands
	41 were removed from their jobs
	100 received warnings

Source: Smolensk Archive file WKP 384, p. 188.

city party organization shows that there were 712 specific statements on various persons. Table 3.2 shows this disposition. Thus, as a result of the investigation of these 712 denunciations, 134 were expelled, or fewer than 18 percent of those accused. Accusations usually did not lead to expulsion. In fact, of all those criticized at the meetings, fewer than a third (223 of 712) eventually received any kind of disciplinary measure.

Examples of the "supported" *fakti*, especially those leading to expulsion, suggest that these proceedings were less arbitrary than one might have thought. Of the 323 supported statements, 71 were disregarded because they were already matters of record or because the member in question had never attempted to hide the fact. According to these statements, mere kulak origins or former membership in another political party were not sufficient grounds for expulsion. Being the son of a kulak or priest may have been a serious matter to some rank-and-file activists, but it did not result in immediate condemnation by the secretaries. However, if the person committed other infractions, such as losing his/her party documents or disciplinary offenses, expulsion usually followed. The only expulsion in which familial or personal connections to "alien elements" was the sole charge involved the member having "hidden this from the party upon entering it."[41]

Again, around one-fifth of the statements were found to be groundless and were ignored. Examples of these included accusations of "suspicious behavior" or unproved charges that factory directors secretly owned land.[42] Accusations of unseemly behavior or alien connections in other localities were dropped when the relevant party committee provided no substantiation or denied knowledge of the member.

The intent of this campaign was to take the *proverka* out of the closed offices of the secretaries and make it a general "party task" for the mass membership. This was an implicit recognition that the local leadership had been so lax in its "party work" that it was unable meaningfully to screen members it did not even know. Only the rank and file could do this, so the verification of party documents and party membership was undertaken "from below." Despite these rebukes and maneuvers, the local secretaries were still in charge of the verification.

Accusations occupied only a part of the meetings of local party organizations after the June 27 Central Committee reprimand. There were at least four other areas of discussion having to do with defective party work: the "formalistic-bureaucratic" handling of the *proverka*, the consequent need for heightened mass participation and criticism of the local leaders, and the weak connection between party leaders and members. The final summaries and reports on the *proverka* in the local organizations would mention these themes first, paying only lip service to the denunciation of enemies and aliens uncovered in the *proverka*.[43]

The meeting in the Smolensk Institute of Marxism-Leninism on July 29, 1935, took a position sharply critical of the leadership.[44] After a denunciation of Secretary Shil'man and ORPO chief Kiselev, the meeting noted that the party's records could be put in order only through the active participation of each member of the party. "Conducting this work of improving the whole system of party work is unthinkable without the broad development of criticism and self-criticism, which in our organizations has been insufficient."

The bureaucratic way in which the *proverka* had been conducted (by Shil'man, Kiselev, and others) was the subject of most of the speakers at the July meetings. Comrade Levenson, of the *Metis* factory, complained that the regional committee conducted the *proverka* "without any care or attention," and one Prushinin, of Bread Factory Number 1, said that Shil'man and Kiselev acted only "mechanically."[45] Speakers at the party meeting in Factory Number 35 made many of the same points, adding in their resolution that the regional and city committees in Smolensk had "perverted the political essence of the *proverka*, conducting this affair only as technical work like *chinovniki*, bureaucratizing [*sic*] the Central Committee decision of May 13 on party management."[46]

Some speakers were merely repeating and paraphrasing the criticisms coming from the Central Committee. However, the tone of many of them reflected real frustration with party affairs. For example, Comrade Fedorova, of the streetcar works, said that when she learned of the *proverka*, she "thought much about what would be asked and how I would answer. But when it happened, they did not even ask me the number of my party card." Also complaining about the local style of leadership in the *proverka*, Comrade Donskoi from the Red State Farm said that "the *proverka* in the City Committee proceeded badly, as many communists had to spend the whole day waiting in the corridors."[47] According to speakers in many organizations, Shil'man, Kiselev, and the entire leadership had committed "fundamental political mistakes" in their handling of the *proverka*. Arkhipov and Rappoport of the city party leadership, although not officially mentioned in the Central Committee rebuke, were also criticized by the speakers.[48]

A call for increased criticism of party organizations was related to the bureaucratic conduct of the *proverka* and meant that party members were to criticize the work of their leaders and check on the "fulfillment of decisions" from below.[49] There was always a tendency to resist *kritika/samokritika*, especially on the part of party leaders who were usually the targets of it, because of the belief that criticism of leaders weakened the prestige of the party. On the other hand, Stalin claimed that lack of criticism was the fatal mistake as it tended to "ruin cadres" by not pointing out their mistakes.[50] Suppression of criticism by leaders was a serious offense, as later events would show.

Speakers frequently bemoaned the suppression of *kritika/samokritika*. Comrade Livin said that, in his organization (*Smolgort*), "We have no self-criticism, which does not mean we do not have any deficiencies," but because criticism is not encouraged "a whole series of communists talked about these deficiencies after [the meetings] to non-party people." Comrade Panchenko, complaining about the self-glorifying speakers at party meetings, said, "The speakers were weak from the point of view of self-criticism of their own work."[51]

The events in Factory Number 35 in the city of Smolensk during the *proverka* are particularly instructive because they show the interplay between various levels in the party. The factory party committee held the required meeting on July 7, 1935. Comrade Zhil'tsov from the city committee gave a report on the Central Committee censure of June 27, after which seven persons spoke. The *uchet*, formal-bureaucratic, *kritika/samokritika,* and party-work themes were more or less mechanically repeated by the speakers. Zhil'tsov had apparently hoped that the meeting would sharply criticize the factory party leadership because, in his concluding words, he complained that there had been very little real criticism at the meeting: "Party meetings for us should not be difficult. They should be school-forums, where we can speak openly. You, here, with respect to party meetings, have not developed self-criticism." At the end of the meeting, a unanimous resolution supporting the Central Committee was routinely taken.[52]

On July 11, Zhil'tsov reported back to the secretariat of the city committee on the meeting at Factory Number 35. On the basis of his report, the city committee resolved

to note that the party committee and aktiv of Factory No. 35 did not sufficiently prepare and conduct its party meeting, with the result that at the meeting self-criticism was not developed and the meeting proceeded at a low level. The mistakes committed by the regional and city party leadership in the conduct of the *proverka* did not receive sharp discussion in the party organizations of Factory No. 35 even after the Central Committee order on this question. The members of the party organizations of Factory No. 35, and first of all the party activists, can not allow the continuation of familyness in the factory and [must] develop Bolshevik self-criticism.[53]

The city committee then ordered Factory Number 35 to hold a new meeting on the same questions. Rappoport, a secretary of the city committee, was to attend, and an instructor from the city (Gavrikov) was to help organize and prepare the meeting. Rappoport was thus given the unenviable task of stirring up criticism of his own (city) party organization at the factory cell meeting.[54]

This second meeting in the factory took place on July 14–15. The space for "those present" showed ninety-seven members in attendance. (The space had been blank for the first meeting.) A special notation stressed that the meeting lasted ten and a half hours. Rappoport and Vasilevskaia (deputy head of the city cadres department) represented the city party.[55]

Rappoport's speech, which was not recorded, must have been a strong one because the long meeting, in the words of some present, raised self-criticism to "new heights." Previously, members had refrained from criticizing either the party leaders or themselves, adopting a "live and let live" attitude; this was "familyness." Leaders also hesitated to denounce (or sack) "their people." However, Rappoport apparently broke the ice because the speakers criticized their leaders and one another at great length. The summary protocol of the meeting, in contrast to its one-page predecessor, covered fifteen closely typed pages and ranged over many areas.

Members were criticized by their fellows for losing their party cards, not attending party meetings, being drunk too frequently, or not fulfilling their work norms. Others were criticized for recommending persons for membership who had subsequently been expelled for some crime or hiding their past. Some of these criticisms and charges were clearly false. The factory director, Ianishevskii, was accused of having served with Kolchak in the White Army. As far as is known, no actions were taken on these statements. (Ianishevskii was subsequently removed, in November, but for incompetence.)[56] At this stage, party masses were encouraged to criticize the leadership but not to overthrow it.

Several speakers decried familyness, which was the "opposite of self-criticism." Comrade Kuz'mina said, "I have not worked here a long time, but the familyness is evident. I live in factory housing and I often hear from the workers that things are bad in the factory." Kuz'mina and other workers complained about incompetent workers who were kept on because nobody complained about anything. Making the point a little stronger, Comrade Cherniavskii said "I think that it is not familyness we are finding here, but the suppression of self-criticism." Comrade Kadolnik said that "I believe that party organizations can really work on people. Ianishevskii does not like self-criticism. Today, we increased self-criticism and I think that the old situation will no longer exist."[57]

Rappoport and Vasilevskaia from the city committee had apparently expected and wanted more at Factory Number 35. Vasilevskaia noted the good general level of participation, but wondered why there was not more criticism of regional and city committee leaders for their conduct of the *proverka*. After that, a few speakers took a more antileadership line in their remarks. The meeting, however, did not satisfy Rappoport. He wanted more criticism of the factory party committee, and in his closing words remarked that "the activists did not show examples of self-criticism."[58]

In fact, during that meeting, there had been opposition voiced to Rappoport's particular line. Comrade Monchinskii, a member of the factory party leadership, attacked Rappoport, Vasilevskaia, and Zhil'tsov (all from the city committee) by name, saying that they had given "no clear direction" in their reports or actions. They said, Monchinskii went on, that things were bad in the factory party organization in general. "That is only because Rappoport put the question thusly: that we did not know the situation in the factory." Such a charge seemed to Monchinskii a little too much like the pot calling the kettle black, and he retorted by attacking the city committee. "The City Committee has become a parasitical organization. Party members, through the leadership of the factory organization, go to the City Committee, but where is the City Committee? Gavrikov has not been seen in the factory, in spite of the fact that he was sent here to organize this meeting."[59]

In his final remarks, Rappoport replied to the attack by accusing Monchinskii of an "incorrect understanding of self-criticism" and an "un-Bolshevik" attitude "by implying that the work of the Factory Number 35 party organization was no worse than most."[60] The resolution proceeding from the factory meeting was typical of the period in that it condemned both the city and the factory party leadership for poor performance in the *proverka* and in party work generally.

The events in Factory Number 35 provide a glimpse into the relations between various levels in the party. The Central Committee had attacked regional and local party leaders for bureaucratism, and the rank and file had gradually joined in. Beset from above and below, the regional and local party staffs then tried to blame each other. The city committee had been obliged to go to the factory and force criticism of themselves as well as of the factory party members and leaders. The factory party committee then counterattacked the city committee for hypocritically demanding action but then disappearing and providing no help. What is interesting here is not so much the often ambiguous targets of *kritika/samokritika* but the alignment of forces and attitudes. The combination of the center and the party masses against the middle leadership *apparat* would appear again.

It is difficult to ascertain exactly how aroused the party masses were in Factory Number 35 or elsewhere. Of course, many of the speakers at these meetings simply repeated appropriate slogans in the words of the party press. But there was also real criticism of leaders by name and to their face, as well as denunciations of particular local conditions. Members were getting things off their chests. What is far more tangible and certain is that the Central Committee wanted to encourage criticism "from below." It was party policy to criticize bureaucratic abuse and sloth, yet this practice had never been advocated as strongly and relentlessly as in 1935. The Central Committee had never before stopped a party operation and denounced the local administrators before the rank and file. The Central Committee had never seemed to turn to the party activists to complete an operation that had been bungled by the regular administrators.

This discussion suggests yet another issue (along with *uchet*, denunciation of aliens, formal-bureaucratic conduct, and *kritika/samokritika*) of

the July 1935 party meetings. This was the oft-mentioned weak connection between party leaders and members. Monchinskii and Rappoport had attacked each other for not knowing what was going on at
lower levels of the *apparat*. Similarly, a number of party members complained in July 1935 that their party leaders did not know who they
were.[61]

The problem was especially serious in rural party organizations. On
July 5, 1935, a meeting of secretaries of rural party organizations was
held in Smolensk. Chaired by Vasilevskaia, the meeting concentrated
on connections between higher and lower organs. Comrade Bubnov,
from the *Kozinskii Kolkhoz*, complained that the city committee only
sent "second-rate people" to help in the country, and they, "[went]
over everything lightly." "Vasilevskaia, Rappoport, and Arkhipov
never happen to be here." Noting that nobody from the city ever
helped with party work or provided necessary materials for political education, Comrade Kazakov said that the leaders of the culture and
propaganda efforts "are always in the city. They have forgotten the
country." At another meeting, Comrade Bel'ianikov said, "The City
Committee meets jointly with the city party *aktiv*. The rural party activists do not approve of these meetings, and it is impossible for us to
attend them."[62]

The problem also existed in urban and factory organizations. One
factory committee, in a resolution on the *proverka*, said that "further
verification of party documents showed that we still badly know the
various communists in our party organization." Leaders' ignorance of
the identities of the communists under them was denounced in the
meetings of the city party committee itself. There, Comrade Lobov
said that "I have been a party organizer for more than a year and have
only seen my City Committee secretary (Comrade Khavkin) once. After that, he does not know me." Comrade Gridin, who worked nine
months as an instructor for the city committee, had "not once been
called into the City Committee–I do not know them and they do not
know me." Comrade Likhachev denounced the city party leadership
for being "separated from the masses" and bureaucratized. "I tried to
see Rappoport for two days and could not. It is easier to see Kalinin!"
(president of the USSR). Other communists complained about not being able to participate in the city committee–*aktiv* joint meetings, or
generally being ignored by the city party leadership. In fact, one of the
workers on the newspaper *Rabochii Put'* said, "We do not know the plan
of work of the City Committee" and complained that "Arkhipov has
never been here."[63]

In the instructions of the Central Committee and in the speeches in Smolensk in July 1935, the question of participation had arisen. The Central Committee, in rebuking the Western Region, had thrown the *proverka* out into the open and demanded the participation of each communist in the verification. Virtually all organizational meetings of the period put forward increased party mass participation, along with *kritika/samokritika*, as weapons against bureaucratism.[64] The *proverka* and related party meetings continued through July and August 1935. Meetings were held every two weeks to discuss the progress of the *proverka*, and after the June 27 censure they were carefully recorded for the files.

On August 8, 1935, the Central Committee issued its second *svodka*, or summary, of the *proverka*, entitled "Second Summary of the Progress in Fulfilling the Closed Letter of the Central Committee VKP(b) of May 13, 1935."[65] Written to summarize the second month of *proverka* activity, it began by noting that, in July, the Central Committee had received 145 written reports from regional party leaders on the *proverka* and had summoned 18 second secretaries and 12 ORPO chiefs personally to account for their conduct, presumably including Shil'man and Kiselev from Smolensk.

The report said that the second month of the *proverka* had been better than the first, but deficiencies still remained. For violating the directives on the *proverka*, four *raion* secretaries had been expelled outright from the party, and eight others had been removed from work with official reprimand. In all, 190 *raions* were repeating the verification – some for the third time.

While the party-work side of the *proverka* seemed to be improving, the pace of the verification was actually slowing down. Whereas 33 percent of the party had been verified in the first month, only 24 percent were processed in the second, brining the total to 57 percent. At any rate, the Central Committee reminded party organizations that they must not consider themselves finished with the verification until their official report (*akt*) was confirmed by the Orgburo in Moscow.[66]

Nationally, in the second month of the verification, 6 percent of the cards checked were confiscated, 45,773 in all. Near or above this average were the problem areas: the Western Region (7.4 percent), Black Sea (11 percent), and Kursk (9 percent) organizations are examples.[67] The favorably regarded organizations, on the other hand, were all below the national mean: Moscow City (1.5 percent) and Region (3.5 percent), Leningrad City (1.6 percent), Donets (3.8 percent), and Georgia (2 percent).

The August report took up the question of "familyness." The report said that one of the problems associated with the second *proverka* was the fact that local communists would not speak out against one another so as not to rock the boat. The situation was improving, though, because of the increased level of popular participation. In fact, the Western Region was given as an example: Across the region, more than 3,000 communists had met in *raion* party meetings to discuss the June 27 censure.[68]

The report ended by noting that, before the *proverka*, many regional secretaries had not been able to give personal descriptions of the *raion* party secretaries working under them. Now, as a result of the *proverka*, this situation was said to be improving. Finally, the report noted that Moscow was actually beginning to learn the membership composition of local party organizations.[69]

The *proverka* finally draws to a close: the summary reports

The May 13, 1935, letter announcing the *proverka* had mentioned a term of two to three months for its completion. Yet, after two months, the verification was only half done and was only beginning in some places. The *proverka*, like all its forerunners, was lagging and dragging – in Smolensk, the verification was only 25 to 30 percent complete by the end of September, one month after the scheduled conclusion.[70]

Nationally, there seems to have been a serious attempt to finish the verification in October 1935. A series of articles and directives suggests that the second or third week in October was a target period. The Moscow Committee, frequently a pacesetter, promised on October 5 to finish in ten days. This was unconvincing, for they were only 58 percent finished on the fifth of the month. Their resolution noted that the *proverka* had been repeated in thirty-three primary party organizations in Moscow Region.[71] The Kursk organization also tried to finish by October 15, but the results were unsatisfactory, and a decision of the Central Committee dated October 19 ordered Kursk to start over again, repeat the *proverka*, and finish by December 15. The decision again denounced the "formalistic-bureaucratic" leadership of the *proverka* in Kursk and fired the local ORPO chief.[72]

The *proverka* was officially completed around October 20 in the Smolensk organizations. Final reports of various party committees show dates of October 18 and 20, November 2, and so forth.[73] For each party organization to consider itself finished with the verification, it had to have its *akt* confirmed by the next highest body. Thus, in the city of Smolensk, the members of the city committee *buro* divided the subordinate organizations among themselves, with each *buro* member visiting a number of organizations, hearing (or sometimes giving) summary reports on the *proverka*, and confirming the results.[74]

The "Summary of the *Proverka*" in Belyi Raion was typical.[75] Dated October 18, 1935, the report began with a short description of the local party organization. Belyi had been a center of kulak resistance and banditry until recently, so party work was "difficult" in some areas. The political level of the 303 party members and candidates in the *raion* was nonetheless "good."

Before the *proverka*, according to Kovalev (first secretary in Belyi Raion and author of the report),[76] the party accounting procedures had been "unsatisfactory." Chronic problems of blank party cards and poor registration had apparently plagued Belyi. However, according to the report, the *proverka* had led to a better system of *uchet* through such new measures as locking blank membership cards in a box, locking the box in a desk, and keeping membership records in one book. Many of the other *raion* and city-party reports began with a discussion of *uchet* and the measures taken to safeguard party records.[77]

The summary reports on the *proverka* written in the fall of 1935 provide the only clues both to the intent of the central party leaders and to the reception of those intentions locally. The similarities among the various reports suggest that the Central Committee may have requested information on party-work subjects in the local reports.[78] On that level, the reports show the specific aspects of the *proverka* that interested the Central Committee and were an attempt to measure the success of the operation in solving its target problem (*uchet*). Although the *proverka* began as an operation to rectify the horrible accounting in the party's files and records, it became an exercise in exposing and correcting bureaucratism and deficiencies in party work, with the party *aktiv* criticizing the local party leaders. This experience was summarized in an article by A. L. Shil'man, second secretary of the Western Region and the explicit target of the Central Committee's criticism:

The development of Bolshevik self-criticism met with opposition in a whole series of party organizations in the Region. This required that the Central Committee clarify to all party organizations that "the second *proverka* is introduced as a consequence of the unsatisfactory leadership of the *Obkom* and the formal-bureaucratic attitude toward the *proverka* on the part of the *raikom* secretaries."[79]

The speed and incidence of the *proverka*

Shil'man's article in November 1935 marked the completion of the *proverka*. Nationally, though, the operation continued until the end of the year. When Ezhov gave his "final" report on the *proverka* to the Central Committee at the end of December, only 81 percent of the party had passed through the verification.[80] The *proverka* lasted for six, rather than the projected two to three, months.

By August, Smolensk had processed only 16 percent of its membership, and, by September, only 30 percent (the corresponding national figures were 58 percent and 60 percent). Progress in Smolensk was so slow because of the necessity to repeat the verification, and very little progress was made until the early fall. By October, Smolensk had jumped to 98 percent and, by the first of December, the operation was finished in the Western Region.[81] The national completion figure was only 81 percent as late as December, suggesting that in more than twice the time allotted for the verification, the party could only finish four-fifths of it. Thus, from an administrative point of view, the *proverka* was hardly a model of brisk and efficient management.

There is only fragmentary information on the numbers and characteristics of those expelled during the *proverka*. No final national figures were ever published. Available data are presented in Table 3.3.

As shown in this table, the national average attrition from the *proverka* was around 9 percent, with problem areas coming in around 11 percent or slightly higher. Expulsion rates in non-Russian areas seem to have been higher. In those cases for which separate figures were given, the rate for candidates was higher than that for members. In the Western Region, 10.1 percent of the members were expelled, and 13.1 percent of the candidates; among transport workers, the figures were 16 and 24 percent; respectively. Partial national figures show the candidate-expulsion rate to be about twice that for members.[82]

Table 3.4 shows the incidence of the *proverka* in comparison with earlier purge operations. If the *proverka* were to be placed in the context of party purges after 1917, it would rank as one of the mildest, even with the addition of figures resulting from its sister operation, the 1936 Exchange of Party Documents (discussed later in this chapter).

The reasons for which persons were expelled varied widely and were never published nationally. The Smolensk Archive does, however, contain fragmentary breakdowns on these criteria. For example, in the

Table 3.3. *Numbers expelled in* proverka, *1935 (members and candidates)*

		Expelled	
	Checked	No.	%
Smolensk			
Entire Western Region	33,944	3,693	10.8
City of Smolensk	4,100	455	11.9
Belyi Raion	303	36	11.2
Factory No. 35	93	9	9.7
Other organizations			
Transport	192,000	35,000	18.0
Novosibirsk	—	—	14.7
Crimea	—	—	13.6
Moscow	—	—	12.1
Azerbaidzhan	—	—	22.0
Ivanov Region	—	—	11.6
Astrakhan	—	—	21.0
National	—	1,800,000	170,000	9.1

Sources: A. Shil'man, "Tekushchie voprosy partiinoi raboty" [Current questions of party work], *Partiinoe stroitel'stvo* [Party construction], no. 19–20, Nov. 1935, 49; Smolensk Archive file WKP 385, p. 155; Smolensk Archive file WKP 89, p. 148; *Moskovskaia oblast'naia organizatsii KPSS v tsifrakh [The Moscow regional organization of the KPSS in figures]*, Moscow, 1972, 28–29; S.S. Deev et al., *Ocherki istorii Ivanovskoi organizatsii KPSS, 1917–1967 [Essays on the history of the Ivanov organization of the KPSS, 1917–1967]*, part 2, Iaroslavl', 1967, 253; A. V. Sokolov et al., *Ocherki Istorii Astrakhanskoi Partiinoi Organizatsii [Essays on the history of the Astrakhan party organization]*, Volgograd, 1971, 365; *Pravda*, Dec. 26, 1935.

Smolensk City Party Committee, 455 of 4,100 members were expelled. Table 3.5 gives the reasons for expulsion.

The vast majority of offenses were nonideological. Lying to the party, having false membership documents, or personal corruption accounted for an overwhelming number of the expulsions. A few well-publicized expulsions were for oppositional activity or espionage. For example, the Smolensk Gorraikom report described one Karl Petrovich Knage who had deserted from the Red Army in the twenties and fled to Latvia. There, he became a gendarme and then headed a punitive detachment that arrested Latvian communists. He illegally entered the USSR and was allegedly still in the service of the Latvian

Table 3.4. *Incidence of purges, 1921–35: expulsion rates (in percent)*

Operation	National	Smolensk
1921 party purge	25	30
1929 party purge	11	13
1933 *chistka*	18.5	2
1935 *proverka*	9	11

Sources: T. H. Rigby, *Communist Party Membership in the USSR, 1917–1967,* Princeton, N.J., 1968, 97, 178; Merle Fainsod, *Smolensk Under Soviet Rule,* Cambridge, Mass., 1958, 44, 216, 222; Smolensk Archive file WKP 384, p. 231; P. N. Pospelov et al., *Istoriia Kommunisticheskoi Partii Sovetskogo Soiuza* [History of the Communist Party of the Soviet Union], Moscow, 1971, vol. 4, part 2, 283; A. Shil'man, "Tekushchie voprosy partiinoi raboty" [Current questions of party work], *Partiinoe stroitel'stvo* [Party construction], nos. 19–20, Nov. 1935, 49; *Pravda,* Dec. 26, 1935; N. R. Andrukhov, *Partiinoe stroitel'stvo v period bor'by za pobedu sotsializma v SSSR* [Party construction in the period of struggle for the victory of socialism in the USSR], Moscow, 1977, 131.

government. Ian Ianovich Diman was the rector of the local Higher Communist Agricultural School and was also expelled in the *proverka*. The charge against him was Trotskyism: He had been giving Trotsky credit for "Socialism in One Country" in his lectures. Examples of such "political offenses" were collected and specially noted in the reports from the localities to the center.[83] The Central Committee apparently wanted such "case material" for publicity purposes. Sketches like those of Knage and Diman were collected by the Central Committee, published, and circulated to party organizations as "supplements" to the monthly Central Committee reports on the *proverka*.[84] However, the vast majority of targets were the usual *razlozhenie* (corruption) and *prostupki* (infraction) offenses.

Belyi Raikom kept a list of the members expelled in the *raion* with detailed reasons for each. Twenty-four members were expelled in Belyi, and each was charged with several offenses. Eight were charged with chronic drunkenness, and seven were charged with stealing, embezzling, or other criminal activity. Nearly all the expellees were charged with violations of discipline. Thus Ivan Borovchenkov, a party member since May of 1932 and the president of his kolkhoz, was expelled for "poor leadership. . .drunkenness and hooliganism." Nikita Petrov, the 41-year-old president of a rural cooperative, was accused of stealing 900 rubles, drunkenness, and a "frivolous attitude toward work." Timofei Vinogradov, director of a school, had "served in Kolchak's

Table 3.5. *Reasons for expulsion in* proverka, *Smolensk City Party Committee, 1935*

Reason	No.	%
Alien elements: White Guards, spies, Trotskyists, etc.	39	8
Class-alien elements who hid their origins from the party	99	22
Altered, forged, stolen party cards; those evading earlier purges	60	14
Criminals, deserters, corrupted	97	21
Untrustworthy, betrayers of party interests	127	28
Drifted away from party: nonpayment of dues, etc.	33	7
Totals	455	100

Source: Smolensk Archive file WKP 384, p. 144.

White Army, was passive in the party, and looked lightly on rules violations."[85]

A careful perusal of these cases suggests that these expulsions were not made for a single isolated offense. It was not enough that Vinogradov had served with Kolchak – but his passivity and poor attitude resulted in expulsion. In Factory Number 35, P. M. Sokolov was expelled for drunkenness, passivity, lack of interest in party affairs, refusing to work on himself, and not fulfilling his work norms. I. N. Kazakov was sacked for refusing to pay his party dues "regardless of the repeated reminders of the party organization and of the party secretary."[86] A careful inspection of these files turned up no case of expulsion for simple familial or personal connection to an enemy or oppositionist.[87]

Clearly, most of those expelled in the *proverka* were "ballast," to use Secretary Shil'man's word.[88] They were similar to the group targeted in the *chistka* of 1933; most of them had joined the party recently. Of the 455 expelled from the Smolensk City Committee, 235 had joined the party in 1929–32. In Belyi, this group accounted for 13 of 24 expellees. More than half those expelled were recruits to the party in the whirlwind years of the First Plan and collectivization.[89]

The social composition of those expelled is not known, but most of the expulsions seem to have been workers or peasants. Table 3.6 gives

Table 3.6. *Smolensk City Party Organization social composition, 1934 – October 1935*

	1934		1935	
	No.	%	No.	%
Workers	3,921	71	3,227	67
Peasants	820	15	891	18
Employees	753	14	735	15
Total	5,499[a]	100	4,853	100

[a]*Discrepancy in original.*
Souce: Smolensk Archive file WKP 384, p. 231.

the social composition of the Smolensk City Party Organization before and after the *proverka*.

It seems that despite the best efforts of the Smolensk secretaries, a number of leading cadres were expelled. Shil'man gave a partial breakdown of those expelled in the *proverka*.[90] Of 1,068 persons described, 485 of them, or nearly *half*, had been involved in what Shil'man called "leading work" in industry, or *kolkhozes,* in the courts and in the soviets. This number included 59 factory or *sovkhoz* directors, 157 *kolkhoz* leaders (mostly *kolkhoz* presidents), and 92 officials in rural soviets. The remainder of the 1,068 described had "worked in various organizations and institutions," were technical or engineering specialists, or were educational employees. Shil'man could not or would not account for 442 expellees. Presumably, they were workers from the bench or *kolkhozniki.* Shil'man was anxious to demonstrate that he and the other Smolensk leaders were not simply deflecting the purge onto the rank and file, despite the fact that only 38 of Shil'man's sample of 1,068 had worked in the party apparatus. Shil'man was trying to show that the leaders were in fact cracking down on responsible bureaucrats, although the few hundred expelled "responsible officials" about whom Shil'man bragged were an insignificant fraction of the tens of thousands of *kolkhoz* and enterprise officials.

Some rather important local party officials were expelled: the head of the Higher Communist Agricultural School (the dubious ideologist Diman), the chief of the ORPO for the Smolensk NKVD, the head of the Western Region Social Security Administration, the director of the city post office, and the chief of a local labor colony.[91] Records in Belyi Raion show that there, one *raikom* instructor, two NKVD workers, two school directors, and three leading workers in *"raion* and soviet work" were among the twenty-three members expelled. Of the thirteen candidate members expelled in the *raion,* there were four *kolkhoz* presidents, three presidents of rural cooperatives, and one president of a rural soviet.[92]

Shil'man's final report on the *proverka* said that two more *raikom* first secretaries had been expelled – one for hiding his former participation in a bandit group and the other for personal corruption. Several more *raikom* first secretaries were removed from their posts for failing to organize the newly demanded party work, and thus "not being able to reorient themselves to these new, higher demands."[93]

So although leading party workers were not the first victims of the *proverka,* they began to fall as the operation increasingly emphasized failures in party work. In the Smolensk City Committee, thirty-seven party secretaries of organizations such as trade unions, farms, and so forth were replaced. Twenty of them were removed from their positions for "not providing leadership," while the rest were transferred to other work.[94] In the city of Kalinin (in Tver' Region), 64 percent of all party secretaries were "renewed" in the *proverka.*[95] It is important to note that these leaders were expelled in most cases for bungling and bureaucratism, not for oppositional activity.

Although the Great Purges are often associated with the decimation of the "Old Bolsheviks," the opposite seems to have been the case in Smolensk in 1935. On the average, party secretaries who were demoted or removed from office had joined the party in 1928, whereas their replacements had joined on the average two years earlier, in 1926. The replacement secretaries were about 3.7 years older as well. Thus those "not providing leadership" were replaced by older and more experienced party workers. New secretaries in the city party organizations included slightly more workers by social origin (30 of 39 compared to the previous 26 of 39) and slightly fewer persons of peasant and employee social backgrounds.[96]

The "lessons" of the *proverka* of 1935

On December 25, 1935, N. I. Ezhov addressed the plenum of the Central Committee on "Results of the Verification of Party Documents."[97] He began by asserting that the *proverka* had proved that the Central Committee was correct in its surmise that many party organizations

were "completely arbitrary in issuing and guarding party documents."
According to Ezhov, the "major result" of the *proverka* (in addition to
the unmasking of alien persons in the party) had been that party organizations "have to a considerable extent overcome their organizational
laxity, have brought order into the registering of party members, have
made a better study of communists, and on this basis have promoted
many new and capable persons to leading...positions."

He went on to claim that it had been a "tremendous advantage"
that the "party organs themselves were directly involved in the verification and did not set up any special commissions." Ezhov was not
suggesting that the party leaders had done a good job in carrying out
the *proverka;* no one could say that. Many of these "leading members"
of the party *apparat* had been "unfit for party work – primarily those
who, despite frequent warnings by the VKP(b) Central Committee,
failed to understand the meaning and significance of the *proverka,* took
an opportunist attitude toward its implementation, and in many cases
directly opposed this most important measure." These had been expelled from the party.[98]

The "principal conclusion" of the experience of the *proverka* was that
party organizations "poorly understood the frequent directions of the
Central Committee on the need for a comprehensive raising of Bolshevik alertness and discipline among party members." The experience of
the *proverka,* according to Ezhov, showed that the Central Committee
had been right to warn against complacency regarding party rules on
admissions and registration *(uchet).* "Only the absence of Bolshevik alertness" (which resulted in complacency) could explain the chaos resulting from mass admissions, unconfirmed transfers from other
parties, lost blank cards, confiscated cards finding their way into the
hands of non-party people, and generally poor accounting. Enemies of
the party and various alien elements had been able to take advantage of
this, "exploiting primarily the opportunistic complacency and idleness
of communists."

Although the *proverka* had allowed party organizations to improve
their organizational work "to a considerable extent," Ezhov never said
that the operation had completely solved the *uchet* problem, as it was
supposed to. That the operation was still going on as he spoke was eloquent testimony to its lack of efficacy. Ezhov took this opportunity to
announce the beginning of yet another *uchet* operation: the exchange of
party documents to be concluded between February 1 and May 1,
1936. The exchange *(obmen)* of 1936 was to be conducted for two rea-

sons. First, the *proverka* had shown that the physical documents themselves were worn and needed replacement. Second, as future records would show, the *obmen* was to reconsider questionable cases of party membership (connected with passivity, low political education, etc.) arising from the *proverka*. Thus members censured (or even expelled) during the *proverka* could be reinstated after "working on themselves," or vice versa.

Not until the completion of the exchange operation were new members to be admitted to the party, and June 1, 1936, was given as a provisional date when admissions might commence. Clearly, the *proverka* had not solved the *uchet* problem. Ezhov was therefore certainly being euphemistic when he described the exchange as the "first step toward consolidating the positive results of the *proverka.*" The very existence of the 1936 exchange suggested that the *proverka* did not complete this work.

The 1936 Exchange of Party Documents

The 1936 Exchange of Party Documents *(obmen partdokumentov)* was a companion operation to the *proverka* of 1935, and the two are often mentioned together in party histories.[99] The exchange was a recognition that the *proverka* had not accomplished its purpose, for the goals of both were "to establish order [in party documents], to study communists, to safeguard party documents in order to exclude any possibility of corruption in party documents or in receiving them for deceptive purposes."[100]

Invoking the name of the Central Committee, the Instruktsiia warned that the exchange, like the hapless *proverka,* was a "serious organizational measure" and that *obkom* secretaries and local chiefs of the ORPO were again "personally responsible before the Central Committee *VKP(b)* for the conduct of this work." Only the *raion* first secretary was empowered to issue new party cards, although in especially large *raions* members of the *buro* were allowed to assist.[101]

Party leaders were apprehensive about the smooth and orderly conduct of the operation by local officials. The instructions for the conduct of the exchange were even more meticulous than for the *proverka*. The exchange was only to begin in an organization when its report on the *proverka* was approved by the Central Committee. The exchange could only take place in the *raion* party committee (that is, in the building itself) and could only be done by the *raion* secretary in the presence of the member and the secretary of the party cell in which the member worked or lived. The member was to fill out a registration form giving biographical and work-record information. The new party documents (party card and report card), if issued, must have the same number as the registration blank filled out by the member. If a mistake was made filling out the cards, the entire set was to be voided by writing "ruined in completion" on all three cards of the same number. The ruined set, with explanation, was to be forwarded to the ORPO for recording. Erasures and smudges counted as mistakes. The member was to sign all three new party documents in the presence of the secretary, who signed them, stamped them, gave the card to the member, kept the registration card in the *raikom,* and sent the report card with all old documents to the *obkom* for confirmation and registration on the party rolls. No deviation from the prescribed procedure was possible.[102]

The instructions paid special attention to the membership cards themselves. New cards were to be sent only to *oblast'* first secretaries by the NKVD courier service, which was also responsible for the transportation of old cards and records between the various committees. Party cards were only to be filled out in special ink distributed by the Central Committee. Moreover, local party organizations were to submit to the Central Committee specimens of the signatures of all whose signatures would appear on them. Each party card was to have affixed to it the photograph of the member – otherwise it was void. No member without a valid party card could receive a new one. These instructions, which embraced eighteen of twenty-three numbered paragraphs in the Instruktsiia, make it clear that the exchange was meant primarily as a bookkeeping measure.[103]

The emphasis in all these instructions was on sound accounting procedures and careful regulation of membership cards. The goal was for each member to have a clean, unerased, unaltered, and uniformly filled in party card that corresponded to an accurate record in the organization's files. The chaos in these matters must have been unbelievable to justify such detailed and careful instructions. Neither the letter nor the accompanying instructions made the exchange a matter of vigilance or of unmasking enemies or aliens – in fact, the opposite order was given.

Referring to the *proverka* (in which the "unmasking" or "denouncing" component was by no means the only aspect), the Central Committee said:

If, in the *proverka,* party organizations paid special attention to the uncovering of hidden penetrations of the party by enemies, rogues, and swindlers, then, in the exchange, they must turn their principal attention toward freeing themselves of passive party members not deserving the high title of member of the party; of the people who accidently find themselves in the *VKP(b)*.[104]

Thus, the exchange was to be primarily a matter of getting rid of passive, accidental, and chance elements who were members but who did not participate in party activities.

The exchange was to run from February through April 1936, and preparations were being reported in the press by the middle of January (about the time the Central Committee and the ORPO issued their instructions.)[105] Although the operation was scheduled to begin on February 1, 1936, the exchange did not begin until the first days of March.[106] In the Western Oblast', First Secretary Rumiantsev had promulgated the decision on the exchange as early as December 29, 1935. Preparations had begun in January, and the exchange itself began on March 7, 1936.[107]

Little information is available on the conduct of the exchange, although, like all previous *uchet* operations, it took much longer to complete than anticipated. On May 24, 1936, three weeks *after* the planned conclusion of the exchange, a special order of the Central Committee ("On the Progress of the Exchange of Party Documents") extended the term for the exchange to August 1.[108] Apparently that date passed by as well, because the first summaries of the exchange (sent from local party organizations and confirmed by the ORPO) did not appear until the middle of November.[109] New admissions to the party had been scheduled to begin on June 1, 1936, but the prolonged course of the exchange forced the Central Committee to postpone them again; this time until November 1936, when they actually began. Even then, the exchange was continuing in many places. Final summaries for many party organizations did not appear until January 1937, and there were pointed warnings at the end of 1936 that old-style party cards (1926 form) would not be valid after the beginning of the year.[110]

Although the exchange of party documents seemed interminable, its toll among the party membership is hard to determine. No national figures on the numbers expelled are available, but some scattered published figures suggest a low incidence. The report of the Smolensk City Party Organization shows that 4,348 new cards were given out to members and candidates. Ninety-seven persons were expelled; this was 2.3 percent of the members, 1.2 percent of the candidates, or 2.1 percent of the entire party organization.[111] In Belyi Raion, of 250 members, 2 members and 4 candidates were expelled – 2.4 percent of the party organization.[112] In Kirov Oblast', the figure was also around 2 percent, and in Uzbekistan it was 1.98 percent.[113] The exchange expelled relatively few persons – fewer, in fact, than in an average year of Control Commission activity in the 1920s.

It seems, however, that the vast majority of those expelled were rank-and-file members. Most of those expelled were workers by social position; 73 percent of those expelled by the city committee, and two-thirds in Belyi. More than half those expelled in the city had joined since 1926. All six of those expelled in Belyi had joined since 1927, and five of them had joined since 1931.[114]

The exchange of party documents in 1936 was not an intensification of the purge, or of anything except the efforts to rectify party norms.[115] It was merely the most recent in a series of operations designed to register and control the party.

Some conclusions on the verification and exchange

The verification and exchange of party documents were begun to rectify problems in the party arising from the 1929–33 period of economic revolution and to complete the work of the *chistka* of 1933. This revolution had demanded the concentration of the party on economic tasks to the neglect of traditional areas of party work: careful record keeping, selective admissions, and political training of cadres. The need for personnel had led to a situation in which non- (or anti-) communists held party cards and in which the party leaders, on all levels, did not even know who was working under them. "Alien elements" (including not only Trotskyists but also ex-kulaks, careerists, and thieves) had come to enjoy the benefits of party membership. "Vigilance'" consisted not only (or even mostly) in weeding out the aliens but also in rebuilding party organizational work and instilling normal, rational clerical procedures in a large organization. In this it failed.

The *proverka* foundered early on the rocks of bureaucratic inertia. It was relegated to a minor place by local authorities, entrusted to subordinates, and conducted behind closed doors. Such complacency resulted from a natural and universal reluctance to "rock the boat" and from the hesitation of local leaders to criticize "their people" or to encourage or allow self-criticism. Ordered in October 1934, the *proverka* was not defined until May 1935. Although it began in some places before May, it was not completed close to the specified time and had not even run its course by the end of the year. The exchange of party documents followed a similar course.

When the *proverka* began to fail, the Central Committee intervened publicly, opening up the verification process to party members in general. The bungling of a *uchet* operation caused its transformation into a matter of party political work. Political issues such as local bureaucratism, the weakness of criticism and self-criticism (familyness), the low level of political participation and education, and the weak connection between organizations (and leaders and members) came to the front as the central authorities encouraged grass-roots criticism of the party *apparat*.

The verification and exchange suggest that confusion, disorder, and inertia were the characteristics of a rather unresponsive political network. Rather than controlling events, the center was trying to respond to them and to improvise solutions. The *proverka* was the third of several variants employed to regulate the membership of the party (the other two being action by the Central Control Commission in 1929 and the special *chistka* commissions of 1933). The fundamental characteristic of party activity in this period was an inability to get things done at lower levels. Moscow was increasingly frustrated in attempts to impose its will on the local *apparat*. It seems that Stalin's political machine neither functioned nor obeyed very well.

What made the *proverka* new and different was the emphasis on fighting the bureaucratism of local leaders. The Central Committee had associated itself with party activists against the conduct of the middle party leaders. The *proverka* clearly shows the thinking of central party leaders and indicates both whom they blamed for the problems and on whom they relied for support.

4

Radicalism and party revival

Party practice must become thoroughly democratic.

Andrei Zhdanov, 1937

Party purges were only half the strategy outlined by party leaders at the Seventeenth Congress in 1934. Stalin and Kirov, along with other high-ranking party leaders, sought a restoration of the party apparatus through education, self-criticism, reorganization, and an attack on bureaucratism at various levels. Stalin had said that the struggle was now for "men's minds"; both he and Kirov claimed that the vast majority of the party's problems could be solved through political education. Because Kirov and his successor Zhdanov would both be identified with this "party revival" program, it is necessary to examine Kirov's assassination at the outset of the campaign.[1]

It is sometimes thought that Kirov was a "moderate" who opposed Stalin's generally hard line on various issues. According to much of the literature, Stalin killed Kirov to clear the way for his policy of terror. In fact, it seems more likely that Stalin and Kirov were allies and that Kirov's death was not the occasion for any change in policy. Indeed, although the Kirov assassination would be dredged up much later (in 1936) to justify an extension of police powers, it had little to do with the problems in the party apparatus at any time.[2]

S. M. Kirov has been identified with a plan of reforms designed to ease social and political conflict and to repudiate Stalin's "policy of general suspicion and universal terror." Boris Nicolaevsky, speaking as the "Old Bolshevik," was the origin of this speculation, believing that Kirov favored a reconciliation with former members of the various opposition groups as part of a general relaxation of police vigilance, or "terror." Kirov supposedly pressed for a "liberal" plan of economic reforms: the abolition of the unpopular *politotdels* in the Machine Tractor Stations, the abolition of the food-rationing system in the cities, and a new statute for collective farm workers called the "Bill of Rights of the Collective Farmer." The entire package of "Kirov Reforms" was to be capped by a new democratic constitution based on universal and equal suffrage and guaranteeing the full equality of all social groups and classes in the new society.[3]

According to Nicolaevsky, even though Stalin, Kaganovich, and their young protege Ezhov were opposed to this plan of reform, Kirov carried that day at the Seventeenth Congress. Stalin supposedly met the challenge of Kirov and his adherents by organizing the assassination of the younger man, thus dealing fatal blows to both a line of policy and a personal rival.[4] Stalin also is said to have used Kirov's assassination as a pretext for the next phase of the "Great Purge" in which he annihilated members of the Old Bolshevik opposition for their alleged complicity in the killing of the popular leader.[5]

The Nicolaevsky scenario suffers from serious flaws. In the first place, virtually no evidence suggests that Kirov favored or advocated any specific policy line other than Stalin's General Line. One scholar has recently concluded that "the problem exists of establishing to what extent the rise of Kirov and the new direction of Soviet policy were connected. As we have seen, they are often so interwoven that it is difficult to single out a line put forward by Kirov which is distinguishable from the official one."[6] The rumor that Kirov favored lenient treatment for dissidents, for example, is offset by opposite contemporary speculations. Trotsky, writing three years after the assassination, called Kirov "a clever and unscrupulous Leningrad dictator, a typical representative of his corporation," and maintained that terrorist acts like the killing of Kirov by "despairing individuals" of the "younger generation" "have a very high significance." Grigorii Tokaev, who was on the receiving end of Kirov's policies toward the opposition, said that Kirov "ruthlessly stamped out" the opposition at this time and was the "first executioner." A contemporary article in Nicolaevsky's *Sotsialisticheskii vestnik* [Socialist herald] labeled Kirov a hard-liner.[7] If Kirov was soft on the oppositionists, the opposition certainly did not know it.

Certainly Kirov's public speeches do not reflect a moderate attitude toward members of the opposition. In his speech to the Seventeenth Congress, he ridiculed members of the opposition, questioning their "humanity" and the sincerity of their recantations. He sharply denounced Trotsky's "counterrevolutionary chatter" and applauded the services of the secret police, including their use of forced labor on canal construction projects. It was upon Kirov's motion that Stalin's speech was taken as the basis for the congress's resolution.[8]

If one leaves rumor and gossip aside, one finds numerous signs that Stalin favored what the Old Bolshevik would have called liberal policies. Indeed, as one scholar has recently shown, Stalin had identified himself with more relaxed social and educational policies as early as 1931. Stalin made conciliatory gestures to the "bourgeois specialists" and relaxed educational restrictions that had excluded sons and daughters of white-collar specialists.[9] In May 1933, Stalin and Molotov ordered the release of half of all labor camp inmates whose infractions were connected with collectivization.[10] The following summer, the political police (NKVD) were forbidden to pass death sentences without the sanction of the procurator of the USSR.[11] The November 1934 plenum of the Central Committee abolished food rationing and approved new collective farm rules that guaranteed *kolkhozniki* the right to "private plots" and personal livestock.[12] The resulting new Kolkhoz Statute represented a considerable concession and retreat from the repressive norms of 1929–32.

The end of the violent class struggle in the countryside, the time for rallying supporters (the winning over of "men's minds" in Stalin's Seventeenth Congress speech), political education, and a fight against bureaucratism had been parts of Stalin's analysis of the situation and are not attributable solely to Kirov. A "policy of relaxation" was also perceived on the literary scene. At the Soviet Writers' Congress in August 1934, the venerable Maksim Gorky contrasted "proletarian humanism" to vicious fascism. This, in the wake of the dissolution of the contentious Russian Association of Proletarian Writers (which, in the name of "proletarian literature" had attacked writers considered too "bourgeois"), seemed to augur a more tolerant attitude toward literature. Previously suppressed artists were now allowed to return and work within the new Union of Soviet Writers.[13] Young Andrei Zhdanov presided over these affairs in the name of the party.

If Stalin and Kirov were antagonists, it would be difficult to explain Kirov's continued rise. Stalin chose Kirov for the sensitive Leningrad party leadership position and trusted him with delicate "troubleshooter" missions to supervise critical harvests (like Kirov's journey to Central Asia in 1934).[14] Kirov was elected to the Secretariat and Politburo in 1934, and Stalin wanted him to move to the Central Committee Secretariat in Moscow as soon as possible.[15] Unless one is prepared to believe that Stalin did not control appointments to the Secretariat and Politburo (despite his alleged practice of manipulating ballots at congresses), one must assume that he and Kirov were allies.

Much more probable than a Kirov-versus-Stalin scenario is one in which Stalin, Kirov, and Zhdanov cooperated. Later in 1934, Stalin, Kirov, and Zhdanov collaborated to overhaul the party educational curriculum.[16] These efforts would eventually result in significant revisions in educational curricula and formed the foundation for the famous *History of the Communist Party of the Soviet Union, Short Course*, in 1938. Such a collaboration would explain the thrust of Stalin's and Kirov's remarks at the Seventeenth Congress, Kirov's promotion to the Secretariat, and Stalin's wish for Kirov to take up his work in Moscow.

More obvious than "terror" in 1934–5 was the continuation of the Kirov–Stalin policy of socioeconomic relaxation combined with the activation and radicalization of party work. Although many of these social and political measures have been attributed to Kirov in opposition to Stalin, it is more likely that Stalin supported the new policies.

The most pronounced political theme of the period preceding and following the Kirov assassination was an increasingly bitter campaign against the officeholders of the Soviet bureaucracy. The summer of 1934 saw a continuation of Stalin's critical attitude toward crime and corruption among middle-level officeholders. On July 9, 1934, the Western Region Committee sent a "Closed Letter" to all *raikoms,* all party and Komsomol organizations, and all *politotdels* in the *oblast'*.[17] The letter dealt with economic crime: speculation, embezzlement, and other economic "disorders" in trade and cooperative organizations; it contained detailed information about thousands of rubles that could not be accounted for. Such crimes were, of course, facilitated by the tremendous economic expansion of recent years which, as in other areas, had caused the party to lose a certain amount of control. The letter posed the following dilemma: How was the party to "struggle to fulfill the production plan while defending the workers from the illegal activities of certain degenerate economic managers?"

Speculation and related crimes had long been a part of the Soviet scene.[18] When discovered, they were punished by imprisonment or death even in peacetime. What was new was the spirit and prescriptions in the letter. Of course, "repression," "trials," and "administrative measures" were to be continued, especially in severe cases. But "it would be wrong to think that the struggle against this social evil can be brought about only through the path of strengthened repression and administrative measures without improving the whole system of mass-organizational work.'' Citing the Seventeenth Party Congress, the letter said that it was necessary for party organizations to "rebuild fundamentally their work along the lines of the Seventeenth Congress.'' Political work was weak, and there was little criticism from the rank and file.[19]

The letter also cited the recent plenum of the Party Control Commission, which had demanded ''mass control over the fufillment of decisions'' in trade and economic organs. Political and mass work was to be used to secure ''active participation'' and the development of ''self-criticism'' on the parts of all party members. This emphasis on mass control over leaders and self-criticism was new and could not have been welcomed by the regional party apparatus.

Moscow's concerns about bureaucratism and weak ideological training were reflected in the high-level personnel changes necessitated by the deaths of Kirov and V. V. Kuibyshev.[20] In plenary sessions of the Central Committee held on February 1 and 28, Vlas Chubar' and A. I. Mikoian, the senior Politburo candidates, became full members. Andrei Zhdanov became head of the Leningrad organization and candidate member of the Politburo (he was already a secretary of the Central Committee). N. I. Ezhov, who has already surfaced as a director of the *chistka* and Central Committee director of personnel, became a Central Committee secretary and chairman of the KPK. When Ezhov assumed these posts, he began to conduct an investigation of the party records in an attempt to restore them to order.[21] For present purposes, Zhdanov the ideologist and Ezhov the security specialist are important figures, and their parallel rises to power symbolize Stalin's dual strategy for the party. Ezhov would face the organizational-accounting-records question, whereas Zhdanov was more in charge of ''party work,'' ideology, and education. The two leaders would ultimately come into conflict over how to reform the party, but both represented a radical challenge to the machines of the party apparatus. Stalin would support both of them.

Zhdanov's promotion was related to the Kirov–Stalin concerns about ideology and bureaucratism.[22] A party member since 1915, Zhdanov had been the secretary of the Tver' and then Nizhnii Novgorod party organizations in the twenties and early thirties. Elected secretary of the Central Committee in 1934, he associated with Stalin and Kirov in the preparations for a new party history textbook in the summer of 1934[23] and was the main party representative at the Soviet Writers' Congress in August 1934. His reputation was associated with literary and ideological questions from his first appearance on the national scene, and he was to become the chief party ideologist. Leningrad, with its radical democratic party tradition, would provide a perfect base from which Zhdanov could press for a revival of "party work."

Zhdanov would become the leading spokesman for more political education and less bureaucratism and thereby continue the party-reform movement begun by Stalin and Kirov. Zhdanov's denunciations of bureaucratism, suppression of criticism, and repression of the rank and file would become sharper and would evolve into a major campaign for populist participation. By 1937, Zhdanov would demand (and get) genuine secret-ballot elections of party secretaries. His brand of radical populism would lead him to vilify the high-handed and authoritarian practices of party secretaries, and he would become one of their harshest critics.

Yet Zhdanov's career as a regional party secretary ultimately made him more sympathetic than some to the problems of regional and local party leaders. He knew that they faced gargantuan problems in their work. Tremendous demands for economic fulfillment, low educational levels, and a shortage of experienced cadres plagued local secretaries, and their authoritarian practices were to some extent understandable reactions to a difficult situation. Zhdanov's remedies were radical but nonviolent. Unlike others, he would never denounce party secretaries as "enemies of the people," even at the height of tension and suspicion in 1937.

Zhdanov wanted the party to become a vehicle for political education, ideological agitation, and cadre preparation on a mass scale. The period before 1934 had seen the party become deeply involved in agriculture, economic planning, and administration. Large numbers of party members at various levels were assigned to oversee the economy, and the party's political functions had atrophied. Zhdanov envisioned an ideologically charged mass party. He consistently fought attempts to prune the party's ranks of peripheral, ideologically unsophisticated, and part-time adherents. He argued for education rather than selectivity and continued to believe that the problems of party committees could be solved through withdrawing them from economic administration, bringing rank-and-file activists into responsible work, and verifying the bureaucracy "from below."

Many of Zhdanov's populist and democratic projects recalled the demands of the Democratic Centralist and Trotskyist oppositions of the

1920s.[24] It may well have been that the forcefulness (and high-level support) behind Zhdanov's campaigns were also responses to the Kirov assassination. The shooting was evidence of the persistence of rank-and-file discontent and even oppositionist sentiment in the party.[25] Zhdanov's efforts may well have represented the Stalinist leadership's attempt to satisfy such grievances and to coopt oppositionist critics.[26]

Zhdanov, Stalin, and "party work"

One of the early signs of a new attitude toward party work was the special decision of the Central Committee on December 17, 1934.[27] Directed against the bureaucratic attitude taken by city party committees toward their own *aktiv*, the decision condemned the existing practice whereby party organizations held meetings that were actually expanded plenums of the party leadership group. Important questions were being considered not by the membership as a whole but by the more narrow leadership group. Such "bureaucratic methods of leadership" "weakened the *aktiv*," which was the backbone of the party and whose meetings were "expressions of the general opinion of the party." Party organizations were ordered to hold improved and lengthened mass meetings of the city activists to serve not only as forums to consider "important questions" but also as a means for attracting more people to leadership work.[28]

There is good reason to attribute this decision to Zhdanov. The decision was first mentioned in a March 1935 resolution of Zhdanov's Leningrad organization that would summarize and amplify these points.[29] Opposition to bureaucratic methods of leadership, encouragement of mass participation in party activities, increased emphasis on political education "on the job" in party work, and better preparation of meetings are all points to which Zhdanov would return.

The opening issue of the party organizational journal for 1935 carried a number of articles along these same lines. An article by A. Stetskii (one of the editors of the journal) entitled "Under the Fighting Banner of Lenin" demanded the observance of "democratic norms" in the conduct of Soviet and state elections. Other contributions in the issue exhorted local party leaders to know their members personally, to educate them, and to "attract them to active work" (i.e., "Toward Raising the Abilities of Each Communist" and "Attract Each Communist to Active Work," both written by local party officials). A piece by V. Nikitin, secretary of the Khabarovsk organization, emphasized the need for the leadership to be "closer" to the masses and to avoid impersonal, bureaucratic leadership. One of the important "weapons in the Bolshevik arsenal" against bureaucratism was self-criticism.[30]

Pravda favorably reported on the meeting of the Kiev committee that had issued a long statement on the necessity for active party work with special attention to education.[31] In March, articles appeared on education, party history, work with youth, preschool education, and expanding work with party sympathizers and "non-party Bolsheviks."[32] Foreshadowing a major Stalin speech on May 4, 1935, a March 26 article in *Pravda* exhorted local leaders to "value party cadres" and strive for a closer relationship with their subordinates. Midway through the campaign, Zhdanov was awarded the Order of Lenin.[33]

These ideas coalesced in an important resolution of the Leningrad City Committee passed on March 29, 1935.[34] Zhdanov's presence before a gathering of *raion* officials from around the city turned the resolution into a guideline for party work everywhere. It was a first statement of Zhdanov's ideas on inner-party affairs. The resolution "On the Tasks of Party-Organizational and Political-Education Work," began by noting that some party workers had put educational work in "second place" behind economic tasks. Educational tasks too often had received only "paper leadership" and were lost in bureaucratic red tape. The history of the Bolshevik Party was an especially important component in ideological work, and the resolution noted that better educational work on party history was especially important in light of the Kirov assassination. Presumably if the assassin had known more about Kirov and the party line, the tragedy might have been averted. Zhdanov did not attribute the assassination to the presence of "enemies with party cards" hiding in the party and did not prescribe membership purges as a solution. Others would.[35]

The resolution stressed the importance of leaders knowing their subordinates' skills, aptitudes, and "styles of work." One way to do this was through keeping more detailed and accurate party records *(uchet)*. Another was through closer contact between party leaders and cadres. Subordinate cadres were to be prepared for and promoted to leadership work, and *raion* committees were to free 50 to 100 party workers for this preparatory work. Mention was also made of the December 17, 1934, Central Committee decision that encouraged participation by the party's activists.[36]

Primary party cells were supposed to be "organs of collective leadership" and "schools for new cadres." The leadership of primary party organizations (such as shop-floor party cells or *kolkhoz* cells) should frequently report on their activities to the membership, "referring to the masses" for answers to questions. Party leaders should consult with members and organizers on the spot to learn the actual conditions of party work. Cells were to serve as training grounds for party cadres who were to be "valued" and "attracted" to active participation.

The largest section of the resolution paraphrased Stalin's and Kirov's speeches at the Seventeenth Congress and exhorted party leaders to raise the educational and theoretical levels of party members. Courses, seminars, lectures, and a select group of propagandists (who were to be freed from all other work) were to expand the educational activities of the party, especially in the area of teaching party history.[37] A new section in *Leningradskaia pravda* was to report on the progress of educational work and two local journals were to be founded to cover the two main areas of party work. One was to devote itself to organizational questions, and a second was to cover mass-agitational work. The resolution concluded with two quotes: one from Stalin on raising the level of organizational work in the party and the other from Kaganovich on the centrality of *party work* to the *apparat*.[38]

The resolution had stressed a number of themes that would appear time and again in the next few years, throughout – and coinciding with the level of – the Great Purge. Zhdanov's emphasis on people, on knowing, valuing, and promoting cadres; on party meetings and mass participation; on ending the inefficient and undemocratic bureaucratization of the party *apparat;* and on mass-educational work would be steady throughout the following years. These points were in line with Kirov's famous assertion that "nine-tenths" of the problems in the party could be solved in this way. One implication of this belief (which Zhdanov would explicitly state later) was that, by comparison, the membership purges were less effective.

The ideas and suggestions contained in the Leningrad resolution of March 29 appeared throughout the spring of 1935 in the party press. Editorials on "Party-Educational Work," "Agitation as an Art," and "Bolshevik Self-Criticism of 'Varnished' Communists" (bureaucrats) pressed the Zhdanov themes, and frequent articles on party history (such as that by the young Boris Ponomarev on April 10) echoed the education theme.[39]

Of course, the mention of this or that theme in the party press is no guarantee that reforms were really implemented. Discussion of increased participation, decreased bureaucratism, or party democracy could have been mere rhetoric. Yet constant denunciation of the apparatus by the center and the incitement of the rank and file against this middle leadership at least show the alignment of forces and the existence of conflict. The calls for inner-party reform would become louder and more frequent in the months that followed and would culminate in 1937. At that time, much of the middle leadership of the party was replaced – mostly through genuine secret-ballot voting by the rank and file and partly "from above" by the police. In both instances, the fallen leaders were denounced for these very failures in party work, abuse of party democracy, and violations of the rights of individual party members.

There is evidence that in Smolensk discussion of party-education issues had begun even before the March 29 Leningrad Gorkom resolution. Perhaps on the basis of the December 17, 1934, Central Committee decision, a plenum (meeting) of the Western Obkom in February 1935 discussed measures for "improving inner-party and mass political work," encouraging active participation in party meetings, and developing work with nonparty sympathizers.[40]

The fleeting mention of the December plenum does not, however, compare with the reception given the Leningrad Gorkom resolution in the party organizations of the Western Region. The resolution was accorded the type of large-scale discussion and promulgation usually reserved for Stalin's speeches or major party decisions. The files of the party committee in Factory Number 35 suggest that a letter had been received from the Leningrad Gorkom plenum explaining its resolution and the points it contained.[41]

Zhdanov's Leningrad resolution also aggravated an existing dispute in the party organization of the Smolensk Institute of Marxism-Leninism. There, a series of mass meetings had been held since March 10, 1935, at which the two principal party leaders of the organization had been sharply criticized by the membership.[42] Baevskii, the head of the institute, and Vasilev, the secretary of the party committee, had been under attack for poor party work, not initiating political educational work, and giving no help to the students at the institute. After receipt of the Leningrad resolution, the rank and file removed Vasilev from his party post and censured Baevskii for political deficiencies. A general meeting of the party members in the institute, held on April 26, 1935, reconsidered and confirmed these measures. Vasilev was singled out for suppressing criticism of himself and for neglecting the "mass" aspects of his job. In encouraging more participation of members in the affairs of their organizations and condemning lax leaders like Vasilev and Baevskii, the party committee of the institute expressly referred to the Leningrad decision.[43]

There is also an important reference to the Leningrad Gorkom decision in the files of the Smolensk City Party Committee. In this organization, the Leningrad resolution was made the basis for the preparation of local "Party Day" activities, upcoming on April 11, 1935. In an "Informational Letter," addressed "To All Party Organizations in the City of Smolensk," the city committee said that "the orders of the Central Committee of the party, Comrade Stalin, and the decisions of the Leningrad Gorkom Plenum are being taken by all party organizations as directives for rebuilding work."[44] In reviewing the activities of several of the city's party organizations, the letter noted that preparatory meetings for Party Day had seen increased participation by rank-and-file members in organizational work. The city committee was no doubt anxious to show some response to the party revival campaign, but events would show that participation in Party Day planning hardly constituted the type of mass participation implied in the Leningrad resolution.

Although there is no evidence that the Leningrad resolution was the basis for any wholesale reorganization, the prolonged discussions in Smolensk indicate that it was regarded as an important decision. Some party officials lost their jobs, at least partially as a result of Zhdanov's resolution, but the movement was not as widespread in 1935 as it would be in 1937. In 1935, the issues in the Leningrad Gorkom resolution represented an early phase of the campaign.

Cadres decide everything

Stalin had mentioned reactivating the party in his speech to the Seventeenth Party Congress in the early days of 1934. He intervened again in an important speech only one month after the Leningrad resolution. In a Kremlin speech to the graduates of the Red Army Academy on May 4, 1935, he initiated a new slogan to coincide with a new period of activity.[45]

He began by briefly reviewing the preceding period, in which industrialization had begun in earnest. Since 1929 it had been necessary "to exercise the most rigorous economy in everything; it was necessary to economize on food, on schools, on textiles, in order to accumulate the funds for rapidly building up industry." Opposition to the course from "some comrades" had necessitated "strong nerves, Bolshevik grit, and stubborn patience," and Stalin admitted that "in pursuing this course, we were obliged to handle some of these comrades roughly. . . . I must confess that I too had a hand in it." That period of industrialization and collectivization was now over. Stalin concluded, "Now we may consider that the road has been traversed," that is, the successes of the General Line are admitted by "everybody." "This means that we have in the main emerged from the period of dearth of technique."

The party had "entered a new period, a period, I would say, of a dearth of people, of cadres, of workers capable of harnessing technique, and advancing it." The old slogan, "technique decides everything," corresponded to the previous period when the buildup of an industrial base was the party's prime task. Now that that had been accomplished and a "vast technical base had been created," "people who had mastered technique" were necessary. "If we had sufficient cadres capable of harnessing this technique, our country would secure results three and four times as great as at present." "That is why the old slogan, 'technique decides everything,' which is a reflection of a period already passed, a period in which we suffered from a dearth of technique, must be replaced by a new slogan, the slogan 'cadres decide everything.' That is the main thing now."

It would seem that Stalin was simply discussing the perennial shortage of technically trained personnel in the party, and, on one level, he was. This had been a problem for the party since the onset of the First Five Year Plan when Stalin had initiated the campaign to promote the growth of a "Soviet intelligentsia." Thousands of Bolshevik engineers were trained since 1929 through a huge expansion of the higher technical education system. In this light, Stalin's speech again supported the training and smooth promotion of the new "Red Engineers." But Stalin was talking about more than this.

Comrades, it cannot be denied that in the last few years we have achieved great successes both in the sphere of construction and in the sphere of administration. In this connection, there is too much talk about the services rendered by chiefs, by leaders. They are credited with all of our achievements. That, of course, is wrong, it is incorrect. It is not merely a matter of leaders.

After his announcement of the new slogan "cadres decide everything," Stalin proceeded to cite a long list of violations of this principle in the daily life of the party. He complained of the "outrageous attitude towards people, towards cadres, towards workers, which we not infre-

quently observe in practice." In a formulation that would be repeated
often in the future, Stalin said,

The slogan "cadres decide everything" demands that our leaders should dis-
play the most solicitous attitude towards our workers, "little" and "big," no
matter in what sphere they are engaged, training them assiduously, assisting
them when they need support, encouraging them when they show their first
successes, promoting them, and so forth. Yet in practice we meet in a number
of cases with a soulless, bureaucratic, and positively outrageous attitude towards workers.

Again making the contrast with the previous economic period of party
activity, Stalin observed,

People have learned to value machinery and to make reports on how many machines we have in our mills and factories. But I do not know of a single instance
when a report was made with equal zest on the number of people we have
trained in a given period, on how we have assisted people to grow and become
tempered in their work. How is this to be explained? It is to be explained by the
fact that we have not yet learned to value people, to value workers, to value
cadres.

Stalin told his listeners that "we must first of all learn to value people,
to value cadres, to value every worker capable of benefitting our common cause. . . . If we do not have such cadres – we shall be lame on both
legs."

In his "cadres decide everything" speech, Stalin had touched on a
number of Zhdanov's themes: the contrast between "economic work"
and "party work," the current need for training and educating cadres,
and bungling in these areas by local leaders. Stalin's remarks, like
Zhdanov's, took the side of "little people," the masses, the party activists, and the young Soviet intelligentsia. The targets were the "leaders," whose insensitivity and high-handed conduct had led to the
problems. Most often, these problems involved a "heartless, bureaucratic attitude" on the part of the leaders toward cadres, a result of the
preceding period when party work was sacrificed for the sake of "technique." Now, according to the new attitude in the party, it was time to
study people.

One of the files in the Smolensk Archive contains protocols of a
number of discussion meetings held in the Western Region in connection with Stalin's May 4 speech. In a number of these meetings, speakers pointed out that party leaders and economic managers were failing
to take the speech seriously and were derelict in their attention to party

work. The Tumanovo Raion *NKVD* party cell received an order from the *obkom* in the summer of 1935 to heed the Central Committee's instructions to end "formalistic" or "nominal" *(formal'no)* bureaucratic methods of leadership.[46]

The party press shows that Stalin's speech and the Leningrad resolution were discussed in the important party committees around the country. On May 27, 1935, a plenum of the Moscow Committee passed resolutions noting that "one can not be a Bolshevik without connections to the masses." A *Pravda* editorial on rebuilding the trade unions stressed that democracy from below was essential to the success of the unions.[47] At about this time, the new collective farm charter was being implemented around the country, and some party leaders were reprimanded by the Party Control Commission in summer 1935 for "high-handed" violations of the new charter.[48]

Massive shifts in population, class warfare, and the fulfillment of economic plans had caused the party to lose its political character and to atrophy. The party had become bureaucratic, economic, mechanical, and administrative to an intolerable degree. Stalin and other leaders at the center perceived this as an ossification, a breakdown, and a perversion of the party's function. Local party and government leaders were no longer political leaders but economic administrators. They resisted political control from both above and below and did not want to be bothered with ideology, education, political mass campaigns, or the individual rights and careers of party members. The logical extension of this process would have been the conversion of the party apparatus into a network of locally despotic economic administrations. The evidence shows that Stalin, Zhdanov, and others preferred to revive the educational and agitational functions of the party, to reduce the absolute authority of local satraps, and to encourage certain forms of rank-and-file participation.

The party machine in the localities did not always obey orders or accept criticism from above or from below. Given the great power of the local party leaders, it was impossible for the rank and file to participate or criticize very much. Without sanction from over the heads of local leaders, it was very risky for the rank and file to criticize their immediate superiors. It was Stalin's intention to inspire action "from below": to conduct a mass political campaign for increased participation and grass-roots criticism. For his own reasons, he wanted to encourage popular hostility and criticism against "heartless, soulless bureaucrats" in the localities.[49]

Zhdanov on the Saratov Kraikom

Because his specialty was not cadre accounting or record keeping, Zhdanov had not been visible in the *proverka* before July 1935. But on July 5–7 1935, he made a speech on the verification campaign and chose the *proverka* in the Saratov Territorial Committee as his subject. Saratov was one of those organizations singled out by Ezhov and Malenkov in their first report on the *proverka* as an example of hasty purging–Saratov claimed to be 62 percent finished after the first month of the *proverka*. His speech in Saratov was entitled "Lessons of Political Mistakes of Saratov Kraikom."[50]

Zhdanov quoted from a Central Committee letter of June 23, 1935, to the Saratov Kraikom that must have been sent in reply to Saratov's first monthly report on the *proverka*. (Many of his comments may therefore pertain to the Western Region, which was reprimanded for many of the same things at nearly the same time.) He began by analyzing the chaos in the Saratov party's files. The city and territorial committees had in their files about ten thousand members who were no longer in Saratov at all. A large number of new Saratov communists were not registered or recorded. Those expelled from the party had been allowed to keep the party cards pending appeal to higher party bodies: a clear violation of the provisions of the May 13 letter. The May 13 letter itself had not even been fully promulgated and discussed – 25 percent of the party members in Saratov had never heard of it. And, typically, the *proverka* had been carried out too fast. Some organizations had verified their entire membership in two days and some in less than twenty minutes. But record keeping was not really Zhdanov's main subject.

He went on to say that "some comrades" had called the *proverka* a "repression" of party members. This, he admitted, was true when the verification was not accompanied by political education. Rather than serving as a vehicle for the political education of cadres, the *proverka* in Saratov had involved "mass repression." "Sadistic methods" of leadership, "violations of kolkhoz law...and collective leadership" had "nothing in common with Leninist leadership" because "mass repressions were opposed by the party." "Mass repression discredits the leadership." He was referring to instances in which members were expelled behind closed doors by a narrow group of officials. Verification was to be done in public, with the member present to defend himself or herself and with others allowed to speak for and against him or her.

Zhdanov was particularly upset about the great number of expulsions and reprimands. In one school, all 1,273 students had received official reprimands in the *proverka*. He also complained that 4,600 persons had been expelled from collective farms since the beginning of the year. One *kolkhoz* had a 50 percent purge rate: "One half of the *kolkhoz* expelled the other half."

Zhdanov then attacked the Saratov leadership in an inflammatory section of his speech on the "dangers of self-assurance." He denounced the local press for failing to expose the territorial leadership and particularly the "personal deficiencies of Comrade Krinitskii [first secretary of the Kraikom] as a leader." Apparently, Krinitskii had counterattacked in his speech by complaining that Zhdanov's intrusion into local affairs undermined the authority of the territorial leadership. Zhdanov's reply shows the heated nature of the discussion:

False self-esteem, famous conceit expressing itself in over-estimation of the successes of the territory, found expression in an incorrect attitude to the correct signals [of the Control Commission.] Comrade Krinitskii and the members of the *buro* launched themselves into a baseless defence of their mistakes, unprincipled shouting, and fundamentally mistaken conversation about dual centers.[51]

Zhdanov's speech contained the sharpest rebuke of the regional party leadership to date. His remarks were a denunciation by analogy of the territorial *apparat* and represented a major escalation of the cold war between the center and the provinces. By implication, though, he had also cast doubt on the entire verification/purge process. He had made it clear that, in his view, the chief value of the *proverka* was as a vehicle for increasing mass participation and political education rather than as a means to uncover "aliens." In addition, he had come very close to agreeing with "some comrades" who regarded the *proverka* as simple bureaucratic repression of the rank and file. Zhdanov could not openly denounce the *proverka* because it was current party policy. (He could and would in 1939.) But he came as close as he could and seemed to make it clear that, although everyone in the Moscow leadership was strongly critical of the regional secretaries, they were not in accord on the remedies.

Chinovniki and passives

The fate of "passive," or nonparticipating, party members became a source of conflict in the leadership in 1936. Debate on this issue showed radical criticism of party secretaries and also suggested nuances and differences among radicals. In the purges of 1929 through 1935, local secretaries had frequently expelled significant numbers of passives. In the *proverka*, Smolensk Secretary Shil'man had gone out of his way to show – somewhat unconvincingly – that this was not the case in 1935. Given the choice, regional leaders preferred a purge of passives, whereas some in the Moscow leadership preferred to scrutinize higher levels.

In his speech to the Saratov Committee, Zhdanov had denounced such wholesale expulsions. Yet the central instructions for the 1936 exchange had specified passive party members as a target group. This arrangement would mean an easy, convenient, and unthreatening purge for the regional secretaries and would appear to be a victory for them. But now, during the exchange itself, other voices in the Moscow leadership were heard, and passives were to be given a chance to "work on themselves."[52] Moscow did not speak with one voice.

From March 7 to 10, while the exchange was still in progress, the KPK had held its third annual plenum.[53] In a passage "On party censures," the KPK plenum had resolved that there had been too many wrongful, hasty expulsions by local organizations on insufficient grounds. Lower party organizations had been far too free in their use of censures, reprimands, and expulsions. Many such disciplinary actions had been taken in closed meetings of the *buro* or party committee rather than in open meetings as required by party rules.[54]

The KPK advised local party committees not to immediately sack those who had been expelled from the party, as all of them were not enemies. The fact that one did not deserve the title of party member was no reason to lose one's job. The Smolensk Archive suggests that, given the shortage of trained personnel, local party committees were confused on what to do with expellees.[55]

Finally, local party organizations were warned to "stay within the Rules" regarding the appeals of expelled members. Noting that many party members had to wait a long time to have their appeals heard, the KPK warned that such "violations of discipline" and "incorrect practices" would not be tolerated; appeals of expelled party members were to be examined carefully, individually, and within the fifteen-day time limit specified by party rules.

Criticism of local secretaries became louder in May. On May 24, 1936, an order of the Central Committee, "On the Progress of the Exchange of Party Documents," noted that far too many party members were being expelled "formally," "bureaucratically," and "mechanically" without proper individual attention.[56] At the end of May, the press highlighted "bureaucratic attitudes toward appeals" in Krasnodarsk, where unjustly expelled party members were unable to have their appeals heard by local party officials.[57]

A history of the Communist Party notes that "certain infringements of the party's policy" were committed during the verification and exchange. Such "distortions" involved "unwarranted expulsions of Communists classed as 'passive.'" "The Central Committee began to receive numerous letters, applications, and appeals from Communists wrongly expelled from the party."[58]

As a result, the Central Committee took up the question at its plenum of June 1–4, 1936. The two main reports were on the new constitution and on the situation in the rural economy. A third topic was also discussed according to "words from Comrade Stalin," although the content of this discussion was not published. It concerned the order of new admissions and appeals from the *proverka* and exchange. The question was referred to the Orgburo for discussion.[59]

Two days after the plenum, a report from a Kharkov *raion* said that ten of eighteen expelled members had been restored to membership and two upgraded to the status of sympathizer. An investigation revealed that they had been wrongfully expelled for being passive.[60] The same week, an article in *Pravda* discussed the Iartsevo Factory in Smolensk where persons were expelled for being passive simply because family and work obligations had prevented them from properly "working on themselves," improving their level of political education, and fully participating in party activities. The article, "How in Iartsevo Communists Are Pushed Aside As Passive," claimed that a "hard attitude" toward such sincere people was wrong.[61] A month later, an article responded that in the Western Oblast' "mistakes were being corrected" concerning passives.[62]

Other articles in the national press in June and July of 1936 suggest the nature of the discussion at the June plenum. "On those excluded from the party and on consideration of appeals" accused many local party officals of being "bureaucrats" and "heartless *chinovniks*" in their attitude toward those excluded from the party. In words later attributed to Stalin, the author wrote that "membership in the party, or expulsion from the party are major turning points in a person's life." The article warned local officials to use care in dealing with these "living people" for whom this was such a "serious business."[63] Although there is no evidence that Zhdanov spoke at the June 1936 Central Committee plenum, the policies that followed clearly recalled his remarks to the Saratov Kraikom a few months earlier.

Proceeding from the June 1936 plenum and the Orgburo's deliberations, the Central Committee issued another of its circular letters on June 24, 1936: "On Errors in the Examination of Appeals from Persons Expelled from the Party During the Verification and Exchange of Party Documents." Its content is remarkable for the eve of the Ezhovshchina, for it shows the intentions of the leadership.

Despite the Central Committee directives, the appeals of expelled persons are being examined extremely slowly. Many expelled persons spend months striving to have their appeals processed. A large number of appeals are examined *in absentia,* without affording them an opportunity to explain in detail the reasons for their expulsion from the party.

Many *raion* party organizations have acted in an intolerably arbitrary manner with respect to expelled persons. for concealing their social origins and for passivity, and not because of hostile activity against the party and the Soviet power, they have been automatically fired from their jobs, deprived of their apartments, etc.[64]

An article in *Pravda* two days later amplified these themes and ordered party organizations to "finally correct these mistakes."[65]

Members had been expelled in batches during the *proverka* and exchange for passivity. In some areas, up to 50 percent of the membership had been excluded.[66] Now, as a result of the June 1936 Central Committee orders, various organizations began to readmit former members in the summer of 1936. In 33 *raions* of the Western Oblast', 212 expelled people were upgraded to sympathizer status; in Brasovskii Raion, of the 17 expelled, 11 were restored to membership.[67] In the Smolensk City Committee, "guided by the instructions of Comrade Stalin at the June plenum," 51 of the 455 previously expelled in the *proverka* were reinstated after having "worked on themselves."[68]

At first glance, the Central Committee appears to have contradicted itself. One of the express purposes of the exchange of party documents had been to purge passive or "chance" persons from the ranks. Those who did not participate in party activities or who had refused to work on themselves were to be expelled. However, the May and June 1936 central orders seemed to castigate local party officials for doing this very thing.

It is likely that this contradiction reflected indecision or disagreement within the leadership.[69] Ezhov was a security specialist and probably backed a policy of maximum expulsions (including passives) in an attempt to "clean" the party. During operations carried out under his supervision, party secretaries were allowed to prune their own ranks as they saw fit. Rank-and-file participation, propaganda, and party work were not themes that Ezhov highlighted.

Zhdanov, on the other hand, spoke for the primacy of "party work," political education, a "soft line" toward passives, and a generally looser membership policy. He had come very close to denouncing purges in general in 1935, and he would do so explicitly in 1938. Zhdanov was an agitation and propaganda specialist who stressed the pedagogic and propaganda functions of the party. He would become a consistent advocate of lighter party penalties and rehabilitation of strayed communists.

There is evidence that Ezhov was under fire for the *proverka* and exchange in mid-1936. Just before the June 1936 plenum, he had delivered an unusual report on the *proverka* to a plenum of the Moscow Committee. He used the occasion to provide a strong defense for the *proverka* (which had ended five months before) when he took the trouble to observe that the operation had begun "at the initiative of Comrade Stalin."[70] (A recent party history also suggests that Ezhov had overpurged the party during the *proverka*.)[71]

The intervention of the Central Committee on the side of the lower party masses and against the *apparat* reflected the *lack* of firm political controls in the party, an inability to enforce local compliance with central directives, and a desire to curtail purging of the rank and file. Warnings against unjust expulsions and the demands to speed up appeals and readmissions intensified in the coming months and years. Stalin spoke to the issue at the February 1937 Central Committee plenum, as did the resolution of the plenum in January 1938. An accompanying press campaign would support these calls, and the effort would culminate in new party rules adopted at the Eighteenth Party Congress in March 1939, which formally abolished mass purges. For now it is sufficient to note that the campaign to restore expelled members and to condemn their treatment at the hands of "soulless" bureaucrats actually picked up momentum before and during the Ezhovshchina.

The Stalin constitution

As early as February 1935, the Seventh Congress of Soviets had decided to study changes in the 1924 Soviet Constitution. By July, a Constitutional Commission had been formed under Stalin's chairmanship.

Zhdanov, Molotov, and former oppositionists Bukharin and Radek chaired subcommittees. Stalin reported on the new draft constitution to the June 1936 plenum of the Central Committee, and the document was formally approved by the Eighth Congress of Soviets in November.[72]

The 1924 constitution had provided for a restricted election of soviets that was to be heavily weighted in favor of proletarian and poor-peasant voters. "Hostile" groups, such as former White Army officers and members of the bourgeois intelligentsia, were disenfranchised. According to Stalin's General Line, hostile classes had been abolished in the USSR since 1929, and the victory of socialism had been assured. Accordingly, the 1936 constitution provided for a democratic "four tail" suffrage. In elections to Soviet bodies (including the newly created Supreme Soviet), suffrage was to be universal, equal, direct, and secret.[73]

Although the Soviet press called it "the most democratic in the world," the introduction of the 1936 constitution did not in itself guarantee full democratization. Until elections we actually held, it was impossible to judge their potential. The real powers of the Supreme Soviet remained unclear, and the constitution made no provisions for democratizing the party apparatus. The coincidence of the new constitution with Soviet attempts to forge collective-security alliances with Britain and France supports the suspicion that the democratic provisions of the Stalin constitution were meant at least in part to provide an acceptable facade for foreign-policy purposes.

But 1937 would see radicals try to realize and even extend the provisions of the Stalin constitution and use it as a weapon against the bureaucracy. These efforts would include attempts not only to stage genuine, contested elections for the Supreme Soviet, but to extend democratic four tail voting to party organizations. As the wave of populist radicalism mounted in early 1937, such attempts helped to provoke a political crisis. The complex political matrix was partly revealed at the February 1937 plenum of the Central Committee, which heard speeches by Stalin, Molotov, and Zhdanov on the situation in the party and state bureaucracies. Before dealing with this important meeting in detail, however, it is necessary to examine a separate chain of developments leading up to the plenum: the hunt for enemies of the people.

5

Radicalism and enemies of the people

> Under present conditions, the inalienable quality of every Bolshevik must be
> the ability to detect the enemy of the party however well he may be masked.
>
> Closed Letter of the Central
> Committee, July 29, 1936

Moderate views on economic planning and the treatment of the opposition had carried the day at the 1934 party congress: A subcommission under Stalin's chairmanship had rejected Molotov's high industrial targets, and Stalin had noted that the opposition had been "smashed" in the party and that "there is no one left to fight." But mid-1936 would see a resurrection of debate on both these issues as N. I. Ezhov and V. M. Molotov reasserted radical solutions to these controversies. Although this resurgent radical current did not at first threaten the party apparatus, its effects eventually created a climate that did.

The assassination of Kirov in December 1934 had seen a brief flurry of diffuse antiopposition radicalism. The Moscow leadership had been unprepared for the shooting, and, at first, *Pravda* did not know whom to blame for the killing. Rather than moving forcefully against key leaders of the opposition, the regime lashed out at White Guards, "former people," and persons already in prison. Such blind rage against traditional class enemies does not suggest a major planned campaign against leading dissidents, and it would be more than a year before the first capital trial of the opposition leadership.[1]

Yet the trial of Zinoviev and Kamenev for moral complicity, combined with certain maneuvers in local party committees, showed that radicals did make a halfhearted and unsuccessful attempt to incite the party against the opposition. The Central Committee issued a secret circular letter on January 18, 1935, entitled "Lessons of the Events

Bound up with the Foul Murder of Comrade Kirov."[2] The letter called for ending "opportunist complacency" and "ensuring revolutionary vigilance" against hostile groups. Although the text of the letter is not available, references to it in the Smolensk Archive and elsewhere suggest that it explained the accusations against Zinoviev and Kamenev and claimed that their adherents were dangerous persons who should be expelled from the party. These followers, "isolated from the masses" and made desperate by their political defeat at the hands of the general line, would clutch at "extreme measures," such as political assassination, "as the only recourse of the doomed in their struggle against Soviet power."[3] Although Zinoviev and Kamenev did not actually order the killing, according to the official formulation, they had encouraged and misled followers who had carried out the assassination.

There are few good data on the effects of the Kirov assassination on local party organizations, but it is clear that the January letter provided the occasion for meetings of various party organizations. Members echoed the points made in the January 18 letter about lax vigilance and the necessity of expelling followers of the two main oppositionists. Various speakers tried to recall past deviations by their fellows and denounced persons who were members of Trotskyist or Zinovievist groups or connected with oppositionists. But most of the charges members leveled against one another concerned class-alien social origins and various alleged civil crimes, rather than ideological deviations or Trotskyism. Those with nonproletarian or nonpoor peasant social origins were particularly exposed, as were those with personal connections to criminals or other malefactors. Class-alien elements included those connected to the prerevolutionary political and social power structure: former gendarmes, kulaks, White Army officers, and traders. These persons were investigated by the party authorities and detailed records were kept of the charges made against various persons. Marginal notations suggest that someone went over these statements later.[4]

These proceedings have been described as a "mass outburst of denunciations and the accumulation of long lists of suspects, many of whom were soon destined to be expelled from the party."[5] Indeed, there was panic in the party, and accusations were made against a number of communists at the meetings. But it is less clear that many were subsequently expelled. Some lower party organizations apparently ignored the vigilance letter and went about their business as usual.[6] Further, the number of expulsions resulting from the January letter seems fairly small.

A list of the Smolensk City Party Organization in connection with the post-Kirov meetings provides the names of those expelled, the reasons for their expulsion, and the dates of the decisions. In the first five and one half months following the Kirov assassination, 21 members and candidates were expelled in connection with "belonging to Trotskyist-Zinovievite groups, putting forth alien ideologies, for antisoviet sentiments, for distorting the history of our party, for slandering the Central Committee, and so forth." Because the total membership of the city party committee was around 5,499 members and candidates, only four-tenths of 1 percent, or four in every thousand, were expelled in the city of Smolensk.[7] Those expelled in December and January tended to be "leaders" or members of "counterrevolutionary organizations," whereas those expelled later were for lesser or associated crimes.[8] The event does not seem to have been used as an excuse for an immediate round of mass expulsions or arrests, at least in Smolensk.

It is difficult to measure the level of post-Kirov repression in the localities, although it is clear that arrests were made. As of April 10, 1935, thirteen persons had been arrested in Belyi District for repeating "counterrevolutionary songs and poems." All were peasants; five were noncollectivized individual farmers.[9] Thirteen arrests (of a district rural population of 85,000) hardly constituted a major dragnet, and the incident illustrates the superficial nature of the regime's reaction. Few oppositionists were arrested, and local police officials were able to demonstrate their "vigilance" by rounding up peasants for incautious singing. Moreover, it seems clear that the wave of repression following the Kirov assassination died out by the spring of 1935. There is no evidence of widespread political arrests between that time and the middle of 1936.

Local indifference cannot alone explain the failure of radical measures against the opposition. If those who favored drastic retaliation against the opposition had enjoyed high-level support in 1935, the opposition leaders could have been discredited or destroyed immediately.[10] The utility of the murder as an excuse for the radical persecution of the opposition was substantially reduced by not taking advantage of the immediate aftermath of anger against the alleged instigators. When Stalin did decide in 1936 to use the Kirov assassination to frame and destroy the opposition, "new NKVD materials obtained in 1936" had to be produced that were not available in 1934–5. What followed the Kirov assassination was not mass violence against the en-

tire opposition, but the Stalin constitution and a campaign for party democracy and increased participation of the party rank and file.

Radicalism in 1936

The opposition issue lay dormant for a year after the Kirov assassination. *Proverka* documents referred to the murder only obliquely, and
"enemies" had not been mentioned at all during the exchange of documents. But in mid-1936, eighteen months after the assassination, the
Moscow leadership decided to reopen the Kirov affair. In a July 1936
secret letter to party organizations, Moscow identified certain leaders
of the former Left Opposition as traitors and assassins. The letter,
probably written by N. I. Ezhov, announced that on the basis of "new
NKVD materials obtained in 1936," it had become clear that Zinoviev
and Kamenev had joined in a conspiracy with Trotsky back in 1932.[11]
The goals of the conspiracy were terror and assassination of Soviet
leaders, and the group had killed Kirov. This 1936 initiative represented an explosive reemergence of the opposition issue and would be
followed by a series of show trials that reviled oppositionists and a campaign of persecution that physically destroyed them. To understand the
origins of this radical offensive it is necessary to consider the activities
and positions of two politicians – Ezhov and Trotsky – whose paths
crossed in 1936.

Who was N. I. Ezhov?

Although Ezhov became the chief agent for the persecution of "Trotskyist enemies of the people," very little is known about him. No official biography was ever published, and there are no works on him in
any language. But the few facts that are available suggest that he was a
radical whose life revolved around class struggle.

Born in 1895 in Saint Petersburg, Ezhov was a metalworker from
age 14 and joined the party in Petersburg in March 1917.[12] He was
therefore 42 years old in 1937 and, by one criterion, an Old Bolshevik
who took an "active part" in the October Revolution. As a Saint Petersburg metalworker, Ezhov found himself among the most radical
and politicized elements of the working class. At 22 years of age, he was
caught up in the political turbulence and sharp class conflict of 1917.[13]

Until 1921 he was a military commander in the Red Army on various fronts, and between 1922 and 1927 he filled several party posts in Semipalatinsk and elsewhere in Kazakhstan. In 1927, he went to Moscow and joined the large staff of the Central Committee, although his specific position is unknown. In 1929–30, he served briefly as deputy people's commissar of agriculture with responsibility for personnel selection during the era of the "liquidation of the kulaks as a class" and took an active part in the initial (and violent) stages of collectivization. In 1930, he headed the Industrial Department of the Central Committee and was simultaneously appointed head of the Assignment and Cadres Department. During the "Cultural Revolution" of the first Five Year Plan, Ezhov was therefore responsible for providing radical proletarian cadres for agriculture and industry while removing "bourgeois specialists." He was closely associated with the utopianism and gigantism of the first Plan, and his location in the Central Committee Secretariat placed him in the nerve center of political radicalism.

Ezhov's radical stand on education emerged in an article he wrote in March 1932.[14] His subject was the proper means for educating the new technical cadres, and, despite growing criticism from moderates, he defended the radical policies of the First Five Year Plan. The radicals had favored the dissolution of the traditional universities and their replacement by more specialized training institutes attached directly to factories. But this "cultural revolutionary" policy had already been challenged by moderates, who attacked such "harebrained schemes and experimentation in the system of university education." A Central Committee order of 1931 had in fact ordered an end to talk of dissolving the traditional institutions of higher learning and asserted "the leading role of universities."

Ezhov counterattacked from the radical side, praising the dissolution of large universities and proudly pointing to the fact that "our higher educational institutes have been transformed into a form of factory." He approved of shorter three-year courses combining practical work with theoretical training. He noted approvingly that 40 to 50 percent of students' time was now spent on practice work in a particular industrial specialty and that "the opposition of reactionary professors to this has been ended." Ezhov criticized only the *quantity* of engineers being produced and advocated continuing the proletarian quotas for admission.

His attack was in vain, however, for in 1932 the moderate view stressing broader and more comprehensive theoretical training became official policy. This was the last time that Ezhov spoke out on economic or production topics for five years. After his unsuccessful sally against the moderates, he seems to have been transferred to other areas of responsibility. From 1930 he had worked in the Cadres (personnel) Department of the Central Committee, and from 1933 he was set to work on the *chistka* and thus removed from educational or economic responsibilities.

At the beginning of 1935, Ezhov became head of the KPK. His activities there seem to have been concentrated on rooting out economic and financial corruption, and the press featured reports on KPK investigations into embezzlement, graft, and bribery. His "vigilance" over economic managers was in keeping with his reputation as a radical specialist-baiter and antibureaucrat. Concurrent with his investigation of corruption and bureaucratism in the KPK, Ezhov organized and administered the *proverka*.

As chairman of the KPK, Ezhov dealt with the "fulfillment of decisions." In practice, this meant investigating cases of bureaucratism, red tape, and financial corruption in the party *apparat*. Discussions of the activities of the KPK in this period clearly indicate that economic malfeasance (embezzlement, speculation, bribery) was the principal line of investigation that resulted in the expulsion of a number of communists. Groups of KPK inspectors were assigned to watch over specific sectors of the economy and government and were so zealous in their surveillance of party leaders and managers that Ezhov received complaints from party secretaries about their "high-handed" conduct.[15] Ezhov's role as activist watchdog over the economic managers is particularly suggestive and may help explain why economic managers and cadres would be particular targets in the Ezhovshchina. Mistrust of economic managers was a habit in the party and had been encouraged or discouraged at various times. Ezhov represented the extreme pole of hostility toward them in this period and stood for a radical sort of antibureaucratism.

Ezhov believed that the party could be defended through loyalty checks, scrutiny of personnel, and purges. He rarely spoke of political education, propaganda, or party democracy. Unlike Zhdanov, who pushed for reform of the party, Ezhov searched for class enemies. But both were radicals who attacked the bureaucracy.

Ezhov's career to 1936 reflects several themes and images: class struggle, attacks on bourgeois specialists (*spetseedstvo*), antibureaucratism, and corruption. He was a puritanical and vigilant investigator who had long been involved against the seamy side of political life.

Ezhov always wore the simple Bolshevik military tunic rather than a necktie and reinforced this formidable and Spartan image when he arrived to receive his Order of Lenin in 1937 with his head shaved in the Civil War style.[16]

Trotskyism in the thirties

Leon Trotsky had been deported from the Soviet Union in 1929 but remained politically active in exile. His contacts with followers in the Soviet Union ran through his son, Lev Sedov. In fact, until his death in Paris in 1938, Sedov was the real organizer of the Trotskyist movement. Regardless of Trotsky's exile location, it was Sedov who maintained contact between the "Old Man" and his followers, organized publication of the *Biulleten' oppozitsii* [Bulletin of the opposition], and provided Trotsky with expert advice on European and Soviet affairs.[17] Sedov maintained a network of friends, contacts, and agents who regularly shuttled information and communication in and out of the Soviet Union. Friendly tourists or members of European communist parties carried letters back and forth between Sedov and various Trotskyists in the USSR. These "special journeys," as Sedov called them, were the main links between Trotsky and the Soviet Union.[18]

Although Trotsky later denied that he had any communications with former followers in the USSR since his exile in 1929,[19] it is clear that he did. In the first three months of 1932 he sent secret letters to former oppositionists Radek, Sokolnikov, Preobrazhenskii, and others.[20] Although the contents of these letters are unknown, it seems reasonable to believe that they involved an attempt to persuade the addressees to return to opposition.

Sometime in October of 1932, E. S. Gol'tsman (a Soviet official and former Trotskyist) met Sedov in Berlin and gave him an internal memorandum on Soviet economic output. This memorandum was published in the *Biulleten'* the following month under the title "The Economic Situation of the Soviet Union."[21] It seems, though, that Gol'tsman brought Sedov something else: a proposal from Left Oppositionists in the USSR for the formation of a united opposition bloc. The proposed bloc was to include Trotskyists, Zinovievists, members of the Lominadze group, and others. The proposal came from "Kolokolnikov" – the code name of Ivan Smirnov.[22]

No doubt excited by such a prospect, Sedov immediately wrote to

Trotsky, who replied in a letter that approved of a bloc but carefully circumscribed Trotskyist participation in it. "The proposition of the bloc seems to me completely acceptable," Trotsky wrote, but "it is a question of bloc, not merger." "How will the bloc manifest itself? For the moment, mainly through exchanging information. Our allies will keep us up to date on that which concerns the Soviet Union, and we will do the same thing on that which concerns the Comintern." Trotsky went on to say that the allies should send materials for publication in the *Biulleten'*, but "we reserve the right to comment on them freely." He also made clear that the bloc would exclude those who capitulated and recanted: Capitulationist sentiment "will be inexorably and pitilessly combatted by us."

While authorizing Sedov to proceed with the formation of the bloc, Trotsky was still unsure of the participants. He asked Sedov about the participation of the Workers' Opposition "and other ultra-left groups." Apparently, Smirnov had relayed the opinion of those in the Soviet Union that participation in the bloc by the rightists was desirable and that perhaps formation of the bloc should be delayed until their adherence could be secured. Trotsky reacted against the suggestion: "The allies' opinion that one must wait until the rights can easily join does not have my approval." Apparently, Trotsky was impatient with passivity on the part of the Right Opposition. "One struggles against repression by anonymity and conspiracy, not by silence."[23]

Shortly thereafter, Sedov wrote to his father advising him that the bloc was organized. "It embraces the Zinovievists, the Sten-Lominadze group, and the Trotskyists (old '[*blank*]')." "The Safarov-Tarkhanov group has not yet formally entered – they have a very extreme position; they will enter soon." After conveying the happy news that oppositional organization had reached this new stage, Sedov was forced to give Trotsky the bad news. It seemed that at precisely the time that the bloc was forming some of its key leaders were being arrested. Ivan Smirnov and those around him had been arrested "by accident." It seems that a provocateur in their midst had denounced them on a separate matter. Zinoviev and Kamenev had been arrested and deported – also in connection with an extraneous affair. Although these events certainly disrupted the bloc, Sedov was not despondent. He was sure that the police had found no incriminating documents or "Trotskyist literature" on Smirnov, and although "the arrest of the 'ancients' is a great blow, the lower workers are safe."[24]

At about this time, Trotsky attempted to contact his "lower work-

ers" directly. During a brief stay in Copenhagen, Trotsky handed a letter to an English tourist (Weeks, by name) who was to deliver it to
oppositionists in Russia. The letter began, "I am not sure that you
know my handwriting. If not, you will probably find someone else who
does." Trotsky went on to call upon loyal oppositionists to become active: "The comrades who sympathize with the Left Opposition are
obliged to come out of their passive state at this time, maintaining, of
course, all *precautions*" (emphases Trotsky's). He went on to give names
and addresses of safe contacts in Berlin, Prague, and Istanbul to whom
communications for Trotsky could be sent and then concluded, "I am
definitely depending that the menacing situation in which the party
finds itself will force all the comrades devoted to the revolution to ac-
tively gather about the Left Opposition."[25]

It is clear, then, that Trotsky did have a clandestine organization inside the USSR in this period and that he maintained communication
with it. It is equally clear that a united oppositional bloc was formed in
1932. In Trotsky's opinion, however, the bloc existed only for the purposes of communication and exchange of information. From the available evidence, it seems that Trotsky envisioned no "terrorist" role for
the bloc, although his call for a "new political revolution" to remove
"the cadres, the bureaucracy"[26] might well have been so interpreted in
Moscow. There is also reason to believe that after the decapitation of
the bloc through the removal of Zinoviev, Kamenev, Smirnov, and
others the organization comprised mainly lower-level less prominent
oppositionists: followers of Zinoviev, with whom Trotsky attempted to
maintain direct contact.

It is equally probable that the NKVD knew about the bloc. Trotsky's
and Sedov's staffs were thoroughly infiltrated, and Sedov's closest col-
laborator in 1936, Mark Zborowski, is said to have been an NKVD
agent.[27] In 1936, the 1932 bloc would be interpreted by the NKVD as a
terrorist plot and would form the original pretext for Ezhov's campaign
to destroy the former opposition. Smirnov, Gol'tsmn, Zinoviev, Kamenev, and Trotsky (*in absentia*) would be the defendants at the 1936
show trial, and the 1932 events would form the evidential basis for their
prosecution.

Sometime in the spring of 1936, the NKVD reopened the investigation of the Kirov assassination. Genrikh Iagoda, as head of the NKVD,
directed the investigation, assisted by Ezhov.[28] The origins of this decision remain obscure. Although the documents suggest that the 1936 investigation was based on "new NKVD materials," they do not

elaborate. The only "new materials" ever produced that changed the 1935 post-Kirov version involved the 1932 bloc. No one suggested that Iagoda's 1934–35 investigation of the Kirov matter had been faulty, but Ezhov's participation in the 1936 review represented an intrusion of the Secretariat into the preserve of the NKVD. This arrangement suggested that hard-liners in the Secretariat did not trust Iagoda to conduct a "proper" investigation of the opposition in 1936.

There are two possibilities. Perhaps Iagoda found out about the 1932 bloc only at the beginning of 1936. Stalin and Ezhov, suspicious about the tardiness of this discovery, attached Ezhov to the NKVD as a watchdog. Alternatively, Iagoda may have known about the bloc for some time (perhaps even since 1932) but covered it up or minimized its importance.[29] Ezhov and/or Stalin found out about it in early 1936 and became suspicious of Iagoda's motives. In either case, Stalin must have initiated or at least sanctioned the proceedings, but later events would show that he neither directed nor approved of the course of the investigation in these early stages.

Party organizations first became aware of the investigation through the circulation of the "Top Secret" letter dated July 29, 1936. Entitled "On the Terrorist Activities of the Trotskyist–Zinovievist Counterrevolutionary Bloc," the letter was written by the Central Committee Secretariat and sent to all party organizations above *raikom* level to inform them of "new NKVD materials obtained in 1936." According to the letter, Zinoviev and Kamenev "in a direct bloc with Trotsky" had actually planned the murder of Kirov back in 1934 and had been "the authors of direct instructions. . .to prepare attempts on the lives of other leaders of our party, primarily Comrade Stalin."[30]

Most of the letter paraphrased and quoted pretrial depositions and confessions of Zinoviev and Kamenev on their organization of "terrorist groups" since 1932. The letter was written immediately after those confessions (Zinoviev's deposition is dated July 25, and the letter was written July 29), and its purpose was to inform local party organizations of the upcoming trial and to acquaint them with "the factual aspect of this affair, as recently brought to light."

According to the letter, Zinovievist and Kamenevist opposition circles in the USSR had established contact with the emigré Trotskyists four years before (in Berlin in 1932 when defendant Ivan Smirnov contacted Sedov) and had jointly plotted the assassination of Soviet leaders. They had done this because the success of the party in industry and agriculture since 1929 meant that opposition politicians had no chance to take power via a political platform. What could they propose, given the successes of recent years? Thus, the opposition had turned to terror and assassination and had become "the organizing force for remnants of smashed classes" and "leading detachment of the counterrevolutionary bourgeoisie."

As a result of this dangerous situation, the party was "to rivet attention on the tasks of the all-around heightening of Bol'shevik revolutionary vigilance." The letter ended with what was to become a slogan of the Ezhovshchina: "Under present conditions, the inalienable quality of every Bolshevik must be the ability to detect the enemy of the party, however well he may be masked."

The July letter and the subsequent August show trial called upon the party to expose oppositionists, not bureaucrats. It called for no purge of the apparatus and did not mention the Right Opposition, whose members still held responsible positions in the economic apparatus. The 1936 letter never mentioned *uchet,* party work, bureaucratism, *kritika/ samokritika,* or any of the themes of the center–periphery conflict. This new campaign against the opposition did not directly threaten territorial party secretaries, and the campaigns against bureaucratism and against the Left Opposition were discrete and mutually independent.

Indeed, the 1936 show trial had a restricted cast of characters. One of the main purposes of a show trial is to define, exemplify, and personify the evil ones: the counterexamples and enemies. Under Iagoda's direction, the NKVD produced a show trial in which Trotsky, Zinoviev, Kamenev, and their followers had conspired to overthrow the Soviet government through assassination and terror. All the accused were connected in some way to Trotsky or Zinoviev, and the trial was a terrifying omen for ex-Trotskyists. Yet there were other more esoteric "lessons" of the trial. Although Ezhov's July letter had mentioned the existence of enemies in certain territorial party committees, the trial testimony made no mention of this and implied that "enemies" were exogenous to the apparatus.[31] No party secretaries were among the defendants, and there was no mention of enemies in the party network, economic agencies, the military, or diplomatic corps. V. M. Molotov (who would later emerge as an advocate of hunting enemies *within* the bureaucracy) was pointedly excluded from the trial's list of alleged assassination targets. Insofar as the "lessons" of the trial defined the current enemy, the definition was fairly limited compared to what it might have been.

Although the use of the death penalty against former party members was unusual, Zinoviev, Kamenev, and other defendants were "former people" from the party point of view. They were repeat offenders who had been prosecuted before. They had been in prison for eighteen months, and their execution seemed to signify the end rather than the beginning of something. The enemies identified at the trial were designated purely as assassins; none was accused of "wrecking" or sabotaging the apparatus. The trial implied that the police had broken the case, cleaned up the treason, and punished the guilty. For purposes of possible future investigations, Iagoda's 1936 script was a dead end.

The trial went according to plan, with Zinoviev and Kamenev confessing to arranging Kirov's assassination. A hitch developed, however, when Bukharin's name surfaced in the testimony–perhaps at Ezhov's instigation. A purge of Bukharinists would cut deeply into the current apparatus and could have unforeseen and dangerous consequences. Mikhail Tomskii, another leader of the Right Opposition mentioned at the trial, promptly committed suicide. Despite Tomskii's "incriminating" act, the press announced that the USSR procurator had found no evidence against Bukharin and company, thus forestalling further accusations. Those who favored an investigation into the activities of the Right Opposition were stymied.[32] Publicly, the enemy had been narrowly defined as the members of the Trotsky–Zinoviev group, none of whom had responsible posts and all of whom were now thoroughly punished.

The July 1936 letter had suggested that enemies had penetrated the party apparatus. But the Iagoda scenario labeled unemployed members of the former Zinoviev and Trotsky oppositions as the exclusive culprits. There is evidence, however, that, even before the August trial, not everyone in the Moscow leadership was satisfied. Before the trial began, *Pravda* published two inflammatory editorials that were commended to the party rank and file for study and discussion.[33] In contradiction to the trial, *Pravda* asserted that enemies had in fact penetrated party organizations. According to these articles, some had argued that the verification and exchange of party documents had weeded the party committees of all enemies. *Pravda* specifically noted that these screenings provided no guarantee that well-masked enemies did not remain in the party. These enemies were hidden; they camouflaged themselves by voicing support for the General Line of the party. It was particularly difficult to discover them because they had fooled local party leaders into protecting them through patronage and nepotism.[34] These editorials, unlike the July letter, called upon the rank-and-file activists to unmask enemies in the party organizations themselves.

In practice, though, the aftermath of the Zinoviev trial did not threaten the position of regional party secretaries. A series of mass party meetings was held in and around Smolensk, at which members accused one another of various nefarious associations with Trotskyists. Some of the speakers denounced the leadership for their faults and for protecting hidden enemies, but because expulsions could only be approved by the leaders (*raikom buros* or *obkom buros*), it is not surprising that most of those expelled in this round of meetings were rank-and-file members rather than responsible officials. Former Mensheviks, "alien elements," former kulaks, and White Army officers were victims, as were ordinary people who were simply related or connected to suspicious persons.[35]

Only rarely did important officials suffer, and when they did the impetus came from outside the local machine. On August 24, for example, *Pravda* published an editorial decrying the lack of political vigilance in party organizations and specifically attacking the editorial staff of the Smolensk newspaper *Rabochii put'* for protecting enemies. The next day, a meeting of the Obkom Buro considered the matter and quickly pronounced *Pravda*'s criticism to be "completely correct." The Obkom then fired the editor and deputy editor of the newspaper for insufficient vigilance. But it was a sign of the power and independence of regional party cliques that the two were not expelled from the party, despite a national rebuke for sheltering enemies of the people. The Obkom protected its own.[36]

Yet the epithet "Trotskyist" now came into common use as a kind of universal designation for the worst kind of enemy. As long as the word was strictly applied to former members of the Left Opposition, its usage did not threaten the regional secretaries, but it could become a two-edged sword. The term was susceptible to many definitions and could be used by anyone against anyone. This new situation would prove disastrous to the secretaries in the long run.

Iagoda and Ezhov seem to have been in conflict over the direction of the investigation. Ezhov's July letter and various press articles had tried to identify enemies in the party apparatus, but Iagoda (and probably the party secretaries) preferred a trial scenario in which enemies were strictly defined as former Left Oppositionists. Ezhov would soon accuse Bukharin of treason, but in September 1936 Iagoda's NKVD gave him a clean bill of health. The result was stalemate.

On September 23, 1936, a series of explosions rocked the Siberian Kemerovo Mines for the second time in nine months. Altogether a dozen mine workers were killed. Any regime or administration that defined its base of support in the working class could not afford to ignore a suspicious industrial accident in which workers were killed. As in the Shakhty case of 1928, suspected sabotage almost certainly produced a Politburo majority in favor of radical action against suspected saboteurs, enemies, and dissidents. Three days after the explosion, Iagoda became commissar of communications and Ezhov was appointed to head the NKVD.[37]

Ezhov brought with him to the NKVD a large number of persons from the Secretariat of the Central Committee to "strengthen" and "mobilize" the police organization.[38] These were "his people," and the NKVD was staffed by party activists, enthusiasts, and radicals like Ezhov himself. Their puritanical conduct of investigations against economic managers and officials in 1937 and the vengeance with which they decimated the strongholds of the economic moderates suggest that 1937, in a twisted way, saw a resurgence of the "cultural revolution."

It could be argued that Ezhov's appointment was part of a Stalin plan to terrorize the Soviet state. In this view, the Zinoviev trial was a planned Stalinist provocation designed to intensify the terror. It involved the execution of former party members and thus represented a clear threat to everyone in the *apparat*. According to this interpretation, Stalin instigated the trial as part of a long-range plan to extend the "purge," and he removed Iagoda when the reluctant police chief dragged his feet and refused to investigate Bukharin. Stalin had to be satisfied with the "limited scenario" of the 1936 trial because he faced "liberal" Politburo opposition to his murderous plans. This view sees Stalin as master planner and active organizer of a well-laid plot.[39]

In addition to the tentative and contradictory initiatives discussed above, the sequence of events in 1936 suggests a number of objections to this hypothesis. First of all, Iagoda's fall does not seem to have been immediately or directly related to a move against Bukharin. When Ezhov displaced Iagoda in the NKVD, the police did not immediately turn against members of the Right Opposition, but rather continued to arrest Trotskyists in the industrial apparatus.[40] Second, there is no evidence of an anti-Stalin bloc in the Politburo. Although Ordzhonikidze and other leaders certainly tried to protect "their people" from arrest, there is absolutely no information on Politburo alignments. More importantly, though, strong circumstantial evidence suggests indecision, confusion, and a reluctance to choose between policy alternatives. Indeed, one could argue the opposite: that Stalin remained undecided. In this view, the dismissal of Iagoda would suggest that Stalin had sided with Ezhov's hard-line views by late September, but not much before. In other words, one could stress that Stalin did not dismiss Iagoda *before* the end of September. If Stalin had been a wholehearted supporter of Ezhov's views from the beginning of the year, he (Stalin) would not have tolerated Iagoda's foot dragging on the Zinoviev investigation, his definition of enemies limited to former Left Oppositionists, or the public exoneration of Bukharin. If he had wanted all along to construct a plot to progressively implicate everyone in a series of trials, he could have done so without embarrassing dead-end investigations, censored and contradictory trial transcripts, and acquittals followed by convictions. Iagoda's dismissal presented no insurmountable political difficulties; Stalin sacked him by telegram while on holiday. It would have been just as easy to remove him at any previous time.

Indeed, it would not be unreasonable to assume that, despite Iagoda's relatively "liberal" attitude and his apparent conflict with Ezhov, Stalin entrusted him with the 1936 Zinoviev–Trotsky investigation. Similarly, Stalin must have approved the 1936 trial's limited definition of the enemy and the subsequent exoneration of Bukharin; such initiatives could not have been taken against his will. One could assert that until late September of 1936, Stalin had not made up his mind about how far or fast to proceed against the opposition, although he did allow Ezhov to begin the process.[41]

Neither the "Stalin as master planner" scenario nor the "undecided dictator" hypothesis can be proved or disproved. Although it can be assumed that Stalin must have approved (at least in principle) the new repression of the Trotskyists, one can know little more because key questions remain unanswered. What did Stalin want, and when did he want it? Could he change the police commissar or other key officials at will? There is almost no evidence on Stalin's role or attitudes until his February 1937 speech, and even then his policies remained unclear. The evidence only shows that a Politburo majority that presumably included Stalin installed the radical Ezhov in the wake of the Kemerovo explosion.

In the fall of 1936, the NKVD concentrated on arresting the rest of the former Trotskyist opposition. These efforts would culminate in the November Novosibirsk trial and the January 1937 Piatakov trial, in which former Trotskyists were accused of industrial sabotage. On one level, these trials were a warning against the mismanagement, sloth, theft, and sabotage that plagued Soviet industry. But the trials also symbolized higher political struggles. The new campaign bore Ezhov's mark. It suggested that (Trotskyist) enemies had indeed penetrated the current economic bureaucracy. It also introduced the accusation of "wrecking" into political discourse and revived the Shakhty image of sabotage by class enemies. In contrast to the Shakhty case, however, the enemy was now said to be hiding behind party cards.

G. I. Piatakov, deputy commissar of heavy industry and a former Trotskyist, was the perfect symbolic target for resurgent radicalism. Piatakov was deputy to economic moderate Sergo Ordzhonikidze, and the new campaign would soon merge with the long-term conflict over tempos. The struggle in the leadership over Piatakov's fate shows the battle lines in the Kremlin and indicates the continuing conflict and un-certainty at the top.

Ordzhonikidze and Molotov, radicals and moderates

G. K. Ordzhonikidze, the commissar of heavy industry after 1932, is often regarded as a moderate who was opposed to Stalin. Indeed, most of his public statements after 1932 were moderate in tone – as were Sta-lin's.[42] Ordzhonikidze was not a professional economist or planner – he was a party activist, and his position at the head of the economic estab-lishment made him a kind of liaison between Stalin (and the party) on the one hand and the economic professionals on the other.[43] Although he supported high planning targets (but not as high as Molotov's), he had to reassure economic moderates that plans would be "realistic." Like Stalin, Ordzhonikidze gave wholehearted support to the Stakhanov movement in 1935–6. He made several important speeches and published a booklet on the subject.[44] He was the perfect choice to oversee the economic establishment, and his ability to pacify the mod-erates and mediate between them and the enthusiasts made him valu-able. He was in complete charge of heavy industry – the most important branch of the national economy – and it is inconceivable that Stalin would leave an opponent in such a position.

Even before Ezhov's formal appointment to the NKVD, attempts had been made to turn the power of the police against "enemies" in the economic apparatus. From the spring of 1936, local NKVD offi-cials had begun to investigate and harass factory managers and low-level economic officials. It seems, however, that these attempts were often frustrated by Ordzhonikidze's successful intervention. Ordzhonikidze had a reputation for protecting "his people" and was able through much of 1936 to prevent police arrests of factory directors.[45]

Ordzhonikidze's opposition to radical *spetseedstvo* and police repression had surfaced in February 1936 when, as a result of his intercession, nine "bourgeois engineers" (including the famous Professor Ramzin) convicted in the Industrial Party trial of 1930 were granted amnesty. The group's petition for amnesty was "supported by the Commissariat for Heavy Industry" as a reward for their invention of a continuously operating boiler. The recognition and liberation of such dangerous "class enemies" could not have pleased advocates of a more radical policy of police vigilance.[46] Similarly, *Pravda* told the story of a factory director who had been readmitted to the party by order of the Central Committee after having been wrongly expelled for Trotskyist associations.[47] Such parries and blocks were merely the tip of the iceberg and suggest the existence of a major struggle within the party and economic leadership over how to proceed. On the surface, the struggle was between Ordzhonikidze and Ezhov, and it would become clear that Molotov was Ezhov's main ally.

Behind these maneuvers was the perennial conflict between advocates of faster economic tempos and those who advised more moderate or "realistic" targets. Indeed, although the outlines of political events in this period are necessarily hazy, it is hard to avoid the impression that much of the radical–moderate conflict in mid-1936 related to the mysterious process of drafting the Third Five Year Plan. Gosplan had begun to draw up the plan in February 1936 and was to report to the Council of Peoples' Commissars by June. No report was forthcoming, however, and it seems that the drafting process collapsed in the middle of the year. The second half of 1936 saw almost no mention of the Plan, and it would be safe to assume that incompetence, confusion, poor economic performance in 1936, or dissent prevented a decision. In April 1937, nearly a year after the draft was to appear, Sovnarkom called for a first draft by July 1, 1937! No report appeared then, and the closing down of the planning journal *Plan* symbolized conflict and chaos.[48]

It is probably not coincidental that, at the precise time the drafting process collapsed, Molotov lashed out against moderates in the commissariats under his control. In the fall of 1936, he carried out a series of radical shake-ups in the leaderships of the economic commissariats over which he presided as head of Sovnarkom. Major leadership changes were made in the State Bank and in the Commissariats of Agriculture, Communications, Forests, Light Industry, and Food Production. These agencies had been criticized in the press; Molotov would shortly identify them as focal points for "underestimators" and "limiters," and he would accuse these moderates of wrecking, sabotage, and treason. Khrushchev-era commentators would call Molotov the "ideological inspirer" of the repression.[49]

Indeed, Molotov had found a way to strike at moderates and avenge his humiliation at their hands back at the Seventeenth Congress. After mid-1936 it was au courant to use "Trotskyism" to identify enemies. It had apparently been impossible for Molotov to move against underestimators as such, but now he could plausibly identify them as traitors according to the current formulation.

Stalin had been a clear adherent of moderate views at the 1934 congress. He had accepted the arguments of Ordzhonikidze and the professional industrialists that slower was better.[50] In the two years following the congress, however, he seems gradually to have shifted toward the opposing camp. It seems probable that part of the reason for his change of mind had to do with opposition to the Stakhanovite movement.

The Stakhanovite movement was a campaign in which individual workers were encouraged to emulate the example of coal miner Aleksei Stakhanov, who had vastly exceeded his work quota in one shift. The campaign got off the ground in 1935 and 1936 and was pushed by Moscow as a way to increase production and raise what Moscow considered to be conservative work quotas. From the moderate point of view, the Stakhanovite shock-workers represented the worst type of voluntarism. Stakhanovite "stunts" required advanced preparation and considerable support staff to "feed" the candidate at his or her workplace. Such special efforts disrupted the routine of production, were hard on the machinery, and often produced substandard finished products. The voluntarist enthusiasm surrounding the movement was too reminiscent of the radicalism of 1929–31. Stakhanovism only became a threat to the moderates, however, because Stalin gave it strong support.[51]

In a November 1935 speech, Stalin said that Stakhanovism was a "profoundly revolutionary movement" that originated "from below," "in spite of the administrators of our enterprises, even in opposition to them." It was "boldly" going forward "free from the conservatism of certain engineers, technicians, and business executives," although "old technical standards, and the people behind those standards...were hindering it." Noting that economic leaders had much to learn from the practical experience of the workers, he asked:

Can it be doubted that leaders who scorn this experience cannot be regarded as real leaders?...Will we really lack the courage to smash the conservatism of certain of our engineers and technicians, to smash the old traditions and standards and allow free scope to the new forces of the working class?

He said that party organizations should "take a hand in this" and help criticize conservative managers. "And if persuasion does not help, more vigorous measures will have to be adopted."[52]

Stalin appeared to be turning to radicalism and voluntarism. Although Piatakov's stand on Stakhanovism is not known, it seems that Stalin had decided by late 1936 to give radical specialist-baiters a free hand. The vehicle was Trotskyism, and the symbol was Piatakov.

Sometime in later 1936, Ordzhonikidze's deputy commissar of heavy industry, G. I. Piatakov, had been arrested.[53] A member of the Trotskyist opposition back in the 1920s, Piatakov had recanted in 1929 and, because of his well-known economic and industrial expertise, had risen rapidly in the administration of heavy industry. Piatakov's speech to the Seventeenth Congress in 1934 had been greeted with "prolonged applause," rather than the silence or polite applause that had greeted the speeches of other former oppositionists. To radicals like Ezhov and Molotov, Piatakov represented a politically suitable target. As a former Trotskyist, his loyalty could always be impeached. His current high position "proved" that enemies had penetrated into high places. His proximity to Ordzhonikidze rounds out the picture of a perfect target for radical attack.

It is clear for several months in 1936, Ordzhonikidze unsuccessfully attempted to save his deputy and to secure his release.[54] The fall of Piatakov would have been a disaster not only for Ordzhonikidze. If Piatakov were to be labeled an enemy or "Trotskyist wrecker," the working definition of enemies would be radically transformed. The "lesson" of such an event would be that top leaders in the party and economic apparatus were now suspect. The evidence is clear that, throughout 1936, central party leaders carried out a heated struggle on how to define the enemy. Although Piatakov remained in detention, Stalin had not yet decided on the disposition of the case. His arrest was not announced or even hinted at until November. Although he was mentioned unfavorably at the Zinoviev trial, the testimony involving him was omitted from the published trial transcript. His fate, an important political issue, remained in limbo until November.[55]

Although Ordzhonikidze was unable to free Piatakov while these struggles and maneuvers took place, his own personal stock and reputation remained high. His birthday on October 28 was greeted with a celebration in *Pravda* as loud and demonstrative as that accorded Stalin. *Pravda* devoted an entire issue to the life and accomplishments of "Our Beloved Sergo," and its pages were filled with letters and telegrams praising his leadership of industry – a leadership his enemies were almost certainly calling into question in light of Piatakov's alleged treason.[56]

Less than a month later, however, the press announced the opening of a trial in Novosibirsk in which a number of heavy-industry officials were accused of having sabotaged mining operations at the Kemerovo Pits. According to the prosecution, various highly placed engineers and technicians had conspired to blow up mine shafts and had caused explosions in December 1935 and September 1936. These "enemies of Soviet power" were said to be connected to German fascist engineers and to local Trotskyist organizations. Most ominously, the conspirators were accused of being connected to the "counterrevolutionary activity of Piatakov," who was denounced as "Trotsky's helper."[57] Press coverage of these grisly events lasted nearly a week and ended with the inevitable announcement that all had been convicted.[58]

The Novosibirsk trial was a major escalation in the campaign against enemies. Clearly, now, the enemy was not just a group of exterior has-beens without power or position. The Kemerovo events showed that current leaders of the economic apparatus had been engaged in sabotage, wrecking, and assassination. *This* trial gave Molotov a place of honor as one of the officials slated for assassination by the conspirators. Trotskyism had now been equated with the enemy in high position.

However, although Ordzhonikidze had suffered a major defeat, his position was not discredited. Bukharin and the rightists, after their exoneration in September, were still not denounced. Although Piatakov had been attacked at the trial, he had not appeared in the dock and had not yet been formally charged. On the day following the trial, the press issued an announcement that the Central Executive Committee had commuted the death sentences of three of the defendants to ten years in prison.[59]

Clearly, though, the tide had turned. The fall of Iagoda, the Novosibirsk trial, and the accusations against Piatakov show that more radical antibureaucratic forces had won the upper hand in Moscow. Finally, in January 1937, Piatakov, Karl Radek, and several other former Trotskyists who had held high positions as late as the fall of 1936 were tried and convicted in another show trial in Moscow.[60]

Like the other Moscow show trials, the Piatakov proceedings have been analyzed in detail and, except for two points, need not detain us here. First, the testimony of Radek directly implicated Bukharin and the rightists in the alleged conspiracy. A number of former rightists still held key positions in the economic apparatus, and Bukharin's fall implicated them as well. This time, *Pravda* did not exonerate the rightists. More importantly, the attack on Bukharin was merely a symbol for an attack on "Bukharinism" – an attack that had important implications outside the circle of the former Right Opposition. Second, shortly after the execution of Piatakov and most of his fellow defendants, Ordzhonikidze committed suicide. Although his power to protect his subordinates had been waning in the final weeks of 1936, Ordzhonikidze's prestige had continued to be an obstacle to those who wanted an unlimited campaign against high officials in the apparatus. Without their protector, officials, planners, and plant managers were exposed to merciless attack from the NKVD.[61]

Two speeches by Molotov in early 1937 demonstrated once again the personal and political animosity that had existed between him and Ordzhonikidze and showed that Molotov had been a prime mover in the campaign against Ordzhonikidze's economic officials. One can suspect that Molotov resented the vast powers of Ordzhonikidze's commissariat, which controlled not only the administration of heavy industry but also matters of supply, housing, personnel, food supply, and construction relating to industrial undertakings. The existence of this superagency under Ordzhonikidze's control must have seemed to Molotov to be a usurpation of Sovnarkom's prerogatives. In the months surrounding Ordzhonikidze's death, his commissariat would be broken up into several more specialized agencies.[62]

As Ordzhonikidze's superior, it fell to Molotov to deliver the speech at the funeral. While praising Ordzhonikidze's personal accomplishments and revolutionary services, Molotov felt compelled to observe that the late leader had been soft on Piatakov. "Comrade Ordzhonikidze did not anticipate that Piatakov, who had been given such a chance, could fall so low."[63] Such criticism in a funeral oration was most unusual and suggests the depth of the conflict between the two.

Molotov's second speech on the situation in industry came at the

February plenum of the Central Committee in 1937. Entitled "Lessons of the Sabotage, Diversionist Activity and Espionage of the Japanese-German-Trotskyist Agents," the speech was a fiery condemnation of the administration of heavy industry.[64] Although Molotov praised Ordzhonikidze for his services to industrial development, the bulk of his remarks systematically denounced the industrial establishment as having been penetrated by swarms of spies and wreckers. Molotov said that Piatakov and at least a hundred of "his people" had "wormed their way" into the Commissariat of Heavy Industry and carried out a policy of wrecking and sabotage. Wreckers had also penetrated the Commissariats of Light Industry, Food Production, Forests, Communications, Agriculture, and the State Bank. He gave numerous examples of such wrecking and, in a scarcely veiled attack on Ordzhonikidze, complained that economic managers were hindering the work of the NKVD by protecting "their people." Economic managers were too caught up in administration, and their "carelessness" had allowed the enemy to function unmolested.

Molotov also noted that the wreckers had espoused a moderate policy toward growth tempos. Wreckers in industry, he said, had tried to "limit the estimates" of what factories could produce. Similarly, wreckers in transport were "limiters" who had claimed that railroad transportation could not increase without new capital investment. Molotov's speech and the accompanying arrests thus represented the triumph of "radical," high-tempo economic policy over moderation. It also showed Molotov's revenge on Ordzhonikidze and the moderates.

Molotov called for increased criticism of industrial leaders by their subordinates. "We must prove the ability to develop Bolshevik self-criticism, however unpleasant it might be for the leaders. . . . It is necessary to liquidate the bureaucratic distortions in leadership, to elevate this struggle to undertake the organization of the economic-production activists." Because of the importance of efficiency to the industrial effort, economic leaders had been virtually autonomous within their spheres.

We must firmly carry out the principle of one-man management, but we cannot reconcile ourselves with such an interpretation of this principle as when leaders oppose themselves to the rest of their workers, when they consider themselves freed from the control of the masses and the ranks of economic workers.

Leaders should no longer think of themselves as functionaries with the ability to dictate to their subordinates. "Self-criticism" was an antibureaucratic, antileader, and distinctly populist slogan that in these times constituted a grave threat to leading officials. Like Stalin and Zhdanov, Molotov was siding with the grass roots against the bureaucracy.

Although it is unlikely, it is still possible that Stalin had a long-range plan. But it would have been a plan in which Stalin, after letting the Kirov assassination cool off for over a year, decided to use a police bureaucracy he did not trust to harass and destroy long-defeated and nonthreatening opponents. Without neutralizing the army, the police, or his regional opponents, he supposedly planned a campaign against an ill-defined group of defendants – some of whom were soon exonerated. Indeed, the hypothetical existence of such a master plan is not implied by the available evidence and is neither necessary nor sufficient to explain the political events of 1936.

Stalin may well have preferred to postpone decisions. This is not to say that he was a "prisoner of the Kremlin," that he was the tool of others, or that he was ignorant of developments. But the evidence does imply that he may have often been reacting to events as much as initiating them. Stalin's interventions (or acquiescence) in March (to reopen the Kirov case), September (to appoint Ezhov), and November (to sanction the Novosibirsk trial) provided impetus for political violence, but none of them were irreversible or unambiguous. Like all skillful politicians, he preferred to keep his options open.[65] He had decided, in principle, to move against the opposition, but the goals and details remained vague, perhaps even to Stalin.

As long as various factions were allowed to contend and maneuver, Stalin's power as arbiter was maximized. His position was deliberately ambiguous, and he seemed reluctant to allow any interest group to gain permanent ascendency, although he gradually leaned further and further in a radical direction. In this light, Ordzhonikidze's suicide was a setback not only to moderate elements in the bureaucracy but also to the system of balances in the Politburo.[66]

Although at this stage the regional party leadership was not directly implicated in the sabotage and treason, their record of opposition to the Moscow leadership left them in a dangerous and ambiguous position. In language that recalled central denunciations of the territorial leaders, *Pravda* would soon denounce "grandes seigneurs" who protected wreckers.[67] November and December of 1936 saw more public attacks on high-handed administrators, and rank-and-file activists were encouraged to criticize leaders of all kinds.[68] These articles, combined with Molotov's references to *samokritika*, suggest that perhaps some in Moscow advocated extending Ezhov's investigations from economic agencies to the party network. Stalin, however, was reluctant to approve this escalation for many months.

The radical–moderate and center–periphery struggles were still discrete and separable. A decision on one did not imply a decision on the other. At the very time that Stalin cracked down on Piatakov and the "Trotskyist wreckers," his Secretariat took the regional secretaries off the hook by finally approving the results of the exchange of party documents.[69] Stalin would emphasize the differences in his speech to the February plenum. Still, the flexible new use of "Trotskyism" and the violent resolution of one conflict created a flammable atmosphere for various other quarrels. Regardless of Stalin's actual plans (or perhaps despite them) the violent conclusion of one factional dispute set a dangerous precedent that would make it easier for other combattants to favor repression. Political violence has a logic and momentum of its own.

6

The crisis matures: 1937

This party *apparat,* which should be helping the party, not infrequently puts it-self between the party masses and party leaders, and still further increases the alienation of the leaders from the masses.

E. M. Iaroslavskii, 1937

The year 1937 saw the February plenum of the Central Committee, which "raised inner-party democracy to new heights." It saw the fall of the entire leadership of the Western Region at nearly the same time as the first genuine party elections in many years. Several radical currents merged in the course of the year to produce a major political upheaval. The February 1937 plenum of the Central Committee is a good place to begin, for the meeting dealt with the radical campaigns of both Ezhov and Zhdanov and saw two rare speeches by Stalin on these matters.

The February 1937 plenum of the Central Committee

According to the laconic announcement of the plenum, the meeting discussed "economic and party construction" and "anti-party activities of Bukharin and Rykov," but no resolutions were forthcoming on these subjects.[1] As one expert pointed out, "the particulars of the proceedings remain mysterious to a substantial extent."[2] Although the details are still obscure, it is known that the plenum lasted ten working days rather than the usual three to five.

Of the five known speeches at the meeting (two by Stalin and one each by Ezhov, Molotov, and Zhdanov), only Zhdanov's was immediately published.[3] Stalin's two speeches, in a unique departure, were published on page two of *Pravda* after a month's delay.[4] Molotov's speech was published in edited form three weeks after that. Stalin's first speech was punctuated by applause only twice (one of these being at its conclusion), and he received the minimum "applause" both times – no "prolonged applause" or "ovations." No resolutions were published "on the basis of" (*po*) Stalin's speech, as was the custom. Taken together, these speeches suggest the existence of considerable discussion and disagreement.

The meeting probably began with the appearance of Bukharin and Rykov before the Central Committee to face Ezhov's report on the charges against them. Ezhov's speech, entitled "Lessons Flowing from the Harmful Activity, Diversion, and Espionage of the Japanese-German-Trotskyist Agents," was never published, although its contents can be partially inferred from the other speeches. Ezhov accused Bukharin of knowledge of the Trotskyist treason and claimed that the threads of conspiracy extended farther than originally thought.[5] Ezhov's report was a justification of the recent Piatakov trial as well as a call for further "vigilance."

Stalin gave two speeches to the Central Committee meeting. The first, "Deficiencies in Party Work and Methods for the Liquidation of the Trotskyists and other Double-Dealers," began by noting that the reports "and the discussion on them" at the meeting had shown that wrecking and espionage were widespread and that not only underlings but "responsible workers" had participated in it.[6] Stalin's theme was simple: "How can it be explained that our leading comrades. . . proved to be so blind and naive in this case that they were unable to recognize the real face of the enemy?" The thrust of his speech was to criticize a number of mistaken opinions and "rotten theories" that some party leaders held. To combine all the "rotten theories" Stalin criticized is to reconstruct the antiradical political line of early 1937. Analyzing his remarks in this way, it seems that moderate defenders of the economic bureaucracy had argued something like the following.

The existence of "enemies" in high places, while unfortunate, is not particularly widespread or dangerous. The stronger socialism becomes in the Soviet Union, the less danger we face from hostile class influences, and, as long as we continue to fulfill our economic plans, we have little to fear from alleged "wreckers." Anyway, there are very few wreckers–they are on their last legs and have no reserves to fall back on. Besides, many of these alleged wreckers do good work.

Stalin noted that such views that benign "enemies would quietly creep into socialism" reminded him of a "belch of the Right deviation." In a sense, Stalin was still fighting Bukharinism, and Bukharin was expelled from the party and consigned to arrest at the same meeting.[7] Stalin rebutted these "theories" point by point and proceeded to lecture the Central Committee on the dangers of foreign spies and domestic saboteurs.

The speech seemed to ramble over several issues, but Stalin's rebuttal to the mysterious discussion can be summarized as follows. Despite long experience (the Shakhty case, the murder of Kirov, the January 1935 vigilance letters on the Kirov killing, the Zinoviev–Kamenev trial, and the Central Committee's letter of July 29, 1936), party leaders had carelessly ignored the calls to improve political and organizational work and thus turn the party into an "impregnable fortress."[8] Party leaders had been distracted and "carried away" by economic campaigns and successes. Foreign threats made their carelesseness more dangerous; the capitalist encirclement was real. In present conditions, the capitalist countries "shower their spies on each other. . . . Why should they send fewer spies, wreckers, and murderers behind the frontiers of the Soviet Union?" Hence the external threat to the Soviet Union should not be minimized.

Party workers, carried away by economic success, "simply gave up paying attention to such things as the international position of the Soviet Union, capitalist encirclement, strengthening political work, struggle against wrecking, etc., supposing all these questions to be second-rate, and even third-rate matters." "Big successes and big achievements not infrequently give rise to carelessness, complacency, self-satisfaction, overweening self-confidence, swell-headedness, and bragging." Sarcastically paraphrasing moderate officials on party work, Stalin said,

Capitalist encirclement? Oh that's nothing! . . . What significance can all these trifles have when we fulfill and surpass our economic plans? The party statutes, the election of party organs, the reporting of the party leaders to the mass of the party members – is there really any need for all this? . . . Mere details! We overfulfill the plans, our party is not bad, the Central Committee of the party is also not bad – what else do we need? They are funny people sitting there in Moscow in the Central Committee of the party. They invent some kind of problems, talk about some wrecking or other, do not sleep themselves, and do not let other people sleep.

In response to the rhetorical question "How are we to liquidate the shortcomings in our work?" Stalin again denounced "rotten theories" that had circulated in the party. "We must destroy and cast aside the . . . rotten theory that . . . the systematic fulfillment of economic plans reduces wrecking and its consequences to naught." Economic progress is no guarantee of success.

Stalin had thus given his strong support to the radical hard line that enemies did in fact exist in the economic bureaucracy and that they had to be "smashed." But, perhaps deliberately, he was vague about the definition of "enemies." Clearly, the former adherents of the Trotskyist opposition were condemned as an "unprincipled gang" of "enemies of the people" who had penetrated "into some responsible positions." Stalin went out of his way to point out that the leaders of the party bureaucracy were not enemies but had simply been careless.

Is it that our party comrades have become worse than they were before, have become less conscientious and disciplined? No, of course not.

Is it that they have begun to degenerate? Again, no. Such a supposition is completely unfounded.

Then, what is the matter?...

The fact is that our party comrades, carried away by economic campaigns and by enormous successes on the front of economic construction, simply forgot some very important facts.

Stalin did not condemn the party bureaucracy. He cast no generalized suspicion on the party apparatus as a whole or, indeed, on anyone except former oppositionists. In fact, he quantified the number of potential enemies and calculated that there were only "about 12,000 party members who sympathized with Trotskyism to some extent or other. Here you see the total forces of the Trotskyist gentlemen." He went on to note that the "total command staff" of the party numbered between 130,000 and 190,000. Accordingly, "Trotskyists" could not account for more than 6 to 9 percent of the leadership.[9]

Stalin had criticized party leaders in his speech for carelessness, but he maintained that "undoubtedly we can" easily improve things. How? He proposed that, in addition to liquidating the "rotten theories" and smashing the Trotskyists, the party needed to retrain (rather than purge) its regional leaders. In fact, ideological and political education were the most important tasks. Closely paraphrasing Kirov's remarks to the Seventeenth Congress, Stalin said,

I think that if we are able, if we succeed in giving ideological training to our party cadres from top to bottom and steeling them politically so that they can find their bearings with ease...if we succeed in making fully mature Leninists and Marxists capable of solving the questions of the leadership of the country without making serious mistakes, then we can thereby solve nine-tenths of our tasks.

Stalin then outlined an unprecedented plan to send the leaders of the party bureaucracy back to school. Secretaries of party cells were to attend four-month Party Courses, regional and local first secretaries were to attend eight-month Lenin Courses, and city secretaries were to study at six-month Courses for the Study of History and the Party's Policy. In addition, regional first secretaries (including those who were members of the Central Committee) were to attend a six-month conference on questions of internal and international policy sponsored by the Central Committee. The various secretaries were to appoint deputies to fill in while they were at school. The deputies would then attend the appropriate course when the regular official returned home.[10]

Stalin had made it clear that, in his opinion, the leaders of the bureaucracy had been careless, complacent, and "carried away by economic success." They were to be "freed from economic details" and politically retrained through education. Zhdanov and Stalin had promoted political education as a solution to the party's difficulties, and during the *proverka* Zhdanov had posed education as an alternative to purges of the party. Zhdanov saw the party as an educational rather than administrative institution and, like Kirov and Stalin, believed in the value of indoctrination.

In his first speech, Stalin had agreed with Molotov and Ezhov that the members of the opposition were dangerous and were to be smashed. Stalin's public sanction of "vigilance against enemies" led to a disastrous increase in the powers and authority of the NKVD. He had also agreed that enemies had penetrated into some high-level positions, especially in industry. But he drew a sharp distinction between the relatively few Trotskyist enemies and the bulk of the leadership stratum. In siding with Molotov and Ezhov, Stalin had stopped short of calling for a generalized *chistka* of the apparatus and had gone out of his way to affirm that it was generally sound. But the apparatus did need reform, and it fell to Andrei Zhdanov to spell out the particulars.

Zhdanov's speech formed the basis for the only resolution produced by the February plenum.[11] The party democracy campaign, attacks on party bureaucrats, encouragement of *kritika/samokritika* at party meetings, and the *uchet* operations culminated in Zhdanov's speech, and the Leningrad secretary lashed out at his *obkom* colleagues. Whereas Molotov and Ezhov had attacked economic moderates and oppositionists, Zhdanov criticized the local party secretaries from a radical point of view.

Inner-party democracy in the Stalin period was defined as (and limited to) "responsibility" or "accountability" of the leaders before the party masses. In practice, this meant the election of party officials as a check on the activity of the leaders and periodic reports by the leaders to the members. Consequently, one of the bases of party democracy was *kritika/samokritika,* which was a "systematic analysis," a means of correcting mistakes, and protection against bureaucratism. Party democracy was also to include promotion of cadres, regular party meetings, verification of fulfillment of decisions, and collective leadership. Primarily, though, it was to be achieved through (and limited by) elections of local party leaders and reports by them to a critical membership.[12]

Zhdanov reminded the plenum that the new constitution had guaranteed direct elections by secret ballot in which all citizens had the same electoral rights and voted for individual candidates rather than lists. These democratic changes would result in stronger political activity by the masses and a "stronger, more flexible" dictatorship of the proletariat. It was time, therefore, for the party to become equally democratic, and Zhdanov proposed extending the provisions of the Stalin constitution to the party.

Party practice must become consistently democratic, the Party must base every aspect of its internal life on democratic centralism . . . enabling all party organs to be electoral, permitting criticism and self-criticism to develop fully, ensuring that the responsibility of the party organs to the party masses is complete, fully activating the party mass.[13]

Zhdanov listed a series of particular violations of party democracy and outlined measures to "rebuild party work." "Many organizations violate the principle, set forth in the party rules, that party organs are to be elected." Organizations had violated the time limit between the required elections by coopting members from lower bodies to serve on higher committees without electoral confirmation. Elections had been transformed into appointment by higher bodies, and this "quite unjustifiable practice" had become widespread. When elections were held, Zhdanov said, there was usually no debate on the various candidacies, and voting was in the open and by list; a "mere formality." He condemned the "intolerable practice" of cooption as a "crude violation of the party rules and of the principles of democratic centralism."

Based on Zhdanov's speech, the Central Committee ordered the immediate abolition of cooption and of voting by list. It insisted that electoral terms be strictly observed and that all elections be by secret ballot.

Primary party organizations were to elect their committees at factory meetings instead of electoral conferences or closed shop meetings. Most significantly, all party organizations from primary to *oblast'/krai* were to hold elections to their leadership organs by May 20, 1937.[14] The 1937 elections were aimed at the regional party networks.

In a few "concluding remarks," Zhdanov replied to what must have been a heated discussion of his proposals. His remarks strongly suggest that two of them, secret-ballot elections and an end to cooption, were subjects for general debate. He noted that although the plenum was now agreed on the use of secret ballots, some comrades had raised questions on actual voting procedures. Zhdanov sidestepped such problems by observing that final rules could be worked out later.

It seems that more Central Committee members objected to the abolition of cooption and appointment to party committees. In a minor concession to this opposition, Zhdanov agreed that party leaders could continue to coopt new members until the elections took place. "Some comrades" were afraid that ending cooption would preclude effective cadres policy, because appointment from above was the only way to pick out the best workers. "Some comrades spoke here about a 'poverty of cadres.'" Party secretaries were clearly worried that without the power to coopt new members to party committees they would find it difficult to keep friends and supporters in power. Zhdanov certainly knew this when he wryly observed that these comrades "forgot about reserves and the ability to promote new cadres" including Stakhanovites and women. Diluting their "family circles" with new people from below was the last thing party secretaries wanted, but Zhdanov's proposals would have forced them to do so.

Zhdanov's speech to the February plenum was similar in tone to Stalin's, but contained a different emphasis. Zhdanov concentrated on the party apparatus and so did not discuss enemies, wreckers, or Trotskyists. But in his approach to problems in the regional party apparatus, Zhdanov's line was identical to Stalin's. While attacking party secretaries in harsh terms, he held out the possibility of reform rather than condemnation.

Apparently the last speech at the February plenum was Stalin's "Concluding Speech in Reply to he Discussion" given on March 5, 1937.[15] These remarks encompassed seven numbered points "on which we do not yet have a completely clear understanding." This speech was vintage Stalin – each point was treated as an attempt to find the mean between two extremes and pursue a pragmatic policy. Many of his

comments tended to temporize some of the harsher words of the first
speech and moderate some of the more extreme statements made at the
plenum. Taken together, the points on which there was not "completely
clear understanding" also suggest the nature of the preceding discussion and opposition to Zhdanov's radical plans to reform the party apparatus. Each of Stalin's points was a criticism of the party's regional
apparatus.

Stalin first discussed shifting the attention of party workers from economic to party-political questions. He said that "voices" at the plenum
had said, "We shall be rid of economic matters, now we can busy ourselves with party political work." On the contrary, Stalin said not to
"get away from economic work":

> You must not jump from one extreme to another. The particular point in the
> draft resolution on the freeing of party organs from economic details and the
> strengthening of party political work does not mean moving away from eco-
> nomic work altogether. It means, simply, no longer to permit the practice of
> supplanting and usurping economic organs.

The party was to get out of the business of running the economy day to
day and was to concentrate on "supporting" economic, soviet, and agricultural agencies by providing "the best people." The logical implication of this reform would have been a party that educated, trained,
and provided politically reliable cadres for administration and industry
while avoiding direct control of society. Although there are signs that
"some voices," including perhaps Zhdanov's, wanted to go that far,
Stalin urged caution.[16]

Stalin again argued for circumspection (if not restraint) on the liquidation of Trotskyists. After noting that, of course, the present wreckers,
spies, etc., had to be smashed, he reflected:

> But here is the question – how to carry out in practice the task of smashing and
> uprooting the German-Japanese agents of Trotskyism. Does this mean that we
> should strike and uproot not only the real Trotskyists, but also those who wav-
> ered at some time toward Trotskyism, and then long ago came away from Trot-
> skyism; not only those who are really Trotskyist agents for wrecking, but also
> those who happened once upon a time to go along a street where some Trotsky-
> ist or other had once passed? At any rate such voices were heard at the plenum.
> Can we consider such an interpretation of the resolution to be correct? No, we
> cannot consider it correct.
>
> On this question, as on all other questions, there must be an individual, dif-
> ferentiated approach. You must not judge everybody by the same yard-
> stick. . . .
>
> Among our responsible comrades, there are a certain number of former
> Trotskyists who left Trotskyism long ago, and now fight against Trotskyism not

worse, but better than some of our respected comrades who never chanced to
waver toward Trotskyism. It would be foolish to vilify such comrades now.

Stalin seemed to be cautioning against uncontrolled witch hunting of
persons with only tenuous connections to Trotskyism. "Voices" at the
plenum had apparently supported such measures, and it seems safe to
presume that they came from two sources. First, Ezhov and Molotov
may have argued for such a root-and-branch approach to Trotskyism in
the party and economic leadership. Stalin warned against vilifying such
"responsible comrades" simply because they were former adherents of
Trotskyism. Second, regional party secretaries frequently sought to
demonstrate their own vigilance by "unmasking" the enemy (currently defined as Trotskyists) among the rank and file. Given this record, it would not have been strange for local officials to protect their
cronies by encouraging the expulsion of rank-and-file members with
remote (or no) connections to Trotskyism. Despite Stalin's strictures,
this practice would continue because it was the obvious way for local
leaders to expel troublesome critics and subordinates while appearing
to be zealous.[17]

Stalin then returned to one of his familiar themes: the selection of
cadres. Workers were to be selected on the twin bases of political reliability and practical suitability for the post, with neither criterion pre-
dominating. However, the real point of these remarks was to attack
"familyness" in the party apparatus.

Most frequently, so-called acquaintances are chosen, personal friends, fellow
townsmen, people who have shown personal devotion....irrespective of
whether they are suitable from a political and a businesslike point of view.

Naturally, instead of a leading group of responsible workers, a family group,
a company, is formed, the members of which try to live peacefully, not to offend
each other, not to wash their dirty linen in public, to eulogize each other and
from time to time to send inane and nauseating reports to the center about successes.

It is not difficult to understand that in such conditions of kinship there can be
no place either for criticism of the shortcomings of the work, or for self-criticism
by the leaders of the work....In addition, when selecting personally devoted
people as workers, these comrades evidently have wanted to create for themselves conditions which give them a certain independence both of the local people and of the Central Committee of the party.

Stalin was joining Zhdanov's criticism of the regional party apparatus.
Cooption, patronage, and familyness are, in any system, the essential
ingredients of political machines. Without them, local cliques could not
function in the traditional way. To end these practices was to uproot the
power of the local notables.

Stalin continued his criticism of party leaders by discussing another familiar topic: the "verification of fulfillment of decisions." This had been the reason for the formation of the KPK in 1934, but here Stalin was not talking only about institutional controls.

There is still another kind of verification, the check-up from below, in which the masses, the subordinates, verify the leaders, pointing out their mistakes, and showing the way to correct them. This kind of verification is one of the most effective methods of checking up on people.

He went on to echo some of Zhdanov's points about democracy: criticizing defects, electing party leaders by secret and direct ballot, and the right of criticism and self-criticism. "The task is to link the check from above with that from below."

There is reason to believe that some in the party leadership openly disagreed with the policy of criticizing leaders.

Some comrades say that it is not advisable to speak openly of one's mistakes, since the open admission of one's mistakes may be construed by our enemies as weakness and may be used by them.
This is rubbish, comrades, downright rubbish. The open recognition of our mistakes and their honest rectification can, on the contrary, only strengthen our party, raise its authority in the eyes of the workers, peasants, and working intellectuals. . . . And this is the main thing. As long as we have the workers, peasants, and working intellectuals with us, all the rest will settle itself.

Borrowing a page from his "Cadres Decide Everything" speech, Stalin noted that slurring over the mistakes of cadres in order to "spare" them from discouragement "means certainly to ruin these very cadres."

We leaders must not become conceited; and we must understand that if we are members of the Central Committee or are Peoples' Commissars, this does not mean that we possess all the knowledge necessary for giving correct leadership. . . . It is necessary that one's experience, the experience of the leaders, be supplemented by the experience of the masses, of the rank and file party members. . . . A correct solution cannot be found unless account is taken of the experience of the masses, who test the results of our leadership on their own backs.

He then gave an example of a "little person," Comrade Nikolaenko, who had warned about suppression of criticism and the prevalence of "family favoritism, the narrow and provincial approach to workers" in the Kiev party organization. As a result of her criticism, she was expelled from the party "as though she were an annoying fly." Upon the intercession of the Central Committee, Nikolaenko was proved right and the Kiev organization wrong.[18]

As you see, simple people sometimes prove to be far nearer to the truth than some highly placed institutions. One could give tens and hundreds of such examples.

Finally, Stalin touched a longtime sore point: the "formal and heartless bureaucratic attitude of some of our party comrades toward the fate of individual party members" who had been expelled from the party. Moscow had denounced the practice on several occasions, but this time Stalin took a stronger stand.

The fact is that some of our party leaders suffer from lack of attention to people, to party members. . . . They have, therefore, not an individual approach to party members. And just because they have not an individual approach when appraising party members, they usually act at random, either praising them wholesale, without measure, or crushing them, also wholesale and without measure, expelling thousands and tens of thousands from the party. . . .

But only people who in essence are profoundly anti-party can have such an approach to members of the party.

Wholesale expulsions based on this "heartless attitude" alienated party members and therefore served the needs of the party's enemies. According to Stalin, such embittered comrades could provide additional reserves for the Trotskyists "because the incorrect policy of some of our comrades on the question of expulsion from the party and reinstatement of expelled people. . .creates these reserves."

Large numbers of members have been incorrectly expelled "for so-called passivity." Such passives were expelled because they hadn't *mastered* the party program. "If we were to go further on this path, we should have to leave only intellectuals and learned people in general in our party." *Acceptance* of the program is sufficient, especially for those working on mastering the program.

It is necessary to put an end to the present blockheaded interpretation of the question of passivity. . . . The fact is that our comrades do not recognize the mean between two extremes. It is sufficient for a worker, a party member, to commit some small offence. . .and in a flash he is thrown out of the party.

No interest is taken in the degree of his offence, the cause of his non-appearance at the meeting. . .the bureaucratism of this is simply unparalleled. . . . And was it impossible, before expelling them from the party, to give them, or administer a reprimand. . .or in the extreme case to reduce to the position of candidate, but not to expel them with a sweep of the hand from the party?

Of course it was possible.

But this requires an attentive attitude toward people. . .and this is exactly what some of our comrades lack.

It is high time to put a stop to this outrageous practice, comrades.[19]

Stalin's second speech had consistently taken the side of the "little person" against the bureaucratism, favoritism, and nepotism that existed in the party's middle leadership. It had stressed self-criticism on the part of this middle leadership and had approved of Zhdanov's democratic procedural reforms. Stalin's reference to the provincial officials who saw the Central Committee as "funny people sitting there in Moscow" confirmed that regional members of the party *apparat* took an "independent" attitude toward the Moscow leadership.

His second speech had renewed the attack on the middle and regional *apparat,* and in his discussion of family circles, fear of criticism, and the "heartless bureaucratic" attitudes toward people, he went further than anyone. However, he had criticized the other group as well. "Some voices here at the Plenum" had suggested an undifferentiated, root-and-branch approach to Trotskyists in general. Such an extreme position was also branded incorrect. His final attack on those who gave out party expulsions "wholesale, and without measure" was both a temporizing of the "maximum" Ezhov position, as well as another slap at the regional *apparat's* handling of the *proverka.*

What happened at the plenum? Publicly, the Central Committee expelled Bukharin and Rykov from the party and passed a resolution on party elections based on Zhdanov's speech. Nearly all sources and rumors agree that there was little discussion about or opposition to the expulsion of Bukharin and Rykov. In March 1937, as in July 1936, party secretaries and officials may have found it easy to sacrifice Zinoviev, Kamenev, Bukharin, and Rykov as exterior, and therefore safe, scapegoats. There was enough talk at the plenum, however, about "some voices" and "rotten theories" to suggest serious disagreement on other issues. The fact that Stalin felt constrained to reply to the discussion and the inability of the plenum to produce a public resolution on the "enemies" question (which Stalin called the "matter under discussion") completes the picture of a divided Central Committee. But the discussion was not about Bukharin. Rather, it seems that the arguments developed over how far to allow Ezhov to proceed against members of the apparatus and about the relative prerogatives of the center and the provinces.

Although no comprehensive resolution ever saw the light of day, there were occasional references to the "Draft Resolution" in various speeches and publications. This secret resolution probably contained elements of the following: "party organizational questions" that pertained to "the freeing of party organizations from economic details";

two paragraphs on the Molotov claim that industrial comrades hindered the NKVD and distorted one-man management;[20] and a paraphrase of Stalin on the heartless bureaucratic attitude toward people.[21] Perhaps the draft resolution remained forever a draft because so many contradictions and disagreements prevented the appearance of a coherent document. Perhaps there was so much opposition to Ezhov's, Stalin's, and Zhdanov's propositions that no single resolution could command a voting majority.

Although Stalin's attacks on the regional party secretaries were severe, the solutions he and Zhdanov proposed were not necessarily life threatening. Regional secretaries were to withdraw from direct economic administration, bone up on political education, subject themselves to new elections, and cease persecution of rank-and-file members. Indeed, such measures, if successfully carried out, would have revolutionized local party administration by forcing local leaders to toe the line in all their activities. But the projected reforms did not imply the destruction of the secretaries. Stalin did not denounce anyone for "protecting enemies" as Molotov had done, and he did not imply that the apparatus was rotten. He urged reform rather than liquidation.[22]

Obviously, though, a warning was implicit in Stalin's attitude. Simply showing economic success with "nauseating reports" was not enough. Politics, not economics, was now in command. Specifically, by agreeing that wreckers and enemies "with party cards" could be anywhere, he was implying that all leaders could be suspect. Although party secretaries were not enemies to Stalin, there was always the chance that the label could be redefined to include them if they failed to reform their administrative machines in the prescribed ways. This carrot-and-stick approach comprised Stalin's policy toward the periphery for the next several months.

After the plenum: local insurrections

The issues arising at the February plenum were reflected in the press in the weeks after the meeting. Articles on inner-party democracy and party work became more frequent, as did pro-Ezhov calls for increased vigilance. Articles on the Trotsky–fascist connection alternated with editorials denouncing the bureaucratic secretaries and advocating party democracy.[23] *Pravda* observed that some local party secretaries thought of their positions as "fiefs." Members were told that they could feel secure in denouncing such "seigneurial attitudes." In fact, rank-and-file criticism should be "severe" and "pitiless," "regardless of person."[24]

The reception given the February plenum in the local party organizations shows the lessons and measures that the Central Committee considered important, and these were reflected in the topics discussed at the meetings.[25] By far the major topic of discussion at these meetings was party work, especially as outlined in Stalin's second speech and Zhdanov's resolution on democracy. The party committee in the Western Oblastnoi Sovet Profsoiuzov (OSPS; regional council of trade unions) was typical. In a series of three meetings on March 22–25, the OSPS saw a torrent of criticism of local leaders by the rank-and-file members based on the February plenum.[26] In a phrase that would become popular in 1937, the party organization noted that the February plenum decisions made it necessary to "rebuild the work of all party organizations." The number of people speaking up at these post-February meetings, and the issues they raised, suggest that there was probably considerable dissatisfaction with the local leaders among the rank and file.

Comrade Kut'ev said that their party leadership had become separated from the rank and file, had introduced a bureaucratic style of leadership, had insulated themselves from criticism, and had committed "massive" violations of the new constitution. Comrade Pantyl' complained that there was no criticism of anything because "in our organization, toadyism and groveling take place, [because of the] suppression of criticism." He went on to attack the OSPS directly, complaining that it provided no real leadership in any of the unions and often illegally transferred elected workers out of the organization to other work.[27] Other speakers at the OSPS meeting complained about cooptions and violations of democracy on the parts of regional and lower leaders. Comrade Zadvorianskii said that in his Komsomol organization there was no criticism. None of the members of the presidum had been elected; they had all been coopted by former members.

There were also criticisms of specific members (for drunkenness, etc.) and the usual complaints about the dismal state of political-education circles, study groups, etc. Although the Bukharin/Rykov subject was mentioned by several speakers, there was surprisingly little on the vigilance theme or on the necessity to unmask spies, etc. Much more space was devoted to condemning specific organizations for not holding elections or allowing criticism, for leaders' forcing members to become "toadies and lickspittles" by not allowing criticism, and for the failure of leaders to be closely connected with their organizations. The OSPS meeting noted that "serious violations of union democracy, a weak level of self-criticism, separation from the masses, violations of class vigilance, inattention to living people still characterize the work of our party organization."[28]

The reception of the February plenum in the party group of the Stalinsk Raion Peoples' Court (Obsud) in the city of Smolensk showed the interplay between central initiatives and local events. Shortly *before* the plenum, on February 2, 1937, the Obsud party leadership had drawn up a report on the work of its party organization. In the areas of party composition of the cell, sweeping its ranks of aliens, and raising the ideological-political level of communists, party work was judged to be improving and morale was considered satisfactory.[29]

Immediately *after* the February plenum, on March 20–22, the Obsud held another meeting to consider the plenum. This time, party work and the general state of affairs were roundly denounced. Secretary Panov came under fire from the first. He and his cohorts had withheld information on the leadership's work, had surrounded themselves with suspicious people, and had withheld information on the arrest of one of "their people" from the members. In contrast to the rosy report of the previous month, members attacked the leadership for "giving only secondary importance" to party work, poorly preparing and promoting new cadres (Stalin was usually invoked here), and frequently suppressing criticism. Several speakers pointed out that new elections of the committee had not been held since February 1935.[30]

In the *Obsud's* resolution, Stalinsk Raikom secretary Vernatskii was denounced for being a bureaucrat. During the entire term of the party committee (two years), the group had never been visited by Vernatskii, who never informed the Obsud of district party decisions.[31]

In some meetings at the *raion* and cell levels, local leaders were denounced so hotly by the membership that they were voted out of office on the spot. Such removal elections had *not* been specifically ordered by the Central Committee. The party elections that Zhdanov had announced were still being organized.

In Belyi Raion, for example, the post-February criticism meetings lasted three to four days.[32] According to the protocols, "little people" spoke at the meetings – people who heretofore were thought to be totally passive. Now criticism was "fully developed," "regardless of person." In the meeting of the Belyi Raikom, 220 of the 240 members attended the criticism meetings, and 77 of them spoke critically of

Raion secretary Kovalev. Party members complained the Kovalev had become a "paper pusher" and had removed himself from the membership. He had falsified enrollment reports for political-education courses and closed reading rooms because he claimed that they were not needed. His methods were "dictatorial and arbitrary" and reflected outmoded and brutal "Civil War methods."[33] Comrade Chemurov complained that "when one is called to the *raikom,* one feels ill at ease. You have to come three or four times to deal with one piece of business, wait a long time, and you still do not get to see the secretary; he is not there, he is busy. This goes on all the time."[34] Demonstrating the alarming new flexibility of the term, some members said that Kovalev was a Trotkyist.[35]

Faced with such a barrage of criticism, Kovalev and his friends in the ruling circle fought back as best they could. In these meetings the leaders closed ranks to protect one another. The chief of the Belyi NKVD, Vinogradov, rallied to Kovalev's defense. He asserted that the members should not be discussing the work of the party organization. According to him, the February plenum implied that members should be discussing the spring sowing.[36] Even before the meeting had begun, Kovalev had tried to limit the damage. He claimed that there were "no great deficiencies" in the work of the party committee. The leadership had made good decisions, and as long as it continued to show good economic results (which were among the best in the region) everything was all right. In self-defense, Kovalev tried the familiar tactic of shifting blame to lower levels. He claimed that *raikom* decisions were sound, but were not being implemented because of the poor work of instructors and primary party cells.[37]

The outburst of pent-up complaints caused Golovashenko, the obkom representative, to attempt to restrain the discussion. He rebuked members who had accused Kovalev of Trotskyism and tried to minimize criticism of the leadership by repeating general platitudes from the February plenum.[38] But members continued to attack Kovalev for coopting various party workers and for dismissing others who had been honestly elected. Members said that they lived in continual fear of being expelled by Kovalev.[39] The meeting concluded by listing all of Kovalev's faults (including "suppression of self-criticism" and "rudeness"), ousting him as first secretary, and electing Comrade Karpovskii as Kovalev's replacement.

This insurrection in Belyi irritated the regional party committee in Smolensk. Two weeks later, the obkom intervened, vetoing Karpovskii and proposing one Boradulin. Another mass meeting ensued, during which the activists rejected Boradulin as being as bad, or worse, than Kovalev, and insisted on their own choice, Karpovskii. Although Karpovskii himself asked the activists to accept the obkom's choice, the activists sent a message to the obkom that insisted that they "orient themselves" toward Karpovskii as first secretary in Belyi. Rather than face the Belyi activists again, the obkom gave in and approved the rank-and-file candidate Karpovskii, withdrawing Boradulin's appointment from above.[40] Kovalev, the defeated secretary, was protected by his Smolensk superiors, who quietly gave him a good job in the personnel department of the obkom.

Thus, even before the official elections, some lower party activists were overthrowing their leaders at criticism meetings. They resisted, apparently successfully, attempts by higher party committees to impose appointed leaders on them, and in the name of the February plenum they began to pick their own party secretaries. No one can read the protocols of the party meetings in Belyi and miss the spontaneous grass-roots anger at the leadership. These meetings were not carefully staged by police provacateurs; in fact, the NKVD tried to defend those leaders accused of misdeeds. The records show that the local police chief was part of the "family circle."

The 1937 elections

Smolensk party secretary A. S. Shil'man wrote in April 1937 that the last *raion* party conference in the Western Region had been back in 1934. As a result, 87 percent of the membership of the *raikom buros* had been appointed rather than elected. Twenty *raikom buros* were entirely nonelected, and in some *raions* meetings of the *raikom* activists had not been called in eight months. In many local party committees, first secretaries had not reported to their memberships in three years.[41] The new party elections that had been announced by Zhdanov would remedy this situation.

A large-scale press campaign was launched to promote and publicize the new party elections. Between March 6 and 25, numerous articles in *Pravda* put forth the slogan "Under the Banner of Self-Criticism and Connection to the Masses!" and described the role of criticism of the leaders by the rank and file.[42] Party democracy was explained in terms of democratic elections, the right to hear reports, and the right to criticize the leaders. Appropriate resolutions from the Moscow Committee and others launched the electoral campaign, and on March 20, 1937, the Central Committee issued a order on the upcoming "Election of Party Organs."[43] The end of March and the beginning of April saw even more articles on self-criticism, democracy, learning from (and being answerable before) the rank and file, and "verifying the leaders."[44]

There were at least two reasons for such a gaudy and noisy election campaign. First, of course, the Moscow leadership was anxious to pose as a democratic force on the side of the common person. Second, and more important, Stalin and Zhdanov feared that local leaders would pervert or manipulate the meetings and the voting. A loud electoral campaign that repeated populist themes might sufficiently encourage the rank and file to truly criticize the leadership and might discourage the latter from sabotaging the process.

The end of March and the beginning of April saw a series of press articles that showed that Moscow was not sanguine about the smooth conduct of the elections. Most significantly, Stalin's speeches to the February plenum were published at the height of the election campaign.[45] Their rambling character plus the delay in their appearance strongly suggest that they were not originally intended for publication. But Stalin's antibureaucratic remarks could be expected to lend strong support for those local members who wanted real elections.

In the days preceding and following the publication of Stalin's remarks, *Pravda* exposed a number of cases of bureaucratic sabotage of the electoral process. Failures to properly organize electoral meetings, suspected ballot fraud, and instances of illegal open voting were denounced in harsh terms. In some places, the local press had been forbidden to publish remarks critical of the local leaders.[46] Thus, even before the voting was completed, Moscow began to suspect the regional and local secretaries of perverting the process and protecting their "family circles."

These concerns found theoretical and doctrinal expression in a fascinating article by the Old Bolshevik historian E. M. Iaroslavskii.[47] Entitled "On the responsibility of the leaders before the masses," the article attacked bureaucratization. In Sverdlovsk, half the presidium members of government bodies were coopted. The Moscow Soviet met only once a year. Leaders did not even know their subordinates by sight. Such "bureaucratic distortions" and violations of the democratic principle had been exposed by the February plenum and needed to be corrected. This could only be done, said Iaroslavskii, through criticism from "little people." Then, in a succinct statement of the inner-party situation in 1937 (and thus during the Ezhovshchina), Iaroslavskii said,

At the meetings of the activists and general meetings of the party organizations, essential deficiencies were revealed in the work of the party apparat. This party apparat, which should be helping the party, not infrequently puts itself between the party masses and party leaders and still further increases the alienation of the leaders from the masses.[48]

Clearly in the preparation for the electoral campaign, the center was trying to unleash criticism of the middle-level *apparat* by the rank-and-file activists. Without official sanction and pressure from above, it would have been impossible for the rank and file, on their own, to organize and sustain such a movement against their immediate superiors. It would have been impossible for local party members personally to denounce their leaders without some protection. The February plenum and electoral campaign provided that official sanction.

On the other hand, the Central Committee did not insist on the removal of all party secretaries – only the bad ones. Election of new party leadership committees by secret ballot from an unlimited list of freely nominated candidates assured the removal of poor leaders but did not guarantee that all leaders would be replaced.[49] It should also be remembered that this electoral campaign was separate from and unrelated to the police activities of the Ezhovshchina. Local secretaries who were voted out in the process described below were not automatically shot. Before the height of the Ezhovshcina in July 1937, bureaucrats were removed by their own activists for poor leadership, not by the police as "enemies of the people." Many of them, like Kovalev, found positions elsewhere where their administrative skills were in demand.

The actual election of new party leadership committees took place in "electoral-reporting" meetings in each party organization in April 1937.[50] Each meeting began with a "summary report" by the leadership committee. Then various speakers at the meeting commented on the report and on the general state of affairs in the party committee. Deficiencies in all phases of party life were brought up, and leaders were denounced face to face for failures of all kinds.

For example, as soon as Comrade Friedlander, party secretary of the OSPS, had finished his summary report, Comrade Genega bluntly declared, "The report does not satisfy me." He went on to describe deficiencies in *kritika/samokritika* and political education. Secretary Friedlander had apparently tried in his speech to minimize criticism of his circle. Genega said, "I do not agree with Comrade Friedlander that it is proper to limit criticism – about what is proper to criticize and what is not." At the same OSPS meeting (April 9–12, 1937), Comrade Iudin complained that simply for asking for help with his work, the committee had tried to exclude him from the party as a troublemaker.[51]

Some, like Comrade Iudin, seemed to have personal grudges against the leaders. Others no doubt were venting grievances of the "have-nots" against the "haves." In any organization, many rank-and-file members resent the petty officials above them, and the archival evidence suggests that the level of resentment was quite high in the Soviet Communist Party in 1937. The center wanted to use this resentment to force compliance by the officials.

Vigilance, *fakti,* and denunciations of specific persons for enemy activity were surprisingly rare at these meetings – even less conspicuous than at the *proverka* meetings of two years earlier. Vigilance was often listed as one of the concerns of the period, and many leaders were blamed for failures in this area, but the overwhelming emphasis in the April 1937 "electoral-reporting" meetings was on criticism of bureaucratism. As Comrade Zadvorianskii said at the end of the first day's meeting of the OSPS,

> The work of the party committee has been unsatisfactory, and that is why the report of the secretary was unsatisfactory. One characteristic which has existed up to this time was self-assurance. There was no criticism of the individual reports of communists. Up to this time, we criticized only "little people" and suppressed self-criticism.[52]

This situation was being reversed.

At the end of the "report" phases of the meetings, the general meeting elected a committee to prepare a resolution summarizing the statements. At the OSPS meeting, this drafting commission comprised five members – Friedlander (the secretary who had been taken over the coals),[53] Levetsov (who had taken an especially hostile and critical attitude toward Friedlander), Gorokhov (another loud critic), and Naidenov and Batov (neutral or quiet). Under their leadership, the meeting debated almost every phrase of the resolution, often voting on linguistic variations in light of the debate. The final resolution listed as its first three points the necessity of following the decisions of the February plenum, a condemnation of "toadying" and "groveling" that had resulted from the leaders' suppression of self-criticism and a call for increased accountability of the leaders before the general meeting. The other seven points dealt with political education, knowing cadres, work with the Komsomol, improving the newspaper, and (9th of 10) vigilance against wreckers.[54]

An election of new leadership followed. There was a conspicuous attempt to follow Zhdanov's guidelines to the letter. The Babaeva Factory in Moscow was said to be an example of ideal electoral practice. First, the party committee met to "study and discuss" the Central Committee order on the upcoming elections and consulted with various members on election matters. Then, four days before the electoral meeting, members received an agenda and were officially notified of the time and place of the meeting. In addition, most members received a copy of the Central Committee order.[55] Democratic procedures were followed as closely as possible in the meetings, and even the size of the future party committee was a matter for lengthy and carefully recorded debate. (At the OSPS meeting, in Smolensk, a seven-person committee was finally approved – five was too few, and nine was more flexible but too unwieldly.) Following the new democratic rules announced by Zhdanov, candidates were freely nominated from the floor. At the OSPS meeting, 34 of the 69 members were on the list of nominees.[56] Then each candidate's merits and faults were discussed openly in the general meeting, and several were asked to withdraw their names if they were not well known. Some candidates asked that their names be withdrawn, and procedures were so careful that this was allowed only after the general meeting approved the withdrawal by vote. Then an electoral committee (*schetnaia komissiia*) was elected from another list of nominees that did not include any of the leadership candidates. Finally, by secret ballot, the new party committee was elected.[57]

Those whose candidacies were withdrawn stepped aside because of inexperience or because of some hostile sentiment expressed against them. In all cases, the candidates were discussed in open meetings, and no prepared slates of official candidates were proposed. At OSPS, thirty-four candidates were proposed for the seven-man party committee, about half a dozen were withdrawn for one reason or another, and the rest remained on the list for the voting.[58]

The extent of the leadership turnover resulting from these elections would be one barometer of the level of democracy in the party, as it would reflect the ability of the rank-and-file membership to select and reject its leaders, at least on a local and regional level.[59] Unfortunately, the Smolensk Archive, although it does provide evidence of the elections (sometimes even preserving the secret ballots), does not reveal the results in terms of turnover – usually because there is no list of the old party committee with which to compare the newly elected group. It is therefore necessary to rely on the press for this information.

Of some 54,000 primary party organizations (PPOS) surveyed nationwide in May 1937, 55 percent of the old leadership committees had been voted out of office in the elections. Over half these party committees had been judged "unsatisfactory" in their work by the membership. In the majority of organizations the range was 50 to 65 percent.[50] Tables 6.1 and 6.2 summarize these results for primary party committees, and Table 6.3 shows the results for primary party secretaries and organizers.

The regional party press in Leningrad Region gave what was probably a typical picture of the electoral campaign as the leadership wanted it carried out. Leningrad was the home territory of Zhdanov and thus must have been a model to be followed in this work.

The elections were the culmination of a twelve-day publicity campaign. The report meetings criticized the leadership for its approach to people. According to the Leningrad reports, there was almost total participation at the meetings from those in the organization. Many who had been considered "ballast" and passive spoke critically at the meetings. Plant directors and party secretaries were said to have been special targets.[61]

Altogether, 41,000 candidates were nominated across Leningrad Region for all party-committee posts. Of these, 30 percent, or 12,300, were withdrawn or removed from the ballot during the discussions of each candidate. Finally, 7,114 of them were elected to party committees; 2,890 (40 percent) of them were elected secretaries for the first time. In one *raion* committee (Vasiliostrovskii), 30 of the 50 elected members of the *raion* party committee were new.[62] Across Leningrad Region, 48 percent of the members of the new *raion* party committees were new. Referring to this as "verification from below," the Leningrad press proudly noted that a great number of the new secretaries were young worker-Stakhanovites or technical workers from various factories and institutes.

Apparently a modest number of *raikom*-level officials in the Leningrad Region were not reelected. Nine *raikom* first secretaries, two second secretaries, and five deputy *raion* secretaries were not reelected. Several Komsomol secretaries were turned out, as were twenty-four newspaper editors.[63] However, it seems clear that the main attrition in the secretarial ranks occurred below *raion* level. Of the dozens of *raikom*

Table 6.1. *Primary party organizations whose work was judged unsatisfactory by the membership, April–May 1937*

Region	Percent of PPOs with unsatisfactory work
Azov-Chernomorsk	50.8
Cheliabinsk	54.6
Chernigov	48.1
Crimea	59.2
Iaroslavl	57.3
Ivanovo	70.1
Kiev	54.0
Kursk	70.8
Odessa	35.7
Omsk	52.7
Sverdlovsk	62.6
Vinnitsa	46.3
National average	50.0

Source: Pravda, May 23, 1937.

Table 6.2. *Electoral turnover of party committees, 1937 (primary party organizations)*

Region	Turnover rate (%)
Chernigov	66
Crimea	64
Donetsk	57
Kiev	57
Kirov	61
Krasnoiarsk	62
Leningrad	47
Sverdlovsk	56
National average	55

Source: Pravda, May 23, 1937.

first secretaries across the region, only nine failed reelection. *Raion* party committees were turned over by half, and most of the replacement was at this level or below.

The campaign in the party and especially in the party press against bureaucratism, mismanagement, weak political work, and violations of democratic norms escalated in the months after the February plenum,

Table 6.3. *Electoral turnover in primary party organizations, 1937*
(secretaries and party organizers)

Region	Turnover rate (%)	Persons elected for the first time (%)
Azov-Chernomorsk	32.3	22.1
Cheliabinsk	35.5	22.9
Chernigov	35.5	18.0
Crimea	46.3	19.1
Dnepropetrovsk	32.7	17.4
Donets	41.2	27.3
Gorky	33.9	16.5
Iaroslavl	36.5	20.6
Ivanovo	37.8	23.4
Kalinin	37.4	21.5
Kharkov	36.7	19.3
Kiev	39.3	27.3
Kirov	38.5	22.5
Kursk	32.8	19.8
Leningrad	38.0	21.7
Moscow	34.2	23.9
Odessa	36.5	21.1
Omsk	38.3	18.3
Stalingrad	40.4	21.3
Sverdlovsk	39.3	20.6
Vinnitsa	35.5	20.6
Western	33.7	19.4

Source: Pravda, May 23, 1937.

and the Leningrad press was in the forefront of this campaign. Every issue of *Partiinyi organizator* [Party organizer] for 1937 carried several articles on violations of democratic rules by party leaders ("The Party Committees Ignore Party Meetings!"), the need for democratic reform in the trade unions, and the necessary connection between upper and lower organizations.[64]

The immediate publication of Zhdanov's speech to the plenum had been accompanied by a spate of articles on the role of the activists, on the necessity of combating bureaucratism, and on generally "rebuilding party work." An editorial in mid-March, "Political Education for Economic Cadres," suggested that political training and knowledge on the part of (moderate?) economic managers was weak and that more political education would decrease bureaucratism. April, the month before the party elections, saw a large number of articles on democracy and electoral control of the party leadership, and these continued into May.[65]

This campaign and these criticisms extended into the party organizations of the Western Region. A March 7–8, 1937, meeting of the KPK had heard a report from Paparde, the KPK representative in Smolensk, which was reported in the national press. Paparde reported that, in his inspection of the situation in Monastyr' Raion, in the Western Region, he had found many cases of bureaucratism and mismanagement and almost no self-criticism on the part of the local party leaders.[66] Many local organizations (as well as regional and territorial committees) were thus featured in *Pravda* in those days, so such an attack was not atypical. It could not, however, have been very comforting to Rumiantsev and his associates to have one of "their" *raions* so vilified in the national press.

The center was stimulating criticism of local leaders on the eve of the elections. "Little people" were being encouraged to speak up. As unofficial accounts and novels of the time show, there were already many of the rank and file complaining about local leaders even before 1937. Both the novelist Kataev and the American worker John Scott described an atmosphere in which there was always grassroots, enthusiast discontent with local leaders. The Smolensk Archive contains many files of complaint letters from average citizens about the abuses of lower and higher officials. These letters were sent to newspapers, prosecutors, and party officials and reflect widespread and often bitter discontent on lower levels.[67] The February plenum awakened and unleashed this sentiment; it did not create it. The meetings after the plenum saw for the first time a situation in which rank-and-file members stood up at meetings and openly disagreed with reports they had just heard.

More than half of the lower-level party leadership was turned out of office in secret-ballot voting that took place after open (and sometimes insulting) criticism from the floor. Even Khrushchev-era party histories and accounts concede that the period after the February plenum corrected many undemocratic abuses, although this period is known in the West only as "the final turn of the screw" in the vigilance-against-enemies campaign.[68]

The party elections of April 1937 seemed a serious threat to local political machines. Free elections threatened family circles that had been built on favoritism, patronage, and cooption. But the threat was more

apparent than real and was much greater at lower levels. More powerful regional officials were in a better position to defend their positions.
Although data about the electoral turnover at various levels are weak, it
seems that attrition of party secretaries was confined to *raikoms* and below. Neither the archives nor the national press contain examples or
evidence of any replacement in a city or regional party committee. In
Smolensk, Ivan Rumiantsev and his entourage seem to have been easily reelected. It is tempting to conclude that once again the regional
"lords" had deflected the heat to lower levels and weathered the storm.

It is not too surprising that the elections failed to open up regional
committees to new people or subject important party bodies to control
from below. Those like Stalin and Zhdanov who wanted to reform provincial party committees must have realized that the regional satraps
would resist reforms that could weaken their positions. Given the ability of the local leaders to control and influence events, it might seem naive of Stalin and Zhdanov to hope that the local machines would reform
themselves. But what choices did they have? Their past attempts to secure "fulfillment of decisions" had included public exhortations by
Stalin, control-commission inspectors, and strong press denunciations
of particular offenders. When these failed, Stalin and Zhdanov proposed reeducation of the secretaries, attempted to strip the secretaries
of their patronage power, and tried to achieve control from below with
new elections. Populist control from below was not naive; rather, it was
a vain but sincere attempt to use the rank and file to break open the
closed regional machines.

Although it is dangerous to speculate on the political calculus of Stalin's decision making, it would be reasonable to suspect the existence of
several factors. Some among his entourage may well have demanded
the heads of *obkom* secretaries; one can be fairly sure that the secretaries
had their defenders in Moscow as well. Stalin seems to have been convinced that something had to be done to guarantee "fulfillment of decisions" and that the situation could not continue unchanged. Zhdanov,
one of the strongest critics of local administration, seemed to offer an
alternative to drastic action. Criticism, education, and internal reform
of local machines through voting and participation were systemic alternatives to massive personnel changes, and Stalin gave his support to
this effort.

Drastic alternatives may have been unattractive for several reasons.
Their faults notwithstanding, the members of the provincial party apparatus had a virtual monopoly on administrative expertise. Their ma-

chines had, after all, carried out collectivization and industrialization and represented the only Bolshevik presence in a tense and divided countryside. Despite Stalin's repeated boasts about the numbers of "new people" awaiting promotion, there were hardly sufficient replacements at hand to restaff the *obkoms* and *raikoms*. Complicating the personnel shortage was the creation of hundreds of new *obkoms, kraikoms, raikoms,* and cells in a new administrative reorganization. All of them required new staffs.[69] Finally, personnel turnover would severely disrupt whatever party work existed in the countryside. The chaos resulting from such sudden replacements would hardly contribute to "fulfillment of decisions," at least in the short run.

The sequence of events in the center–periphery struggle suggests that Stalin was trying a series of tactics to force compliance and regularized procedures from the regional secretaries. The election–control-from-below tactic may not have seemed too promising in the spring of 1937, but, in the light of the available alternatives, it was worth a try. The populist campaign makes sense as one of a sequence of options, but not as part of a lengthy, planned liquidation.

The democracy campaign, *uchet,* antibureaucratism, economic tempos, party elections, and the controversies surrounding these issues were not parts of the same, single crescendo that culminated in the Ezhovshchina. They were related to the violence only insofar as they show us aspects of the same complex political landscape from different angles. That political situation, conditioned by economic, social, and ideological issues, consisted of a network of blocs, alliances, "factions," and loyalties. Although this situation tells us nothing about plans or premeditation, it provides the matrix in which the war and Bonapartism scares of 1937 took place. Political events between February and July 1937 were fast moving and developed on a day-to-day basis in an atmosphere of crisis, chaos, shifting loyalties, and mounting tension.

The fall of the Western Oblast' leadership: the June coup

The last chapter in the center–periphery struggle of the 1930s began in late May and early June of 1937. It was the time of the annual regional party conferences, at which *obkom* leaderships traditionally reported on their work. Normally, these conferences had been forums to celebrate the accomplishments of the region and had attracted little attention and no negative comment in the press. But because of the growing friction between the center and the provinces, the 1937 round of conferences was different.

The *obkoms* were besieged by criticism at the conferences, and they fought back as best they could. Moscow hoped that the rising tide of criticism in the press and in recent party meetings would carry over into the regional conferences where *obkoms* would be in an exposed position. The regional administrations had traditionally been able to defend themselves against such threats, so this time Moscow introduced a new tactic: emissaries from the Central Committee. High-ranking visitors from Moscow attended some of the June conferences, and their presence tipped the scales against the entrenched leadership. Regional party secretaries and their staffs are known to have been removed at four of twenty-five conferences reported in the press.[70]

Yet most key leaders showed remarkable tenacity. Despite tough tactics from Moscow, the vast majority of regional party cliques managed to stay in power during the conferences. Zhdanov had sharply denounced A. I. Krinitskii, first secretary of the Saratov Kraikom during the *proverka*, and Saratov had come under attack in the press since. Yet Krinitskii was not only reelected, but the political line of his committee was judged "correct" and its work "satisfactory."[71] In Armenia, First Secretary Amatuni had been denounced in the national press for several days before the convening of the Armenian Party Conference. His work was judged "unsatisfactory," and he was forced to criticize himself severely at the meeting. Nonetheless, he was reelected.[72]

Even more impressive was the reelection of First Secretary Vrublevskii of the Mari Obkom. Vrublevskii was sharply criticized at the conference, and *Pravda* observed that even then Vrublevskii "had not been self-critical." Worse, the head of the Mari Soviet Executive Committee (*ispolkom*) had been expelled from the party the previous day for protecting enemies of the people. Despite such threats, Vrublevskii was reelected first secretary.[73]

According to custom, regional conferences judged their *obkoms* or *kraikoms* on two criteria: their "political line" and their "work." Of the twenty-five conferences for which information is available, only five were judged "correct" in political line and unreservedly "satisfactory" in work. The work of four *obkoms* was judged "unsatisfactory," and another eight were accused of "serious mistakes."[74] The work of the remainder was not publicly characterized. But even the unprecedented hostility of many party conferences was not enough to dislodge most secretaries.

The Western Regional Party Conference reflected the rising criticism. The delegates to the conference were various *raion* secretaries, instructors, propagandists, and activists from around the entire region: probably a few hundred persons in all. The conference's final resolution, although taken unanimously, reflected anything but unanimity.

The resolution began with a section outlining the great economic successes of the preceding period. The Second Five Year Plan was said to have been fulfilled ahead of schedule, the "mass" number of Stakhanovites was increasing daily, and agricultural production was growing.[75] A flowery passage on the new Stalin constitution noted that it increased democracy and political activity from the masses. This two-page optimistic section on economic and political improvement concluded, "Having heard the summary report of Comrade Rumiantsev on the work of the *Obkom,* the Fifth Regional Party Conference recognizes the political line of the *Obkom* as correct and the work satisfactory."

But then, a nine-page section of the resolution began to attack the "practical leadership" of the Obkom:

However, the party conference notes that in the practical leadership of the *Obkom* were committed a series of mistakes and omissions, and in the work of the buro of the *Obkom,* its departments, city, and *raion* committees of the party there are serious deficiencies.

First came a series of general radical criticisms, beginning with the Obkom's handling of the *proverka* and exchange in 1935–6. According to the now familiar story, the local leadership in Smolensk had used "formalistic" and bureaucratic methods in the *proverka*, had badly used the operations to raise the level of activity of the party activists, and had allowed a situation to develop in which there were large numbers of baseless exclusions. The Obkom leadership in its day-to-day activity had neglected party political work, had countenanced wide violations of democratic centralism, had used cooption instead of election, and had not insisted on the answerability of the party organs before the membership. *Kritika/samokritika* had been suppressed and "in the recent period were at a low level," the leaders having frequently displayed a "scornful attitude" toward worker complaints. Key leaders were responsible to the Obkom, not to mass control, and thus "covered themselves with the authority of the Obkom – the deficiencies of their work were not exposed to criticism by the party organizations who could not bring them to party responsibility." Protected by the Obkom, economic and union leaders could thus afford a "scornful attitude toward workers' complaints."

Then, in a flat contradiction to the first pro-Rumiantsev part of the document, the resolution attacked the leadership of the Western Region for economic failures. The Stakhanovite movement in the region was "weak," as were efforts in the "leading branches of industry." There had been "completely unsatisfactory fulfillment" of the 1936 (and part of the 1937) economic programs. Rural collective-farm administrations were weak and had made poor use of available facilities; cadres were moved about clumsily.

Most of these criticisms, whether aimed at failures in party political education, promotion of the cadres, or economic administration, were traced to the "weak connection" between higher and lower party organizations.

> The direct, living connection between the *Obkom* and the series of *raions,* which is especially important, was insufficient, and thus insufficient was the help of the *Obkom* organizations to these *raions.*
>
> The Conference thus notes serious deficiencies in the work of the departments and instructors of the *Obkom,* insufficient help to the *raions* in raising the quality of party and political work, in teaching, promoting, and elevating the cadres of activists.

When, on rare occasions, emissaries came from regional party bodies, they talked only to local leaders. The resolution insisted that higher party leaders visit the localities in person and talk to rank-and-file activists, rather than listen to formal reports. It demanded that they investigate conditions, find fault, and prepare reports, not just listen to them. The leadership was enjoined to "talk to the masses" in a more systematic way.[76]

The resolution of the Fifth Regional Party Conference in Smolensk was a compromise document. The first part supported the leadership group, whereas the much longer second part took a different view of things and effectively contradicted the first section. It is important to note, however, that Rumiantsev had the last word. He commanded enough support to win approval for his report (and thus for his continued tenure in office), and his political line was ultimately considered "satisfactory."[77] It was still very difficult for local party activists to remove regional party secretaries on their own.[78] But the compromise document clearly shows a trend – one looks in vain in party history for such strong manifestations of criticism "from below." The antibureau-cratism campaign was gaining ground and "verification from below," as Stalin had called it, must have made the middle party *apparat* nervous.

Yet Rumiantsev was still in power, and five days after the conference he submitted a "Plan of Work" for the Obkom, according to party procedure.[79] The neatly printed plan mentioned the points raised at the conference, but simply listed them perfunctorily in a long list with neither dates to consider them nor specific measures to improve the work.

In the five days between the conference and Rumiantsev's plan, an event took place that would spell the end for him and many others in his position. On June 11, 1937, *Pravda* announced the arrest and trial of Marshal Tukhachevskii and the leading generals of the Red Army on charges of espionage, treason, and participation in a conspiracy to overthrow the Soviet government.[80] Army Commanders Tukhachevskii, Iakir, Uborevich, Eideman, Kork, Putna, Feldman, and Primakov were arrested.[81] I. P. Uborevich, commander of the Western Military District and candidate member of the Central Committee, was a member of the Western Obkom Buro in Smolensk. Rumors have suggested that military members of the Central Committee had joined a group denouncing Ezhov at the February plenum, but there is no supporting evidence.[82]

Although Tukhachevskii and the generals had been under suspicion since early May, it took a month for Stalin to make up his mind about what to do. On May 4, the British government was advised that Marshal Tukhachevskii would not be attending King George's coronation (as previously announced) for health reasons. On May 11, the press announced that he had been removed from his post as deputy commissar of defense and transferred to the backwoods Volga Military District. On the same day, Ian Gamarnik, deputy commissar and head of the Main Political Administration of the Red Army, was relieved of his duties and replaced by Mekhlis, the editor of *Pravda*. Associated with Mekhlis's assumption of the army political office was a May 8 announcement that restored the system of "dual command" in the military. Higher officers would be assigned a watchdog political commissar from the party, whose signature was necessary for any military order to be valid.[83] This Civil War–era system maximized communist supervision of the military and reflected the party's traditional fear of "Bonapartism."

There are many rumors and speculations about the Tukhachevskii affair. In the absence of primary sources, speculations of memoirists and politicians have variously accused Hitler and Stalin of framing Tukhachevskii. Others have suggested that the generals were actually plotting a coup against Stalin, who beat them to the punch. With no creditable sources and so many contradictory rumors, the entire affair must remain mysterious.[84]

The Soviet Army was a territorial military force, and the removal of army officers affected the regional party leadership. The army command was dispersed into various military *okrugs*, or districts, around the vast country. Therefore, although personal links between military officers were strong, so must have been the connections between various Generals and the *local* party authorities with whom the military commanders had close contact. Uborevich was a member of the *obkom buro*, so his "treason" naturally cast suspicion on those party leaders with whom he worked on a day-to-day basis. The destruction of the territorial military commanders, for whatever reason, could involve much of the local and regional party *apparat.*

Calls for the death penalty for "traitors" were the immediate reactions in Smolensk. A party meeting in the OSPS was held for this purpose as early as the night of June 11 – the same day as the *Pravda* announcement.[85] The acknowledgment of this event by local party committees, and their unanimous calls for the death penalty, were the only immediate reactions in Smolensk, and many doubtless considered the matter closed.

However, only a week later (June 19–21), an extraordinary plenum of the Western Obkom discussed the "party leadership of the Western Region." The occasion was the arrival in Smolensk of L. M. Kaganovich, who "participated" in the meeting. Although the transcript of this three-day meeting is unfortunately unavailable, accounts of the meeting delivered to local party organizations contain discussions of the events surrounding the removal of Rumiantsev and his people. June 1937 marked the first time that the formulation "enemy of the people" was applied to regional party secretaries.

One account of the meeting suggests that Rumiantsev and his associates in the leadership were arrested before the meeting, which was held to "confirm" the event.[86] Rumiantsev's arrest and simultaneous expulsion from the party were "ordered" by the Central Committee and carried out by the NKVD.[87] Two accounts maintain that Rumiantsev and his associates were directly connected to Uborevich. In the Smolensk City Militia meeting on July 1, 1937, Comrade Glotov said that Uborevich had implicated Rumiantsev.[88]

Kaganovich chided the local party members for not uncovering Rumiantsev's wrecking and for being hesitant to criticize and denounce the former leader. At this point, several party members apparently admitted their laxity in vigilance. Comrade Lepin, of the region court cell, said, "I worked in the *KPK* and carry more responsibility than others. I saw a series of mistakes in the *Obkom*...but failed to draw the proper conclusions."[89] Kaganovich had noted that the Western Region was a frontier region, sharing a border with "Fascist Poland." Germany, Japan, and Poland were clearly preparing an intervention against the USSR and, toward that end, wanted to link up with the fifth columns inside the country. The plan, to which Uborevich, Rumiantsev, and others were parties, allegedly involved the arrest of the Soviet government coincident with the invasion of the country from abroad. Kaganovich said many comrades had forgotten Stalin's warnings about the capitalist encirclement at the February plenum.[90]

In the meetings held in local party organizations to discuss the removal of the leadership, many of Rumiantsev's failings were for the first time characterized not as deficiencies but as conscious sabotage of party work. Rumiantsev and his associates (Shil'man, Arkhipov, Makarov, Sheinin, Kovalev, and "possibly Rakitov") were accused of using their high positions for wrecking in economic and party work.[91] They protected each other. Their tactics were "to install their own people in the apparat – kindred souls....These people artfully created a false authority and occupied themselves with toadying and strangling criticism. It is necessary to choose comrades who work well politically, rather than friends."[92] One example was Kovalev, the former first secretary of the Belyi Raion party committee, who had come under attack by his own activists after the February plenum and had been removed from his position by the local membership. When Rumiantsev fell, Kovalev fell. As Comrade Bupev said, "In Belyi, the former *Raikom* secretary Kovalev was carrying out a wrecking policy directed by the enemy of the people Rumiantsev, and when the party organizations exposed him as an enemy, then the *Obkom* took him into itself."[93] Although it is improbable that either Kovalev or Rumiantsev were "carrying out a wrecking policy," the relationships are clear. Kovalev was one of Rumiantsev's "own people." By using such familyness and patronage, Rumiantsev had "suppressed criticism and self-criticism, creating a circle of 'his people.'" Many of these people were now accused of bureaucratism – for "sitting in his office and doing nothing," "staying in their *dachas* rather than working," and not caring about people and their problems. Many of these bureaucrats and "careerists" actually took sanctions against their critics and made whatever criticism that actually existed "formal, one-sided, and un-real." Moreover, Rumiantsev and his associates, according to one tantalizing but brief passage, had tried to blame the party leadership for his own shortcomings in that he "used criticism of the Central Committee to shield himself."[94]

In the course of these discussion meetings, Rumiantsev and his circle were denounced for the failures in party work that had been spelled out so clearly in the regional conference resolution of the preceding week, and there is therefore no need to reiterate them here. A poignant final criticism of Rumiantsev came from one Comrade Klimkin and probably tells more about Klimkin and the general level of political culture than it does about Rumiantsev: "It was the case that the enemy of the people Rumiantsev while in Plokhinskii *Raion*, threw money to children and kolkhozniks from his moving car."[95]

Rumiantsev and the entire regional Buro were removed and arrested no later than June 19. Protocols for the next meeting of the Obkom on June 26 show Paparde as the new acting regional secretary.[96] Paparde was the former representative of the Party Control Commission to the Western Obkom, and he therefore may have been Ezhov's man on the spot. By the fall of 1937, D. S. Korotchenkov had become "Acting Secretary" of the Western Obkom, having been transferred from the Moscow party organization.[97]

The decimation of the Rumiantsev circle in Smolensk suggests one pattern to the Ezhovshchina. Rumiantsev was removed "from above" for connection with the alleged military plot. The timing of his fall, and even explicit statements, tied him to Uborevich's demise. However, in spite of the fact that the blow came from the Central Committee, Rumiantsev's fall occurred during the most vituperative antibureaucracy campaigns the party had ever seen. This campaign had not been able to unseat Rumiantsev "from below." A regional secretary who was also a Central Committee member was so firmly entrenched that it took direct intercession from the party's central leadership to remove him. Although a *raion* secretary like Kovalev could be ejected from office by discontented activists, an important satrap such as Rumiantsev who ruled an area the size of a European country was answerable only to the Central Committee. The criticism from below showed that rank-and-file party activists were probably not unhappy to see the first secretary fall.

The two radical currents of the 1930s had converged in July 1937, and the resulting turbulence destroyed the bureaucracy. Zhdanov's party-revival campaign and Ezhov's hunt for enemies fused to create a chaotic "populist terror" that now swept the party. Party revival became the vehicle for vigilance. The demands of party revival meant that party committees met regularly and often (sometimes for days at a time) for criticism sessions. But party secretaries were no longer criticized solely for bureaucratism. The atmosphere of Ezhov's vigilance campaign and the "treason" of the generals now injected a new element into the process. Criticism was transformed into unmasking of enemies, and the new equation was poor party work = wrecking.

The secretaries' power had been stripped away, and many of them were imprisoned or shot. More than that, the very duties of the office now exposed its occupant to suspicion. When Belyi secretary Kovalev closed reading rooms because of poor attendance, he did not know that populists would interpret his rational measure as criminal sabotage. Any exercise of power, any mistake, could bring charges of "bureaucratism" or "treason" from above or below. Antibureaucratic populism and police terror destroyed the offices as well as the officeholders. Radicalism had turned the political machine inside out and destroyed the party bureaucracy.

7

Epilogue: the Ezhovshchina

Ils sauront bientôt que nos balles
Sont pour nos propres généraux.

"The Internationale"

Unfortunately, continuous archival coverage of local events in the Western Region ends in the middle of 1937. After that time, it becomes very difficult to trace the interplay of central and peripheral forces, and knowledge of the period of the Ezhovshchina must remain sketchy and incomplete. In the absence of other sources, one must rely on the press and fall back upon the older methods of Kremlinology and text analysis in an attempt to piece together events, disputes, and policy changes relating to the center–periphery struggle. Interpretation of events from late 1937 through 1938 must therefore be hypothetical and incomplete. Despite the essentially speculative nature of any analysis of the politics of the post-1937 period, certain patterns emerge that suggest the contours of the Ezhovshchina.

Observations on incidence

The Ezhovshchina was a maelstrom of political violence that involved all bureaucratic factions and interest groups. Stalin used police repression of "enemies of the people" to settle old scores and to destroy anyone he chose. Others in the Moscow leadership turned the police tool to their own advantage as well. Kaganovich used terror to sweep transportation agencies of those he mistrusted. When he took over the Commissariat of Foreign Affairs, Molotov used the police weapon to wipe out the clients of former commissar Maksim Litvinov.[1] In fact, through denunciations to the police or to Stalin, any leader could use the vigilance campaign to destroy members of rival groups. Even officials who would soon be arrested as "enemies" were able to secure their opponents' arrest.[2]

Regional and local officials of the NKVD were caught up in the momentum of the vigilance campaign and were under pressure to produce results (discover enemies) in order to further their careers; it is certain that local scores were settled this way in 1937–8. One arrest led to another because no police official wanted to be accused of not vigilantly following all the threads of "conspiracy." Acquittals and releases were rare for the same reason. Many of the arrests seem to have resulted from chains (sometimes family circles) of personal connections. Those under interrogation were always encouraged to implicate and denounce others in a prophylactic attempt to destroy possible circles even remotely connected to the main targets. The intensity of the arrests increased when some victims eagerly implicated others in an attempt to stop the Ezhovshchina by helping it become absurd.[3]

Impressionistic data (which are all there are on the Ezhovshchina) suggest that most arrests of key provincial (and other) leaders took place in the summer or early fall of 1937 – coincident with or immediately after the military affair.[4] The fall of the military officers was somehow crucial to the extension of the Ezhovshchina to party committees. As in Smolensk, the arrest of an important military "conspirator" (Uborevich) led to the arrest of those regional party leaders with whom he had worked. According to Trotsky's calculations, all regional party secretaries were removed and replaced by the end of 1937.[5]

The Smolensk pattern seems to have been repeated across the country. In the wake of the fall of the generals, other regional party organizations were "cleaned out" by emissaries from the center. In June, Malenkov went to Belorussia and elsewhere and oversaw the removal of the party leadership there. In July, Beria did the same in Georgia. August would see emissaries Molotov, Ezhov, and Khrushchev go to the Ukraine, and Malenkov and Mikoian went to Armenia to engineer leadership changes.[6]

After the arrest of the Red Army commanders, the number of arrests mounted as the NKVD pulled in clusters or circles of suspects whose centers were former Trotskyists, Bukharinists, army officers, regional leaders, or other targets. These arrests would continue at varying levels for a little over a year, although July to December 1937 seems to have been the worst time. It was in this period that Khrushchev says that

Stalin began to approve lists of persons for arrest whose names had been submitted by Ezhov as a result of his investigations. Khrushchev claimed that the 383 lists contained thousands of names.[7]

Space and a lack of sources do not permit a detailed study of the incidence of the Ezhovshchina among various groups. It seems clear, though, that former members of the opposition movements and officials working in economic-related fields were particularly exposed. The conflicts between radicals and moderates over planning, combined with the milieu in which the plans were carried out, made a clash between rigid, puritanical investigators and economic administrators inevitable. Any reader of accounts of industrial affairs in the thirties knows of the "scrounging," under-the-table bartering for scarce materials, the petty bribes and favors, and the technically illegal "private deals" between various managers. Such "clever fellows," as they were sardonically called, were often forced to keep two sets of books – the real ones and the ones they showed to investigators to avoid suspicion. Their activities may have even increased production, especially when they ironed out deficiencies in the plan, but in the highly charged political atmosphere of the thirties such covert dealings were regarded as "wrecking." John Scott, John Littlepage, and others have also described how the perennial shortage of trained personnel and experienced administrators led to untold mismanagement, accidents, and destruction of valuable machines through sheer stupidity and ignorance. How could one convince an NKVD investigator that this was not deliberate sabotage? A puritanical police, impatient party enthusiasts, and even less comfortable workers were unwilling to understand economic disorder as incompetence. The concerns of the economic and production specialists were always practical and "expert," the emphasis of the radical party activists was ideological, heroic, vigilant, and "red."[8]

There are strong signs that the pattern of Ezhovshchina arrests was one in which *leaders* (rather than simply "Old Bolsheviks") were especially vulnerable to repression. Rank-and-file expulsions, although numerous, were proportionally fewer than during the previous *chistki*. Like the membership purges of 1933–6, the Ezhovshchina highlighted the tension between center and provinces, leaders and led. But in its incidence at various levels of the party, the Ezhovshchina seems to have been the opposite of the mass purges in that leaders were much more likely to fall than rank-and-file members.

The second half of 1937 saw local party meetings in the Western Region in which members denounced or accused one another for connections with enemy elements or indeed for being enemies of the people themselves. Hysterical accusations were made for defacing Stalin's portrait, having a brother who was under arrest, or for being the offspring of kulaks or priests (a traditional denunciation). There were frequent checks of the biographical information supplied by the members on themselves. Such "loyalty checks" often resulted in the digging up of suspicious behavior or activity from ten years before – such notations were gathered into lists, investigated individually, and categorized into files.[9] The few continuous series of meeting protocols in the Archive provide no information on the rate or total number of expulsions, although a few points do stand out.

First, in all the organizations for which archival information exists on the Ezhovshchina, (Belyi, OSPS, Obsud), most of those expelled were from the leadership circle. In Obsud, eight persons (17 percent of a cell membership of 47) were expelled during 1937. Of these, four were members of the Obsud Buro, the group of ten that led the party organization. The remaining six members of the Obsud Buro were in turn investigated, but the charges were "unsupported" and apparently no action was taken.[10]

A survey of the records in Belyi Raion supports the impression that leaders (*raikom* officials, administrators, party secretaries) were the main targets of repression. Of 244 members and candidates of the Belyi party organization, 36 (14.8 percent) were expelled in 1937. (Seven cases were still pending at the end of the year.) Twenty-nine of those expelled (80 percent) were in leading positions. They included two *raikom* first secretaries, one chairman and two deputy chairmen of the district soviet executive committee (*raiispolkom*), a Komsomol district secretary, the district prosecutor, the chief of the district NKVD and one of his fellow officers, the directors of the three largest schools in the district, the head of the district land office (*raizo*), the director of the Belyi Machine Tractor Station, four heads of industrial undertakings, two heads of trade organizations, five collective-farm chairmen, and five chairmen of rural soviets.[11]

Older persons were often more likely to be arrested, primarily because they held the senior positions.[12] A leadership position in any field increased one's risk of being a victim, especially in the economic or party *apparat*. But a recent study of Old Bolsheviks of Stalin's generation suggests that they were not specific generational or generic targets. Of a sample of 127 Old Bolsheviks who had been active participants in the October Revolution in Moscow, death information was available for 109. Of these, 2 died in the October Revolution, 16 in the Civil

War, and 6 of natural causes before the Ezhovshchina. Of the Old Bolsheviks alive in the mid-thirties, 38 were victims of the Ezhovshchina and 38 survived to die naturally. Thus, only 50 percent of this sample of prominent Old Bolsheviks fell in the police operations.[13]

Back in 1934, at the Seventeenth Congress, Ezhov had said in his report for the credentials commission that 10 percent of the party had joined in 1920 or earlier.[14] In 1939, Malenkov would say that the figure then was 8.3 percent.[15] Computing on the basis of the total party membership at the two times (about 1,826,000 and 1,514,000 full members, respectively), the total numbers of such Old Bolsheviks were 182,600 in 1934 and about 125,000 in 1939. This means a net loss of 57,000, or a decrease of about 31 percent, from all causes during the period of the Ezhovshchina. Old Bolsheviks fell because of their leadership positions in 1937, not because of their age or past experience.

It seems that the incidence of the Ezhovshchina in the party – as measured by party expulsions[16] – was not as great as in previous operations. The total number of persons expelled from the party in 1937 was smaller than the number expelled nationally in the *proverka* in 1935, or indeed in any previous year of official "purge." Table 7.1 summarizes this material.

According to one authoritative calculation, the total number of expulsions during the period November 1936–March 1939 (nearly two and a half years) was fewer than 180,000, or about the same as the *proverka*.[17] In Belyi District, 11.2 percent of the membership had been expelled in the 1935 *proverka*, whereas 14.8 percent were expelled in 1937.[18] If the national *Ezhovshchina* expulsion figure is broken down over time, one arrives at a figure of about 10,000 expulsions per month, comparted with 21,250 per month for the 1935 *proverka*. Thus the rate of expulsion during the Ezhovshchina was less than half what it had been two years previously.

The scanty archival material on the Ezhovshchina at the lower or local level is inconclusive but suggestive. It seems clear that, like previous radical campaigns, it had an antileadership, antibureaucracy bias, and the police terror was directed against the same targets as previous pronouncements and efforts.

Criticism and terror had not only liquidated the regional leaders but had cast doubt on the nature of leadership and power in general. What were the powers of local leaders in relation to the rank and file? How was the work of party secretaries to be verified? What were the differences between good decisions, "mistakes," and "wrecking"? What

or control of the phenomenon. In fact, considerable confusion and bungling accompanied the terror. Frequently, important officials were promoted to powerful and important positions, only to be arrested shortly thereafter.[22] Although such shifts might serve a variety of hypothetical purposes, they also would appear to be administratively dysfunctional and needlessly disruptive. In 1937, 1,143 celebrities were officially nominated to the Supreme Soviet in October, but by the time of the voting less than two months later, 5 percent of them (54 persons) had disappeared. They included one deputy chairman of Sovnarkom, 11 regional party secretaries, 10 chairmen of regional soviet executive committees (*ispolkoms*), and 8 senior military commanders.[23] Why had these worthy candidates been publicly put forward if they were targets? Apparently, there was considerable day-to-day indecision and confusion about whom to arrest; there seems to have been little detailed planning or coordination and a good deal of spontaneous violence.

The literature is also replete with cases of NKVD inefficiency. Officials slated for arrest could go on vacation or move to another town and avoid repression altogether. Pavel Kuznetsov, editor of a Kazan' newspaper, was charged by the NKVD as an "enemy of the people" but moved to Kazakhstan. He later translated odes to "Father Ezhov," which were published in *Pravda*. Similarly, when the NKVD came for Colonel Kutsner at the Thirty-Eighth Regiment in Minsk, he took a train to Moscow. Presenting himself to the Main Personnel Administration of the Red Army, he asked for a job anywhere but Minsk and was assigned to teach at the Frunze Academy in Moscow. The warrant for his arrest was "just local stuff," and he was safe in Moscow. According to survivors, "a person who felt that his arrest was imminent could go to another town and, as a rule, avoid being seized."[24]

This highly charged and chaotic political atmosphere reopened old wounds and plunged the party into disarray. Members denounced leaders (and each other) for dubious class origins, long-forgotten sins, and current misdeeds. Secretaries defended themselves and proved their vigilance by expelling and denouncing batches of rank-and-file members. *Spetseedstvo*, antibureaucratism, and class hatred reemerged in strength against the backdrop of a full-blown spy scare. Panic-stricken local party officials even resorted to filling administrative positions with politically "safe" employees of the NKVD.[25]

Although Stalin certainly supported the liquidation of highly placed "spies, wreckers, and enemies" and the promotion of "control from below," there is no reason to believe that he intended for the fusion of the two campaigns to produce the chaos it did. Almost immediately,

Moscow began a series of unsuccessful attempts to limit the chaos while continuing to support investigations of highly placed "enemies."

Even as the press continued to push antibureaucratic and mass-criticism themes, Moscow warned against excesses that could lead to chaos. Thus, in the first two weeks of May, the press reported on party meetings in the Donbas. The articles lauded the efforts of local activists to unmask opponents of the Stakhanov movement and other enemies but complained that the continuous series of party meetings (some of which lasted several days) was disrupting production. By the middle of the month, *Pravda* was complaining about uncontrolled *spetseedstvo* and unwarranted arrests of technical specialists. The office of the USSR procuracy was instructed to investigate incidents of false arrest.[26]

In June, the press continued to criticize radical "excesses." *Pravda* complained that criticism of leaders had sometimes gone too far. Production and labor discipline had suffered as rank-and-file activists criticized their leaders and managers. The press warned that such excesses were dangerously reminiscent of the antiparty activities of Trotsky-ists.[27]

On October 2, the Central Executive Committee of Soviets took the unusual step of publishing a change in the law. According to the announcement, the law formerly provided a sentence of ten years for espionage and a sentence of death for more serious offenses. The new law provided an alternative sentence of twenty-five years. Although the change was said to be part of the "struggle against such crimes," the announcement specifically stated that the change was to provide courts the "possibility to select for these crimes not only the highest measure of punishment (shooting) but also deprivation of freedom for a more prolonged term." The immediate publication and wording of this decision suggest an attempt to limit and restrain local death sentences.[28]

Later in October, Stalin made one of his rare Olympian pronouncements, which esoterically condemned radical excesses. In a reception for lower- and middle-level leaders of industry from the Donbas, Stalin toasted the leaders of Soviet industry. Although he did not directly denounce radicalism, he went out of his way to explain that Soviet technicians and economic leaders, unlike their prerevolutionary counterparts, deserved the trust and respect of the Soviet people. Stressing that members of the Soviet intelligentsia and management cadre were drawn from the proletariat, he defended such leaders *(khoziaistvenniki)* and warned that it was wrong to persecute *all* leaders. It would have been unnecessary for him to make such remarks had radical specialist baiting not been out of control.[29]

The lengthy preparations for elections to the Supreme Soviet also show that Moscow was reacting to and trying to channel events rather than creating them and illustrate the political confusion, indecision, and apprehension among party leaders. In late June 1937, the press had announced the decisions of the June plenum of the Central Committee that had approved detailed "Regulations on Elections to the Supreme Soviet of the USSR."[30] According to this widely publicized electoral scheme, candidates for seats in the Supreme Soviet were to be nominated without restriction. Each seat was to be contested. Free and open nomination procedures were to produce several candidates for each position; all nominated candidates who were qualified could run; and the candidate who received a majority vote would win the seat. If no single candidate received a majority, a runoff election between the top two would decide the winner. This radical electoral scheme was confirmed a week later by the Central Executive Committee.[31] On paper, the electoral system seemed democratic. But by the time the voting took place in December, new rules were issued that voided the widely-publicized democratic June scheme and substituted a system that allowed only one candidate per seat.

Why did Moscow contradict itself and retreat from contested posts in the election? It is possible that the fears of local party leaders may have lent support to those in Moscow who opposed populist mobilizations and input from below. As early as March 1937, some local activists had expressed apprehension about free elections in the countryside.

One member in Belyi worried that, in an uncontrolled election, priests and "alien elements" could easily be elected.[32] Another activist pointed out that the elections had to be managed in such a way that "the masses know whom to elect so they will not send enemies of the people to office." Comrade Ivanov noted that rural party control and political work went so badly that "if we act this way in the elections then we will undoubtedly suffer a defeat." At a series of party meetings in June, Belyi activists again expressed alarm at the effects of free elections on the soviets. One official worried that "alien elements, enemies, and friends of Hitler" could be elected. Other speakers reported confusion in the countryside over the meaning of the Stalin constitution and the upcoming elections to the Supreme Soviet. A *raion* prosecutor reported that many peasants thought that the new constitution meant the end of collective farms and the return of individual farming. Some peasants, anticipating a Bolshevik defeat in the elections, had even begun to confiscate pasture land from the collective farms for private use.[33] At an August meeting, a member asked if voters could write in candidates during the voting. Confusion was so great that one official answered yes while another answered no.[34]

Local activists were clearly worried about the possible effects of secret ballots and contested seats, and there was considerable fear that nonparty candidates would defeat party candidates in head-to-head contests. If *Pravda's* exhortations are any gauge, local activists not only complained about the voting system but refused to expend much energy preparing for and organizing the voting.[35]

On October 13, *Pravda* announced the conclusion of an "Extraordinary Plenum of the Central Committee" that had met in the preceding days. According to the announcement, the Central Committee discussed the upcoming elections and "took decisions" on the matter. The discussion and the decisions were secret. Although no official resolutions were forthcoming, it is clear that the plenum revoked the June electoral system and ordered the nomination of one candidate per seat.[36] Accordingly, a resolution of a Belyi party meeting that had convened to discuss the October plenum called for single candidates.[37]

On December 7, less than a week before the voting, the Politburo announced that party and nonparty candidates were to "enter the elections in a bloc." That is, all candidates would run as if they belonged to the same party and all would appear on the same ticket.[38] Because members of the same "bloc" would not want to run against one another, each seat would have only one candidate. *Pravda* repeatedly stressed that party members were to enthusiastically support nonparty candidates and vice versa. Although presented as a sign of the unity of the Soviet people and of the confidence the electors had in their candidates, the results were clearly a retreat from the democratic procedures spelled out in June.

Some time between June and October, party leaders had become frightened about the implications of truly democratic elections.[39] They may have feared that party presence in the countryside was so weak that party candidates might lose their electoral contests. It may well be that the opinions of fearful bureaucrats had forced Moscow to back away from populism. In either event, the contradictory pronouncements on Supreme Soviet voting demonstrate indecision, confusion, debate, and a lack of planning in the highest leadership. Moscow leaders were making decisions at the last minute in response to developing conditions.

Confusion and disorganization continued to characterize local party activities as well. Two weeks before the voting, activists complained that even party workers poorly understood the electoral system. A meeting in Belyi the day before the voting revealed that preparations were poor: Electoral lists had not been circulated, and many people did not know the names of their candidates. No voting booths had been installed in many rural areas. One official was so worried about the outcome of the voting that he proposed the stationing of a 24-hour armed guard at each rural voting point.[40]

Although sources on this period are weak and vague, there are signs that Stalin may not have been entirely satisfied with other events in mid-1937. He certainly favored an offensive against disobedient, suspicious, and corrupt members of the bureaucracy, but it is by no means certain that he was comfortable with the accompanying excesses. For whatever reason, he seems to have tried to reduce the cult of the NKVD by putting a certain distance between himself and the radical efforts of the police.[41]

Indeed, the second half of 1937 had seen the growth of an Ezhov–NKVD cult in the press. A dramatic increase in publicity for the NKVD that flooded the national press included poems about Ezhov and the police, articles about espionage techniques, and photographs of police officials. This tide of glorification included frequent reports of ceremonies honoring NKVD officials. In the month of July alone, NKVD officers received at least 40 Orders of Lenin and more than 63 other decorations, and a town was renamed for Ezhov (Sulimov became Ezhovo-Cherkessk).[42] Presumably, this glorification was at least partly a reward for Ezhov's "services" in unmasking the plots of Tukhachevskii and other officials. In October, Ezhov became a candidate member of the Politburo.[43]

In the first two weeks of December, however, members of the Politburo gave highly publicized speeches in connection with their nominations to the Supreme Soviet. These speeches are particularly interesting for their attitudes toward the police. Of thirteen published speeches, only seven mentioned the accomplishments of the NKVD.[44] Speeches by top-rank leaders Stalin, Molotov, Zhdanov, Voroshilov, Mikoian, and Kalinin made no mention of the police at all.[45]

The Politburo speeches were printed in full, with one exception. Ezhov's speech was censored. After saying a good deal about Trotskyist–Bukharinist spies and wreckers, Ezhov observed that "yes, and now comrades, the struggle is not finished. In our path we meet no few difficulties." Then, in the middle of his speech, there was a unique editorial cut:

Further, Comrade Ezhov, discussing the history of the party's struggle with the Trotskyist–Zinovievist–Bukharinist band, gave a profound characterization of the Trotskyist–Bukharinist gang in the service of the foreign bourgeoisie. He spoke of the hatred which the Soviet people feel for the fascist–Bukharinist agents of foreign intelligence services. At the end of his analysis of the struggle with the Trotskyist–Zinovievist and Bukharinist–fascist bands, Comrade Ezhov exclaimed "Our Soviet people are destroying each one of the contemptible henchmen of the capitalist lords, these foul enemies of the working class and of all toilers!"[46]

If Ezhov's "characterization" of the enemy was so profound, why was it not published? It seems that his views were for some reason considered inappropriate; the enemies question and the role of the NKVD were again disputed issues. Ezhov was in trouble and was probably being blamed for excessive repression.

During the third week of December 1937, the NKVD celebrated its twentieth anniversary. Taken together, however, the events of the month did not suggest an unqualified success for police interests. On December 20, *Pravda* announced that, in connection with the NKVD's anniversary, 407 police officials had received medals or decorations, and the following day it announced an unprecedented celebratory meeting in the Bolshoi Theater in honor of the NKVD.[47] A number of prominent party and police officials addressed the gathering, and their speeches were published in *Pravda,* as well as under separate cover.[48]

According to several of the speakers, Ezhov and his NKVD were comparable to Feliks Dzerzhinskii and his Cheka–both were the "unsheathed sword" of the revolutionary common people in time of extreme peril to the Soviet state. Quotes from Dzerzhinskii on his "fire" and "passionate soul" in defending the republic were followed by previously published exhortations from Stalin on the danger of capitalist encirclement. There were citations from Lenin on how "a good communist is at the same time a good Chekist." These were followed by claims that those Bolsheviks who worked for the NKVD in 1937 were the most devoted Bolsheviks; they were responsible before the Soviet people and prepared to give their lives for communism. The Soviet intelligence service, whether Cheka or NKVD, was in the "vanguard of party and revolution" and of "class self-defence."[49]

The most interesting theme at this meeting and in press coverage of the police was the alleged close connections between the NKVD and the common people. Dramatizing this theme, many of the speakers at the meeting were workers, foremen, and the like form Moscow factories who quoted Ezhov's statement:

In the world, there is not one state where the organs of state security, the intelligence organs, are so closely connected with the people, so clearly express the interests of that people, and guard the interests of people.

In the capitalist world, the intelligence organs are the most hated part of the state apparatus for the broad masses of the laboring population, because they stand guard over the interests of the ruling group of capitalists. Here, on the other hand, the organs of Soviet intelligence, the organs of state security stand guard over the interests of the Soviet people. That is why they deserve the respect, deserve the love of the whole Soviet people.[50]

It seems that the leaders and supporters of the NKVD felt the need to emphasize the relationship between police activities and the needs of the common people in order to give police activities a radical populist or democratic gloss. The championing of the interests of the masses by the NKVD against highly placed criminals was not unlike Zhdanov's radical attack on bureaucratism, at least in point of view and tone. Both incited the rank and file, the party activists, and the common people against the officeholding establishment. Both stressed maximum activist participation against the elite. Both claimed to be "mobilizations."

Ezhov certainly had radical credentials, and the wholesale destruction of economic planners and administrators, combined with the annihilation of the regional party *apparat* under an ideology of antibureaucratism, strongly suggests that the politics of the 1929–32 "cultural revolution" conditioned the Ezhovshchina. Previous chapters showed how Molotov and Kaganovich took fierce measures against "limiters" and "counterrevolutionary limit-setting" in 1936–7. Ezhov had destroyed virtually all the targets of radical-activist criticism during the preceding decade.[51] But, unlike the Stalin–Zhdanov mobilization tactic, police control necessarily came from above. The point of the December Bolshoi meeting seems to have been to point out that the activities of the police could also be understood in a populist context. Police officials invoked the Dzerzhinskii tradition, mobilized supportive quotes from Lenin, and reiterated that the police "deserve the respect, deserve the love of the popular masses."

These assertions seemed defensive and reactive, and the attempt to boost the prestige of the police fell flat. First, the meeting was chaired by Anastas Mikoian, a secondary figure who had not seen fit even to mention the police in his electoral speech eleven days before and who had no known connection to the NKVD.[52]

More significant was Stalin's boycott of the meeting and attempts by police supporters to hide the embarrassment. The commemorative volume published about the Bolshoi meeting contained a photograph of

Stalin and Ezhov smiling at one another from behind a podium.[53] Yet the press announcement of the meeting shows that Stalin did not attend, despite the fact that all other members of the Politburo were present. Indeed, *Pravda* esoterically highlighted Stalin's absence from the NKVD meeting. At the close of the police celebration in the Bolshoi, there was a short intermission followed by a musical concert. Although Stalin did not attend the meeting, *Pravda* reported his arrival for the music.[54] Stalin's absence stood in sharp contrast to the glorification of the NKVD – the previous day's *Pravda* had been almost totally devoted to the police – and it is hard to imagine a greater insult to the police or to Ezhov, whom the press had earlier called a "Stalinist pupil" and "Stalinist commissar."

Mikoian's chairmanship and Stalin's conspicuous absence reduced the importance and prestige of the ceremony. In recent months, Stalin had attended receptions and meetings for heroic aviators, polar explorers, and collective-farm women. He had recently addressed meetings of industrial managers and Supreme Soviet voters. Why was Stalin not present for such an important celebration as the anniversary of the police? Perhaps he chose to disassociate himself from the nefarious activities of the NKVD to make it easier for him later to condemn the repression he authored.[55] Yet it is just as reasonable to believe that Stalin was unimpressed with the chaotic effects of police activities and unwilling to grace the commemoration with his person.

There were other signs that the power and prestige of the NKVD were perhaps in decline. At the end of December, one of Ezhov's deputy commissars of the NKVD was transferred to a post in the Commissariat of Forests, and another became deputy commissar of communications.[56] In the following weeks, a third deputy commissar of the NKVD was transferred to other work.[57]

On February 20, 1938, *Pravda* published a signed letter from the Politburo congratulating the participants in a polar expedition. The fourteen signatures were led by Stalin, Molotov, and Voroshilov. Ezhov appeared eleventh, ahead of only Petrovskii, Eikhe, and Khrushchev.[58] Three months later, Ezhov was appointed commissar of water transport.[59]

The January 1938 Central Committee plenum

According to some accounts, the resolution proceeding from the January 1938 Central Committee plenum constituted a "signal" for the winding down of the Great Purge by blaming the "excesses" of the Ezhovshchina on overzealous, careerist, and "enemy" officials who had expelled and arrested far too many innocent people in the preceding period.[60] This hypocritical shifting of the blame from himself to other officials meant that Stalin was preparing to "purge the purgers," to rid himself of any blame for the terror and take credit for bringing the culprits (including Ezhov) to justice. Yet the situation was more complicated than this explanation would suggest.

Shortly before the plenum, the press attacked the "false vigilance" of party secretaries who had victimized rank-and-file members to cover themselves.[61] The January 1938 plenum produced a resolution that took a hard line against "certain careerist Communists who are striving to become prominent and to be promoted by recommending expulsions from the party, through the repression of party members, who are striving to insure themselves against possible charges of inadequate vigilance through the indiscriminate repression of party members." This type of person "feels it unnecessary to make an objective evaluation of the accusations submitted against the Communist," "indiscriminately spreads panic about enemies of the people" and "is willing to expel dozens of members from the party on false grounds just to appear vigilant himself."[62]

According to the resolution, such persons adopt "a completely incorrect approach, and expel Communists from the party in a criminally frivolous way."

There have been many instances of party organizations, without any verification and thus without any basis, expelling Communists from the party, depriving them of their jobs, frequently even declaring them enemies of the people without any foundation, acting lawlessly and arbitrarily toward party members. . . .

It is time to understand that Bolshevik vigilance consists essentially in the ability to unmask an enemy regardless of how clever and artful he may be, regardless of how he decks himself out, and not in indiscriminate or "on the off-chance" explusions, by the tens and hundreds, of everyone who comes within reach.

The resolution gave several examples in which many expulsions from 1935–6 had been reversed by the higher party bodies or the Party Control Commission (KPK).[63] The "heartless, bureaucratic attitude" on the part of the local party leaders allowed this to take place. Leaders were not considering their people on a "careful individual basis" and instead were "acting in an intolerably arbitrary manner." Such "formalistic'' behavior had been mentioned before, in June 1936 and at the February plenum.

The bureaucrat ''shouts louder than anyone else about vigilance, hastens to 'unmask' the greatest number possible, and does all this to cover up his own crimes before the party.'' He and his people assumed that ''once a deposition has been submitted against a party member, regardless of how incorrect or even provocational it may be, this party member is dangerous for the organization and must be got rid of immediately in order that he himself will be proved vigilant.'' Unfortunately, people ''frequently surround them with the halos of vigilant fighters for the purity of party ranks.''

Such accusations were only esoterically directed against Ezhov. Actually, the resolution gave the NKVD credit for *reversing* unjust expulsions. ''In many *raions* of Kuibyshev *Oblast'*, large numbers of communists have been expelled from the party on the grounds that they are enemies of the people. But the organs of the *NKVD* found no grounds for arrest.'' Nowhere in the resolution is there the slightest criticism of the police, Ezhov, or even of the campaign against enemies of the people. In fact, it actually exhorted the party to increased vigilance.[64]

The specific targets of reproach were *party* organizations and leaders. ''The *VKP(b)* Central Committee considers it necessary to direct the attention of party organizations and their leaders to the fact that... they are committing serious mistakes.'' ''Party organs,'' ''*raion* party organizations,'' ''party leaders,'' ''some party organizations and their leaders,'' and ''*oblast'* and *krai* organizations'' were the culprits.

The January 1938 decision was in direct line of succession with other radical critiques: the June 1935 rebuke of the Western Oblast', Zhdanov's Saratov speech of 1935, the plenum of the KPK in early 1936, the June 1936 Central Committee letter on appeals, and Stalin's remarks about inattention to people at the February 1937 plenum. It was not only filled with the same language as these decisions, speeches, and letters, but quoted from them directly to reinforce its point and to show that the abuses were continuing in spite of instructions from the center. The resolution was the sixth high-level statement that bureaucrats, not common people, were the targets.[65] The repetition of such high-level demands says more about Moscow's continuing inability to limit rank-and-file expulsions than it does about an alleged need by Stalin to cover his tracks.

The resolution identified certain secretaries as ''enemies of the people" and "provocateurs" and criticized their "false vigilance" in no uncertain terms. Although it suggested that the actions of these enemies would now be put right and that excessive vigilance was a thing of the past, a *Pravda* editorial the day after the plenum advised members that the struggle with enemies was not yet over. "On the contrary," one must not weaken vigilance. Three days later, another editorial clearly identified some local party secretaries as "enemies of the people" and pointed out that the January resolution provides a "sharp new weapon" in the struggle with the enemy.[66]

Taken together, Moscow's statements of December and January suggest attempts to limit grass-roots chaos and repression of the rank and file by panic-stricken party secretaries. The police had been implicitly insulted and criticized in late 1937, particularly when they tried to associate themselves with rank-and-file interests. Yet Ezhov's NKVD establishment remained strong despite transfers and Ezhov's simultaneous duties at Water Transport. Stalin wanted to stop local chaos without totally discrediting the NKVD, for he supported continued investigations and repression of oppositionists and other "suspicious" persons. So it was no paradox that the trial of Bukharin followed the January criticisms of excessive local vigilance.

The public trial of Bukharin and Rykov in March 1938 showed that oppositionists were still enemies. This trial has been thoroughly studied, but a few points are worth noting.[67] The chief evildoers presented were Bukharin and Rykov, the former leaders of the Right Opposition. Their trial was almost anticlimatic from a political point of view. Bukharinists had been declared "enemies of the people" more than a year earlier, and, because most of them were under arrest already, the trial represented the formal liquidation of the movement's symbols. The trial was a piece of theater designed to give the coup de grace to Bukharinism and publicly to redefine the enemy.

All the other defendants (save one) were figures in the central or national republic hierarchy. There were three diplomats, two from agriculture, three from nationality areas, two from the NKVD, and one each from finance, domestic trade, and foreign trade.[68] The defendants in the 1938 morality play were foreign spies, secret agents, assassins, and skilled saboteurs who had wormed their way into high positions since the 1917 revolutions. These were the enemies.

Police arrests of high-ranking "enemies" continued into 1938 even as Ezhov's star began to set. He had been under a cloud since his appointment to Water Transport and had been out of the public eye. On

December 8, the press announced that he had been relieved of his duties as head of the NKVD "at his own request."[69] Four days later, the Moscow Regional Court reversed the first of many convictions of former "enemies."[70] The declaration noted that the Supreme Court had not only released five construction engineers but had recognized that the five had actually tried to thwart "real enemies."[71] Ezhov was last seen in public on January 22, 1939, at a memorial ceremony honoring Lenin. After that, he completely disappeared, and his name was never again mentioned in print during Stalin's lifetime.[72]

Although some arrests still took place in 1939, nearly all accounts agree that the police operations were essentially over. Several Khrushchev-era memoirs remember that, when Beria took over, those who had not signed confessions (and against whom there was therefore no "evidence") were released and restored to their previous positions. Furthermore, it seems that there was another wholesale turnover in the ranks of the NKVD, with Ezhov's people being replaced by a Beria staff. In this process, the old police were frequently prosecuted (and sometimes shot) for misdeeds in the preceding period. Evgeniia Ginzburg, who was in Iaroslavl' Prison and who saw no newspapers, said that the prisoners could tell when Ezhov fell: The draconian regime in the prisons (frequent solitary confinement and deprivation of all privileges) was relaxed one day. The timing was confirmed a few days later when Beria's name began to appear on official prison notices.[73] Although one does not know much about the internal Kremlin struggles in this period, one can also observe that as Ezhov's stock collapsed Zhdanov's visibility rose.[74]

The abolition of mass purges

Even as a weakened Ezhov continued high-level arrests of such leaders as Politburo members Eikhe, Chubar', and Kosior in 1938, new attempts were being made to protect and readmit rank-and-file members. The forceful resolution produced by the January 1938 Central Committee plenum caused a decrease in the expulsions of party members and an increase in the number reinstated. Moreover, in the six months after the plenum, the number of new members taken into the party tripled over the number of the preceding half year. Fragmentary data suggest that, before the January resolution, party committees were confirming around 87 to 97 percent of all expulsions. After January, party committees and *buros* upheld only about half as many.[75] The press in 1938 contained frequent references to appeals from expelled party members.[76] Writers complained that not only were appeals being processed slowly but that some regional administrations continued to expel rank-and-file members in large numbers. Old habits die hard. In August, a *Pravda* editorial summed up the progress to date. It noted that, before the January 1938 plenum, there had been 53,700 appeals under consideration. Since the plenum, and additional 101,233 had been submitted, making a total of 154,933. Of these, party committees had so far examined 85,273, and 54 percent (46,047) of those appealing had been readmitted. The editorial exhorted party committees to continue the process and to speed up reconsiderations.[77] Throughout 1938, writers continued to criticize the regional party leaders for wrongful expulsions and "unbolshevik situations" in various administrations.

It is possible, in light of Zhdanov's previous utterances on these points (and the ones he would make at the Eighteenth Party Congress in 1939), to attribute some of the arguments in the January 1938 resolution to him. He was the first to speak out against the abuses, mistakes, and trampling on individual rights that accompanied the *proverka* in 1935, and much of the January 1938 resolution sounds like his speech to the Saratov *Kraikom* and his remarks to the February plenum in 1937. He pressed his point about defending the rank and file in his speech to the Eighteenth Party Congress in 1939 when he gave an important speech on changes in party rules.

The Eighteenth Party Congress convened in Moscow between March 10 and 21, 1939. It had been five years since the 1934 "Congress of Victors," and the reports at the 1939 meeting provided a sort of overview of the preceding period. Major speeches were given by Stalin ("Report on the Work of the Central Committee to the 18th Congress of the CPSV(b)"), Zhdanov ("Amendments to the Rules of the CPSU(b)"), and Molotov (on the Five Year Plan).

Speaking strictly of the membership operations *(chistki)*, Stalin for the first time reviewed the entire problem and its solution.[78] In a section of his speech entitled "Regulating the Composition of the Party," he described the problems the party had encountered due to the mass influx of 1930–3: chance and careerist elements, poor political education, and the accounting difficulties. At the time of the Seventeenth Congress, it had been decided to continue the *chistka,* which had begun the previous year. Because of the seriousness of the problems (and because of the failure of the *chistka*), the operation "actually continued until

May, 1935.'' The assassination of Kirov ''showed that there were quite a number of suspicious elements in the party.'' This, in addition to the unsolved *uchet* chaos, led to the *proverka* and exchange, which were completed in September 1936, at which time readmissions commenced.[79]

Stalin's discussion of the *chistka* had a defensive tone. He was anxious to give the most favorable characterization to operations that no doubt he had supported, and he twisted the facts to do so. He failed to mention that the *chistka* had rambled on until its final abolition in December (not May) of 1935 and that the exchange of party documents dragged on into early 1937 (not September 1936), at which time the party had to threaten to invalidate the old cards to get the operation completed. In spite of these failures, which were freely discussed in private channels, Stalin claimed that the party had succeeded in weeding out the hostile and unreliable persons, having ''strengthened itself by clearing its ranks of dross.'' ''Our party is now somewhat smaller in membership, but on the other hand it is better in quality. That is a big achievement.''[80]

Everyone had agreed, however, that the *chistki* had caused problems resulting from a careless, ''heartless,'' ''formal-bureaucratic'' approach to party members, and as a result many innocent or simply passive communists had been wrongfully expelled. Zhdanov in particular had condemned these mistakes more and more strongly since August 1935. Responding to these problems, Stalin said,

It cannot be said that the cleanings were not accompanied by grave mistakes. There were, unfortunately, more mistakes than might have been expected. Undoubtedly, we shall have no further need to resort to the method of mass cleanings. Nevertheless, the cleanings of 1933–1936 were unavoidable and their results, on the whole, were beneficial.[81]

Stalin thus concluded that, although the *chistki* had involved ''mistakes,'' their effect had been positive and successful in weeding out the ranks.

Zhdanov was more critical of the regional bureaucracy and made a much harsher assessment of the screenings in his speech to the congress. In practical contradiction of Stalin's view, Zhdanov said that the mass cleanings were ''of very little effect and did not achieve their purpose.'' As part of his speech on changes in the party rules, he proudly announced that provisions for such mass cleanings were being removed from the party rules and that such operations were officially abolished.[82]

In contrast with Stalin's view, Zhdanov characterized the *chistki* as negative, ineffective, and unsuccessful in weeding out the party.

Zhdanov told the congress that the *chistka–proverka* operations had been failures not because of "mistakes" but because of their very essence. Referring to the period 1933–6 (before and not including the Ezhovshchina) as the "mass purge," Zhdanov said:

> The objectionable feature of the mass purges is that, bearing as they do the character of a campaign, they are attended by many mistakes, primarily by the infringement of the Leninist principle of an individual approach to people.
>
> By establishing a definite standard and measuring everybody by one criterion, the method of the mass purge encourages a formal approach and does not permit the full observance of the party principle that members must be treated with careful attention, and in practice it often leads to the infringement of the rights of party members.[83]

Zhdanov went on to abolish the practice of "mass purges" in the future, removing this provision from the party rules where it had been inserted in 1934. In effect, he had said that the very method of "sweeping" the party involved so many mistakes, by its nature, that it was not worth the trouble. By their very design, mass purges were bound to lead to excesses and perversions at the hands of their administrators.

Zhdanov gave a number of examples of the mistakes and persecutions involved with the *uchet*-cleaning operations. For example, Comrades Sedenkov and Tolstikov (from Stalingrad and Voronezh, respectively) had been maliciously expelled in absentia because they had criticized the work of local party officials. "Instability" and "mistakes" were the reasons given, and their expulsions were bureaucratically confirmed by the *oblast'* committees. In both cases, bureaucratic sloth and outright hostility from the local party leaders held up the appeals for months. Finally, at the initiative of the Central Committee (the control commission for Tolstikov), their expulsions were reversed, and the secretaries involved were expelled and removed.[84]

He then turned to the passives who had been wrongfully expelled by heartless bureaucrats.

> It was in relation to them that most mistakes were committed by the party organizations. It frequently happened that honest and devoted people, exemplary workers in their factories, were classed among the passive elements. Under this category were comrades who did not have some trifling and futile assignment of duty, who were tied by large families, or who several times missed attending a study circle, or who failed to answer some brainwracking or pigheaded question at a political examination.

After noting that Stalin had condemned such "outrageous practices" at the February 1937 and January 1938 plenums, Zhdanov turned his attack on those who had slandered innocent people "under the flag of 'vigilance.'"[85]

Sometimes, as in the case of "the slanderer Priluchnii," more than a hundred communists were expelled as a result of one person's charges. Sometimes more than half the membership of an organization was expelled as the result of false denunciations.[86] According to Zhdanov, a person would try to ensure himself or herself against charges of insufficient vigilance through the maximum number of denunciations against other people.

Zhdanov then discussed a practice that had perhaps accounted for the majority of expulsions.

Expulsions from the party on the grounds of "connections" with enemies at one time assumed very large proportions and are still to be met with.

On these grounds, honest people were expelled from the party wholesale, their only fault being that they were brought into contact with enemies of the people by their work – "passed them on the street," so to speak.[87]

This fashionable formula – "connections with enemies of the people" – . . . was employed in such a broad and vague sense as to include all sorts of things – ordinary acquaintanceship, contact with enemies at work owing to official duties, actual connections with enemies. . . – without any graduation whatever, all covered by one general formula.[88]

In his final comment on the mistakes of the cleaning operations, Zhdanov cited the decisions of the February plenum and the January 1938 plenum, saying that those decisions "resolve themselves to this, that *expulsions from the party must be reduced to a minimum*" (emphasis in original). "Expulsions from the party at one time became a sort of small change in many party organizations, while such measures as caution, rebuke, reprimand, strict reprimand, and final warning – all that fairly flexible scale of measures. . . was forgotten."[89]

It might seem that such righteous indignation *after* the operation was at least hypocritical and that, by speaking out at this late date, the leadership was trying to shift the blame for the repression that they themselves had encouraged or tolerated. This is the general explanation for these remarks given by most students of the period.[90] Its flaw, however, is that these criticisms had been voiced many times before, even during the cleaning operations themselves. The Central Committee had taken a stand on these errors at least as early as March 1936 (when, according to Khrushchev-era party histories, the first complaints from party members reached *Pravda* and the Central Committee).[91] Indirect evidence even suggests that the matter was discussed in the Central Committee as early as December 1935, in connection with Ezhov's report on the *proverka*. Stalin associated his name with the criticism as early as June 1936 and strongly condemned the "outrageous practices," including even indiscriminate approaches to Trotskyists, in his speech to the February plenum in 1937. An attack on the local leaders responsible for these mistakes was the main topic at the January 1938 plenum, whose resolution finally led to a reversal of many of the errors. It was not that the Central Committee had been silent all that time, but rather that its admonitions had been ignored by local secretaries.

Again, it must be noted that Stalin and Zhdanov were discussing the *chistki* and not the Ezhovshchina. Although both, in varying degrees, admitted to problems and mistakes in the former, the latter continued to enjoy a clean bill of health. Stalin attacked those abroad who argued that "ridding ourselves of spies, assassins, and wreckers like Trotsky, Zinoviev, Kamenev, Iakir, Tukhachevskii, Rosengoltz, and Bukharin had shaken or demoralized the Soviet system." On the contrary, he said, the trials and arrests had strengthened the Soviet Union by ridding it of enemies whose guilt was unquestioned.[92]

Zhdanov, for his part, supported the Ezhovshchina. Referring to the "enemies of the people" arrested in the police operation as "enemy scum," "vile" agents of fascism, spies and diversionists, he said that their arrest had strenghened the country and had been necessary. Comparing the cleanings with the Ezhovshchina, Zhdanov said that the latter had been successful whereas the former had not: "By far the most important work of purifying the ranks of the party of enemies of the people, traitors, treason-mongerers and fascist agents was performed after the mass cleanings" (that is, in 1937-8).[93] No more eloquent contrast could be drawn between the 1933-6 purges and the 1937-8 Ezhovshchina.

In the end, nothing had succeeded in making the party more obedient or efficient or in changing the patterns of power at the various levels of the territorial apparatus. Poor (or no) fulfillment of decisions in the provinces remained a necessary evil. The goals of the regime, the size and backwardness of the country, low levels of education, inadequate communications, and a shortage of political trained cadres all conspired to force a particular power distribution on society. Under such circumstances, it is hard to understand what "centralization" would have meant and difficult to imagine any transformational regime except one in which local bosses exercised relative autonomy, patronage power, and freedom from close control from above or below.

If the party wanted to stay in power, govern a vast country, and carry out its "historical tasks" of economic modernization, it had to make each party secretary into an autocrat. By doing so, the party paradoxically made it more difficult to guarantee overall obedience. This structure discouraged effective participation by the rank and file in local decision making or controls. "Control from below" and effective "answerability before the masses" had proved themselves hazardous to the regime's foundations in the thirties, and the lesson was not lost on those who came to power in those days.

It is perhaps ironic that the party democracy and vigilance campaigns were originally intended to improve the functioning of the apparatus. Their catastrophic fusion and mutual reinforcement destroyed what little discipline and order existed in the party. Because both political currents were explicitly populist and antibureaucratic, leaders at all levels were subjected to merciless attack from above and below. But repression and chaos hit the party at all levels. Frightened or malicious party secretaries tried to deflect the heat downward (as they had in the *proverka*) with rank-and-file expulsions of "enemies." Rank-and-file activists also lashed out at one another as class and personal hatreds were aggravated by the spy scare.

Although Moscow politicians, including Stalin, tried to channel and control political campaigns, the evidence shows that they had great difficulty doing so. As in the cases of the Shakhty trial, collectivization, and membership screenings, Moscow had to intervene forcefully to limit and defuse movements it had unleashed. The repeated but unheeded demands to halt expulsions of passives between 1935 and 1939 are examples of Moscow's inability to control local events. "Fulfillment of decisions" remained as elusive as ever.

In 1937 and 1938, Stalin and company tried to contain radicalism through press articles, speeches, revised electoral plans, and deglorifying the police. That they had to take such measures shows their lack of tight control over events. None of this means that political terror and violence erupted independently of the actions of top party leaders. It is clear, for example, that Stalin sanctioned the destruction of the opposition. But the limited evidence suggests that Stalin, like Mao Zedong thirty years later, found it easier to initiate campaigns than to control them.

Conclusion: some observations on politics in the thirties

We see, therefore, at first the picture as a whole, with its individual parts still more or less kept in the background; we observe the movements, transitions, connections rather than the things that move, combine, and are connected.

Friedrich Engels

One should hope that the anonymous NKVD official was lying to Isaak Babel's widow when he told her that the police had burned much of their archive as the Germans approached Moscow in 1941.[1] Until and unless such sources become available, it is impossible for a study of the Great Purges period to be definitive, and it is dangerous to venture many firm conclusions about the politics of the 1930s. Yet the press, Smolensk Archive, and other printed sources do make it possible to see the outlines of politics in the Communist Party in the period and to make some observations, suggestions, and hypotheses. This effort may well have raised as many questions as it answered, but because of the need to reexamine and rethink the Stalin period, new questions should not be out of order.

This analysis has concentrated on the center–periphery conflict within the party apparatus. This struggle is important to the political history of the thirties; and it was a substantial part of the background of the Great Purges. In addition to the material presented above, a look at Central Committee membership in the thirties highlights the importance of this tension. Indeed, the trend of representation of regional party officials in the Central Committee illustrates the rise and fall of the territorial secretaries in this decade.

Table C.1 shows the rise in power and influence of the regional secretaries in connection with industrialization and collectivization, as

Table C.1. *Full Central Committee membership of regional party secretaries, 1927–39*

	1927		1930		1934		1939	
	No.	%	No.	%	No.	%	No.	%
Obkom and *kraikom* secretaries	3	4.2	11	15.5	12	16.9	3	4.2
National party secretaries	2	2.8	2	2.8	7	9.9	4	5.6
All regional secretaries	5	7.0	13	18.3	19	26.8	7	9.8
Size of full Central Committee	(71)		(71)		(71)		(71)	

Source: J. Arch Getty, William Chase, and Charles Wetherell, "Patterns of Party and State Office Holding in the Soviet Bureaucracy, 1929–1931," paper presented to Third National Seminar on Russian Social History in the Twentieth Century, Philadelphia, January 29–30, 1983 (based on quantitative study of Central Committee membership, 1927–39).

well as their catastrophic decline in the Great Purges. The relative political weight of territorial party officials was clearly an important part of the background of the Great Purges.

Of course, the center–periphery conflict in the party was not the only important issue of the period, and the Great Purges do not resolve themselves simply into an administrative struggle between centralizing forces in the capital and peripheral power centers. Foreign policy, Stakhanovism, the timely promotion of "new men," nationality questions, education, social conflict, and Stalin's personality have all strongly influenced the politics and history of the decade. Other scholars will prefer to emphasize the primacy of one or another of these issues and conflicts. Study of the organizational struggles within the territorial party apparatus represents only one approach (albeit an important one) to the cataclysmic history of the 1930s. One can only welcome the illumination of other dimensions and topics.

For example, the crisis of the thirties had a social component. Moscow's demands that leaders accelerate the promotion of new men highlight the tensions between Soviet and "bourgeois" specialists, old and new Bolsheviks, reds and experts. It is just as clear that the cataclysm had beneficiaries. New men, red experts, and others of the

Khrushchev–Brezhnev generation benefited from the political turn-over. Students will decide for themselves the extent to which society and politics influenced each other. Although social issues and conflicts were important, this study has suggested that the crisis in the party was basically a political one that cannot entirely be explained in genera-tional or class terms.

Keeping the obvious source caveats in mind, the present analysis has suggested a number of conclusions about Soviet political history in the 1930s. First, it seems that the Bolshevik Party was not the monolithic and homogeneous machine both totalitarian theorists and Stalinists would have us believe. Administration was so chaotic, irregular, and confused that even Merle Fainsod's characterization of the system as "inefficient totalitarianism" seems to overstate the case.[2]

Although the Soviet government was certainly dictatorial (or tried to be), it was not totalitarian. The technical and technological sophistica-tion that separates totalitarianism from dictatorship was lacking in the thirties. The primitive texture of the Smolensk Archive, the real weak-ness of the central government in key areas, and a certain degree of political pluralism argue strongly against any totalitarian characteriza-tion. On a local level (where most of the population interacts with the government), political administration was marked by incompetence, sloth, inertia, and real cultural backwardness. The system had the dis-advantages of bureaucratism without the corresponding benefits of effi-cient bureaucracy. Administration on a local level often resembled a popular peasant culture that was trying clumsily and sometimes half-heartedly to be a modern bureaucracy.

This chaos, although historically important in its own right, has im-plications for political conflicts. The confusion and disorder in local party membership files and the inefficient fulfillment of central direc-tives served to augment and protect the powers of local officials. The less the center knew about local affairs, the less it could intervene and control them, and Moscow party leaders spent much of their time try-ing to find out what was happening in the provinces. Conflict erupted as the center tried to streamline, regularize, and ultimately control lo-cal political organizations.

An inefficient and clumsy bureaucracy also meant that the effects of campaigns and orders from Moscow could be either minimized or ex-aggerated as they reverberated down the chain of command. Because chaos implied a certain local autonomy, some tasks (like the *proverka* of 1935) died a bureaucratic death without being completed. Inefficiency, confusion, and local self-protection also meant that other campaigns (like the populist *kritika/samokritika* effort or the *Ezhovshchina*) could easily run out of control.

In addition to the ramshackle and unresponsive nature of its bureaucracy, the party was also split by conflicts between factions, strata, and key personalities. There were local frictions between leaders and led, middle-level struggles between regional and district committees, and higher-order battles between provincial bodies and the Moscow center. At the summit, personal fights among key leaders were so bitter that they leaked into the staid and usually restrained Stalinist press. The competitions between Molotov and Ordzhonikidze and between Zhdanov and Ezhov were only the most obvious struggles – future researches will uncover others. Such struggles among courtiers (who were themselves powerful political actors) are not new to historians and should not surprise students of even the Stalin period. As Timothy Dunmore recently noted, "Few are now prepared to accept too literally Milovan Djilas's picture of senior Politburo members obsequiously following Stalin about and taking his orders down on a convenient note pad."[3]

There was a lively politics in the party during the 1930s. Indeed, open controversies on broad policy options were forbidden, and no alternative grand strategies could be proposed in public. But although there were no more open arguments about what to do, there were many options and disagreements about how to do it. The strategy (the General Line) had been set, but the tactics of implementation were undecided; this, too, was politics. Anyone who has worked in a large organization knows that the politics of implementation is at least as important (and personally bitter) as the politics of grand strategy. It was easy to forge broad public agreement on general strategy and even on the nature of the problems facing the apparatus, but it was next to impossible for various factions and strata to agree on or coordinate solutions.

Although the inner politics of the Kremlin still eludes us, it is clear that in the thirties Stalin's lieutenants represented policy alternatives and options. It is surely significant, for example, that V. M. Molotov always advocated fast industrial growth and the need to destroy "underestimators," oppositionists, and other "enemies." It is just as clear that Sergo Ordzhonikidze represented opposite policies.

As far as the struggles within the party apparatus proper are concerned, the views and policies of A. A. Zhdanov are important. He believed that most of the party's problems could be solved through indoctrination, propaganda, and the sound political education of new cadres. Zhdanov always defended the rights of rank-and-file activists and was a consistent advocate of *samokritika* and criticism from below. He wanted to involve the activists in the work of party committees, to protect them from abuse and expulsion by local secretaries, and to promote them to leadership work. Even passive and peripheral members were to be salvaged.[4]

Zhdanov's advocacy of a "new, more flexible dictatorship" and his conception of the party as an educational institution and vehicle for indoctrination put him in conflict with those party security specialists who traditionally controlled personnel assignments. He clashed with cadre chiefs Ezhov (1934–9) and Malenkov (1939–48) over party tactics and strategy. Whereas Zhdanov believed that reeducation and reclamation of party members could solve every problem from bureaucratization to continued political opposition, Ezhov, the mandate checker turned personnel specialist, advocated more stringent selection and security measures. He favored pruning the party through purges and expulsions that inevitably removed the passive and "ballast" elements that Zhdanov the ideologist sought to preserve and educate.

This and other studies have shown that Zhdanov ascribed primary importance to the pedagogical and ideological functions of the party. During the period when his influence was ascendant (1939–48), the party Secretariat was organized along "functional" lines, according to which personnel assignment and verification were concentrated in a single cadre department. When his opponents' influence was strong (1934–9, 1948–60), the Central Committee Secretariat was organized along "production-branch lines." According to this plan – which Zhdanov sharply denounced – there were separate cadre departments to provide personnel for each branch of industry. Most of the Central Committee departments became personnel agencies, and the cadre specialists (Ezhov, then Malenkov) benefited accordingly. Zhdanov's scheme meant an apparatus more concerned with noneconomic functions (agitprop, schools, culture). The Ezhov–Malenkov plan implied close party supervision of the economy: an orientation Zhdanov opposed.[5]

Zhdanov ultimately failed to withdraw the party from economic administration and to convert it into a more pedagogically oriented organization. But his influence remained strong, and his partisans continued to be highly placed until his death in 1948. The subsequent massacre of his followers by cadre chief Malenkov and secret policeman Beria demonstrates both Zhdanov's personal clout while he was alive and the depth of his dispute with his opponents.

But in the mid-thirties, Zhdanov and Ezhov could agree on one thing: The middle-level party bureaucracy needed reform. Ezhov blamed party secretaries for the chaos in party records, for the bungled membership screenings, and eventually for treasonable conspiracies. Zhdanov denounced local secretaries for bureaucratism and repression of the rank and file. Although Zhdanov and Ezhov sharply disagreed on the appropriate reforms, they were both baiters of the bureaucracy and critics of the secretarial network. Stalin supported both of them.

This study of the structure of politics in the thirties has, in turn, suggested another conclusion. The traditional view of the events of 1933–9 – which sees them as related and incremental parts of the same terrorist crescendo – needs revision. Merle Fainsod and others described the 1933–9 period as an "almost continuous purge" in the Western Region, and his conceptual framework has dominated nearly all views of the period. It is based on the idea that after 1933 (or 1934) there was a constantly increasing level of "purging" accompanied by a similarly rising curve of fear and panic. According to this view, the continuous purge began in 1933 with the *chistka*. The assassination of Politburo member Sergei Kirov in December 1934 "touched off a new round of almost continuous purges," which expanded in "everwidening circles." In the months after Kirov's murder, "the net was spread wide," leading to a hailstorm of indiscriminate denunciations and a "rich haul" of victims. The Central Committee, however, was "apparently dissatisfied" with the haul and issued the letter of May 13, 1935, calling for a "new purge under the guise of a check-up on party documents" (the *proverka*). But because of a "lack of ardor" on the parts of local authorities, the Central Committee (always read Stalin here) rebuked the Western Region with its order of June 27, 1935, and demanded increased purging. The "mounting hysteria" of the "heresy hunt" increased as the "axe of the purge" swept through the ranks of the party.

According to Fainsod, the Central Committee instigated more terror when it ordered the exchange of party documents in early 1936. "Hard on the heels" of the completion of this "third purge operation" came "yet another signal for the continuation and intensification of the purge": the letter of July 29, 1936, which, in preparation for the up-coming trial of Zinoview and Kamenev, called for increased "vigilance'' and led to a ''holocaust of denunciations'' and ''rising panic and disarray.''[6]

This view is weakly supported by the available primary evidence. Aside from particular errors (the *uchet* problems were hardly a ''guise''; the June 27 Central Committee rebuke was for expelling too many, not too few), this interpretation suffers from grave phenomenological problems. First, in terms of their attrition to the party the 1933–6 membership screenings were actually a *decrescendo,* in that each operation expelled fewer members than the previous one. Indeed, these purges were milder than their direct ancestors of the 1920s. Second, most expulsions were for nonideological and nondissident infractions: violations of party discipline, theft, abuse of position. Simple nonparticipation accounted for more of those expelled than did political crimes. The screenings were hardly ''heresy hunts,'' and to associate the benign exchange of party documents with the ''axe of the purge'' is at least inaccurate.

The *chistki* were different from the Ezhovshchina, although Ezhov was involved in both. They had different targets and were conducted by different agencies for different reasons. In fact, the membership purges ended before the Ezhovshchina began, and readmission upon appeal began before, and continued during, the terror. It would be a mistake to confuse the monotonous repetition of membership screenings (caused by bungling and sometimes intentional local mismanagement) with an alleged planned attempt to steadily increase terror in the party. The relation between *chistki* and Ezhovshchina was more complicated and was a function of the interplay among various strata and constituencies in the party. All political events of the thirties were not simply related parts of the same Great Purges crescendo.

The ups and downs of the central–regional struggle do not coincide with some of the other familiar Great Purges events associated with the persecution of the opposition: the Riutin affair, the assassination of Kirov, and the show trials. These traditional landmarks of the Great Purges do not seem directly related to the main events of the conflict within the apparatus. If one were to graph the increases and decreases in tension between the center and the provinces and compare the curve with one charting the peaks and valleys of the more familiar struggle with the opposition, the curves would not match. The Seventeenth Congress saw a public reconciliation with the opposition, but it also saw a violent attack on the regional secretaries. Central–regional conflict heated up in 1935 (with the *proverka*), but after the brief post-Kirov repression, 1935 was a relatively calm year for the opposition. In 1936, oppositionists were being arrested and imprisoned, but regional secretaries seemed at the height of their power. Only in 1937 did the various struggles and lines of development converge in the Ezhovshchina.

The traditional Riutin–Kirov–show-trial periodization is not wrong, but it is only one of several discrete political developments in the thirties. There were rising and falling levels of conflict on many issues: Stakhanovism, relations with the old "bourgeois specialists," promotion of new cadres, and the speed of industrial development. It would be dangerously reductive to press all the issues, debates, and campaigns into one historical stream of events.[7]

Some will feel that this study has taken a naive view of Stalin's role as planner and perpetrator. There is no doubt that he had chief responsibility for political leadership, but the present account has more than once failed to conclude that the events were part of a coherent plan. Evidence of high-level confusion, counterproductive initiatives, and lack of control over events has not supported the notion of a grand design. Careful analysis of archival, documentary, press, and creditable memoir sources neither supports nor disproves the existence of a plan. It is still possible that the events of 1933–9 were parts of a devilish and devious strategy, but the evidence indicates that a master Stalin plan must remain an a priori assumption, an intuitive guess, or a hypothesis. It can be suspected but not established on the basis of the presently available classes of evidence.

Stalin did not initiate or control everything that happened in the party and country. The number of hours in the day, divided by the number of things for which he was responsible, suggests that his role in many areas could have been little more than occasional intervention, prodding, threatening, or correcting. In the course of a day, Stalin made decisions on everything from hog breeding to subways to national defense. He met with scores of experts, heard dozens of reports, and settled various disputes between contending factions for budgetary or personnel allocations. He was an executive, and reality forced him to delegate most authority to his subordinates, each of whom had his own opinions, client groups, and interests.

It is certainly dangerous to take the speeches of Soviet leaders at face value. All politicians dissimulate about their roles and plans. Yet it is not naive to assume that the speeches and articles of Soviet politicians reflect real conflicts, struggles, and policies. After all, in the political culture of the thirties, Stalin's speeches were taken as revealed truth.

They were widely publicized, memorized, discussed, and taken as directives by local party committees. Stalin's word was law, and for this reason alone his pronouncements are worth studying as a certain reflection of political reality.

The problem is to separate Stalin's "real thoughts" from the needs of the "cult of personality." A look at his theoretical pronouncements shows that, like all skilled politicians, he spoke out of both sides of his mouth. Throughout the thirties, Stalin publicly tried to synthesize several points of view. Diametrically opposed moderate sentiments (the period of struggle and repression is over) and radical prescriptions (class struggle and vigilance should increase) were both incorporated into Stalin's public statements.

For example, in his 1934 speech to the Seventeenth Congress, Stalin defended the theory that "intensifying the class struggle" was necessary to build a classless society. In the same speech, though, he proclaimed the "complete victory of Leninism" and observed that opposition in the party had been "utterly demoralized and smashed." "There is nothing to prove and, it seems, no one to fight." The only remaining problem was that "remnants of their [oppositionists'] ideology still live in the minds of individual members," producing "confusion on a number of questions of Leninism." Despite the intensification of struggle, Stalin said that the only necessary measures were those designed to raise the ideological level of the party.

Even in 1937, when he said that "the further forward we advance...the greater will be the fury of the remnants of the broken exploiting classes, the sooner they will resort to sharper forms of struggle...and...clutch at the most desperate means...as the last resort of doomed people," he was not technically contradicting his previous assertions on the victory of socialism. The enemy was "broken," "desperate," and "doomed." The means of struggle (assassination) became sharper, but the *level* of class struggle (mass violence and class conflict) was being lowered in the country.

Stalin's facile theoretical combination of the radical and moderate points of view was, to say the least, a flexible one. The synthesis was plausible, appropriate, and optimistic in 1934; but by 1937, after Stalin's gradual swing from moderation to radicalism, it could be used as a theoretical justification for terror.

His vague, Olympian pronouncements demonstrate one use of the "cult of personality": to downplay conflict at higher levels. All Bolshevik politicians conjured up Stalin's approval in support of their particular views. Zhdanov could press for the primacy of party work; Ezhov could call for more vigilance; Molotov could demand faster industrial tempos; Ordzhonikidze could call for moderation; and all of them could invoke quotations from the great Stalin in support. This arrangement not only tended to cover up political disputes but also maximized the dictator's freedom to maneuver.

Nothing could be allowed to jeopardize the facade. When in 1938 Stalin criticized the cult of personality, it was necessary to suppress his remarks. In a letter to a minor publishing house, Stalin advised against the publication of a hagiographical *Stories About Stalin's Childhood:*

> The book abounds in a mass of factual improbabilities, alterations, and unearned praise. The author is led astray by lovers of fables, by impostors (even by impostors "in good faith"), by flatterers...the book tends to instill...the cult of personalities, of leaders, of infallible heroes. This is dangerous and harmful. The theory of "heroes" and masses is not a Bolshevist theory...I recommend burning the book.[8]

His denunciations of the "cult of personalities" can be understood as simple assertions of the well-known modesty of the supreme leader. But if that were all that was involved, it is hard to understand why the letter was not released or published until after the dictator's death. More likely, statements condemning the cult of Stalin from the leader himself were too subversive to the regime's operating principles and norms to be published in the thirties.[9]

Curiously, Leon Trotsky had put his finger on the issue in a particularly lucid analysis of Stalin's role. In arguing that Stalin's personality was not crucial in its own right, Trotsky noted that Stalin was the front man, the symbol, of the bureaucracy. In Trotsky's view, Stalin did not create the bureaucracy but vice versa. Stalin was a manifestation of a bureaucratic social phenomenon: "Stalin is the personification of the bureaucracy. That is the substance of the political personality."[10]

Yet Western scholars have remained hypnotized by Stalin's cult of personality, and their obsession with him has led to studies of the Great Purges period that provide no detailed investigation of the political, institutional, and structural milieu of the phenomena. Rather than placing events in these contexts, scholars have often discussed the Great Purges only against the background of Stalin's personality and categorized Stalinism simply as the undisputed rule of an omniscient and omnipotent dictator. Contradictions and confusion are seen as manifestations of Stalin's caprice, and too often the political history of the Stalin period has merely been the story of Stalin's supposed activities. An understanding of the thirties based on Stalin's personality is as limiting and incomplete as an explanation of Nazism derived primarily from Hitler's psyche.

It is not necessary for us to put Stalin in day-to-day control of events to judge him. A chaotic local bureaucracy, a quasi-feudal network of politicians accustomed to arresting people, and a set of perhaps insoluble political and social problems created an atmosphere conducive to violence. All it took from Stalin were catalytic and probably ad hoc interventions at three pivotal points – early 1936 (to reopen the Kirov investigation), November 1936 (to condemn Piatakov),and June 1937 (to unleash Ezhov) – to spark an uncontrolled explosion. That he did so intervene speaks for itself.

Actually, the question of Stalin's role as planner was – or should have been – a secondary one in this analysis, which has, rather, tried to show that the party before World War II was a certain type of disorganized and cumbersome machine. The existence of high-level personal rivalries, disputes over development or modernization plans, powerful and conflicting centrifugal and centripetal forces, and local conflicts made large-scale political violence possible and even likely.

The evidence suggests that the Ezhovshchina – which is what most people really mean by the "Great Purges" – should be redefined. It was not the result of a petrified bureaucracy's stamping out dissent and annihilating old radical revolutionaries. In fact, it may have been just the opposite. It is not inconsistent with the evidence to argue that the Ezhovshchina was rather a radical, even hysterical, *reaction* to bureaucracy. The entrenched officeholders were destroyed from above and below in a chaotic wave of voluntarism and revolutionary puritanism.

The radicalism of the thirties did not last. Although ritualized *kritika/ samokritika* became a regular part of party practice, it would never again have the impact it did in 1937. Although politics in the thirties was often populist and even subversive, the exigencies of World War II combined with the practical demands of running an increasingly complicated economy meant that radicalism and antibureaucratism would fade into the past and be replaced by a new respect for authority. In the thirties, Stalin was often a populist muckraker, and his image, as Avtorkhanov remembered, was of someone who hated neckties. The real petrification of the Stalinist system set in during and after the war, when commissariats became ministries, when the party leader became premier, and when the man who hated neckties became the generalissimo.

Appendix: the Kirov assassination

It is widely asserted that Stalin conspired in the assassination of Serge Kirov in December 1934. Yet the evidence for Stalin's complicity is complicated and at least secondhand. In fact, if one traces the assertion that Stalin killed Kirov to its origins, one finds that, before the Cold War, no serious authority argued that Stalin was behind the assassination.[1] The KGB defector Alexander Orlov was the first to make such a claim in his dubious 1953 account.[2] Boris Nicolaevsky repeated the story in his influential 1956 essays (his 1936 "Letter of an Old Bolshevik" had not accused Stalin), and it has since been widely accepted in Western academic and Soviet dissident circles.[3]

Equally interesting is a list of those who did not believe Stalin organized the crime. Neither the Old Bolshevik of 1936 nor Nikita Khrushchev implicated Stalin. Khrushchev only said that there was much that was "mysterious" about the incident. At the height of his power, he could easily have charged Stalin with the crime had he wanted to.[4] He blamed Stalin directly for the deaths of Rudzutak, Kosior, Eikhe, and other Politburo members, but not Kirov. Leon Trotsky, like Grigori Tokaev, believed that the assassination was really the work of misguided young oppositionists.[5] G. Liushkov, an NKVD defector who outranked Orlov and Krivitsky, told his Japanese protectors that Stalin was not involved.[6] Most recently, Adam Ulam noted that Stalin had little to gain from the killing.[7]

Turning from possible sources (or lack of them) to the circumstances of the assassination, one finds more ambiguity. As Khrushchev noted, much in the situation suggested police complicity. Neither his bodyguard nor anyone else was with Kirov at the time – a probable breach of security rules. The bodyguard (Borisov) was killed in an automobile accident *before* he could be questioned by Stalin and the Politburo, who rushed to Leningrad to conduct the investigation. Finally, it seems that the assassin (Nikolaev) had been previously detained by the local NKVD and released, even though he carried a revolver and a map of Kirov's route to work.[8]

Although this evidence may implicate the police, it does not necessarily point to higher involvement by Stalin or others. The NKVD officials in Leningrad who had been responsible for Kirov's security received light sentences in Siberia at the hands of their fellows on an NKVD board and remained alive for a few years. They would hardly have survived at all if they could have connected others with the crime. Similarly, the head of the NKVD at the time, Genrikh Iagoda (to whom Stalin allegedly gave instructions to kill Kirov), confessed in open court in 1938 to having killed Kirov at the instigation of the opposition. If Stalin had used Iagoda to assassinate Kirov, it would have been very dangerous to allow him to appear later before the microphones of the world press. Iagoda knew that he would be shot anyway, and it would have been easy for him to let slip that Stalin had put him up to it. Stalin would not have taken the risk of such a damaging assertion's coming to light.

Many have commented on Stalin's unusually prompt reaction to the shooting. As noted, he and other Politburo members rushed to Leningrad to oversee the investigation. Hours after the crime, the Central Executive Committee, at Stalin's suggestion, issued an extraordinary order that speeded up investigation, sentencing, and execution of people accused of terrorist crimes and denied appeals from such convictions.[9] The shooting was certainly an extraordinary blow to the Soviet government, and the reactions suggest panic. The killing was perceived as the first shot in a coup against the leadership. Such wartime measures are not really surprising, and it would have seemed incongruous if the leadership had not reacted in such a way. Finally, the "Law of December 1, 1934" (which Stalin rammed through after the shooting) was subsequently rarely used.[10]

Other circumstances surrounding the assassination point away from Stalin's involvement. When the assassin was apprehended seconds after the shooting, he was carrying a diary that incriminated no one and asserted that he was acting alone.[11] If Stalin had organized the assassination to blame the opposition, an incriminating diary would have been priceless written evidence, and, if Nikolaev had not kept one, an appropriate document could certainly have been manufactured. If the assassination had been planned by Stalin or one of his supporters, a diary implicating the opposition would have been preferred. No diary at all would have been better than one exonerating the opposition. Finally, if Stalin had planned these events, he would hardly have allowed this "dead end" diary to be mentioned in the press. It only weakened an accusation against the opposition. Circumstances suggest that Stalin and his partisans were not in control of this situation.

The immediate official response to the assassination was ad hoc and confused, showing few signs of advance planning. In the days after the killing, the government identified Nikolaev variously as a lone assassin, a tool of a White Guard conspiracy, and finally a follower of the Zinoviev–Kamenev oppositions in Moscow and Leningrad.[12] It was not until December 18 that the regime hinted that the Zinoviev opposition might be involved.[13] Five days later, the secret police announced that Zinoviev, Kamenev, and thirteen of their associates had, indeed, been arrested on December 16. But "in the absence of sufficient evidence to put them on trial," they were to be administratively exiled within the USSR.[14] It was not until a month later, on January 16, that an official announcement said that Zinoviev and Kamenev were to be tried for maintaining a secret oppositionist "center" that had indirectly influenced the assassin to commit the crime.[15] The changes and contradictions in the official characterization of the assassin suggest that no story was ready to hand and that the authorities were reacting to events in a confused way.

It is often thought that Stalin and company planned the crime to have a pretext for crushing the opposition. Yet the aftermath of the crime suggests confusion and mindless, unfocused rage. The repression directly following the assassination was diffuse and spasmodic. There was an immediate wave of arrests in Moscow and Leningrad. Many of these were of Komsomols and junior members of opposition groups, and their numbers were quite small, at least in comparison with the arrests of later years. Several dozen persons already in prison (and identified as White Guards) were executed in blind retaliation for the crime.[16] In one of the stranger episodes of the aftermath, a number of "former people," including nobles and former merchants, were ejected from Leningrad for violations of residence permits.[17] (According to Leningrad rumors, the police scanned the city directory in an attempt to find *someone* to repress in the wake of the killing.) It seemed that the regime, unprepared for the crime and unclear about who should be punished, lashed out in a violent but ad hoc way at traditional enemies of Soviet power. These reactions were reminiscent of the knee-jerk responses of the Cheka during the Civil War, when hostages were arrested and executed in blind retaliation for White actions. Such responses suggest neither a careful plan nor discriminating identification of more important target groups. Stalin would not have needed the killing of Kirov to justify this type or level of repression.

Although Zinoviev and Kamenev were arrested after the killing and sentenced to prison, their crime involved only "moral complicity."[18] It would be eighteen months until the first major trial of the opposition leaders and the first mass arrests of even middle-level oppositionists. Key leaders of the opposition (such as Piatakov, Radek, Bukharin, and Rykov) continued to work unmolested until 1936. No mention was made of major opposition conspirators in the press after January 18, 1935, and no campaign followed.[19] The violence of the Ezhovshchina, with its spy scare, fear of war, and campaign to unmask traitors, was two years away; and the lull suggests that hard-liners were politically unprepared to use the Kirov assassination. When they finally were able to use the assassination against the opposition, it would be on the basis of "new NKVD materials obtained in 1936." No one was able to capitalize on the situation in 1934–35 by striking at the opposition while the iron was hot.

Neither the sources, circumstances, nor consequences of the crime suggest Stalin's complicity. The lack of any evidence of political dispute between Stalin and Kirov, discussed earlier, would appear to refute any motive for Stalin to kill his ally, and it is difficult to disagree with Khrushchev's laconic remark that much remains mysterious about the crime. Based on the sources, there is no good reason to believe that Stalin connived in Kirov's assassination, and all one can say with any certainty is that Leonid Nikolaev, a rank-and-file dissident, pulled the trigger.

Bibliographic essay

It seems to me not amiss to speak of the danger of trusting to the representations of men who have been expelled from their country...such is their extreme desire to return to their homes that they naturally believe many things that are not true, and add many others on purpose; so that with what they really believe, and what they say they believe, they will fill you with hopes to that degree that if you act upon them you will incur a fruitless expense.

Niccolò Machiavelli

Readers familiar with previous writings on the Great Purges of the thirties will have noted that the present work is based on a rather different source base. Archival and press sources predominated here, and the vast corpus of émigré memoirs and Soviet underground (*samizdat*) writings played little role in the present account. This choice was deliberate and was based on methodological grounds.[1]

Soviet history has no tradition of responsible source criticism. Scholars have taken few pains to evaluate bias, authenticity, or authorship. Specialists have accepted "sources" that, for understandable reasons, are anonymously attributed ("Unpublished memoir of _____ _____"), and treat them as primary.[2] Given the source difficulties, this tendency is understandable but not defensible. Because so much of the writing on the "Great Purges" is descended from, and based on, a rather uncritical acceptance of these accounts, it is important to examine some of the more influential ones in detail.

Probably the most fundamental and basic "source" on the plans of Stalin and the inner workings of Ezhov's NKVD is that by Alexander Orlov. *The Secret History of Stalin's Crimes* is his "inside" account of the Great Purges.[3] Orlov is the source of the first and most-cited account of Stalin's participation in and direction of the Kirov assassination and

the subsequent show trials and is the "smoking gun" of the Kirov killing. Orlov was an NKVD operative in the organization's "Foreign
Department," and one would therefore expect his information to be
firsthand. However, during the entire period of the "Great Purges,"
Orlov was an NKVD chief in Spain during the Civil War. He was in
the Soviet Union only twice for brief visits of a few days each, and his
"information" is based on corridor gossip he picked up among some of
his NKVD friends during those brief visits. By his own admission, he
knew little about what was happening in the Kremlin. He heard about
the execution of Tukhachevskii on French radio.

Most of Orlov's information is of the form "Pauker told me that Stalin...," or "Agranov said that Ezhov...." None of his information
on the decisions and workings of the inner leadership can be considered
firsthand primary source material. The fact that Orlov was called home
in 1937 to almost certain arrest and death at the hands of his "confi-
dants" makes one wonder how highly placed he was during the Ezhovshchina.

All this is aside from any consideration of possible political bias. In
Orlov's case, even a defender would admit that his credibility is im-
peachable. First, there is nothing in Orlov's memoir about his major
occupation at the time – NKVD operations in Spain. The rather sordid
role of the police in Spain in executing oppositionists and deviants
among the Republican forces is well known, and one observer has suggested that Orlov's hands were as red as Ezhov's. After Orlov defected
to the United States, he worked for American intelligence, testifying
before various congressional committees in the early 1950s on the techniques of Soviet espionage in Cold War Europe.[4] Because his book was
written in this period, one might legitimately wonder whether his new
friends, loyalties, and perspectives colored his account. Normally, the
testimony of a sometime Stalinist agent, mass murderer, and former
spy would be subjected to at least a modicum of critical attention and
doubt. But the question of political bias only compounds the main
problem with the Orlov source – the lack of proximity to events.

Similar to, but less influential than, Orlov is the work by Walter
Krivitsky. Krivitsky was purportedly a Soviet military intelligence chief
for Western Europe. Because of his position abroad, he too is unable to
provide much firsthand information on events in the Soviet Union.
Like Orlov, Krivitsky reported corridor gossip he heard during trips to
Moscow.[5]

Another Soviet official who escaped to the West was Alexander Barmine, the Soviet ambassador to Greece. Like Orlov and Krivitsky, Barmine was only in the Soviet Union for short periods during the 1930s, for all his assignments were abroad. Barmine's gossip pipeline was the diplomatic service, however, not the police. He received nearly all his information through conversations with diplomats (Soviet and foreign) who passed through the Soviet embassy in Greece during the Ezhovshchina. Barmine can hardly be considered a primary source on the "Great Purges" – not even *his* sources were primary. Considerable differences between the various editions of Barmine's "memoirs" also raise doubts about the sources of his speculations.[6]

A more useful defector account of the 1930s is Victor Kravchenko's *I Chose Freedom*. Unlike the above raconteurs, Kravchenko was in the Soviet Union during the 1930s as a factory worker, engineer, foreman, and finally economic planner. He was a party member and a squad leader during the collectivization campaign. He went through the verification and exchange of party documents in 1935–6 and passed through the Ezhovshchina in 1937. As one who was becoming more and more alienated from the party, he knew what it was like to be under suspicion, to be on the receiving end of an investigation. Even more than the others, Kravchenko was nowhere near the center of decision making. He was a low-level, sometime protégé of Ordzhonikidze, never a confidant. Unlike the others, he made little attempt to speculate on or infer the intentions of the leadership, and he is content to describe his own personal experiences.[7]

There is another group of émigré–defector accounts that reproduce prison-camp rumors and gossip among imprisoned victims of the "Great Purges."[8] Although much of the "camp" information has the ring of truth about it, it is the literature of persecuted victims. Although there is nothing inherently false about such sources, the authors, by definition, were on the "outside" of the decision-making process. They can tell us what the camps were like but not why they existed. Their guesses and observations about political decision making may be interesting but can hardly be taken as primary source material.

Among the émigrés, the Trotskyist and Menshevik-oriented authors and presses in Europe have also provided a large part of the basic account. Emigré contact with events in the Soviet Union and with its leadership was tenuous and relied on "correspondents" either living in the Soviet Union or traveling around Europe on official business.

Trotsky's main organ in this period was his *Biulleten' oppozitsii,* edited by him and his son Sedov and published in Berlin and Paris. Its commentary on events in the Soviet Union was based on interpolations from *Pravda,* which Trotsky continued to read as assiduously as a modern Kremlinologist. Trotsky was at least sometimes supplied with information by other sources, as when Ivan Smirnov passed along secret Soviet reports on the economy in 1932.

Trotsky's location far from events always made him a dubious source for anything except biting editorials on the Great Purges. Because he was held up as the arch-conspirator to the Soviet people (and his friends and family were killed by Stalin), there is reason to wonder about the objectivity of his analytical judgments. Robert McNeal has also shown how frequently Trotsky's analysis of the USSR changed and contradicted itself along with the Trotskyist party line.[9] The partisan works of Western pro-Trotskyist memoirists such as Ciliga and Victor Serge suffer the same problem.[10] From the point of view of source criticism and reliability, Trotsky was a skilled, knowledgeable, but biased Kremlinologist.

A more serious and influential group of émigré commentators were Menshevik leaders Rafael Abramovich, David Dallin, and Boris Nicolaevsky.[11] The most important Menshevik publication was the *Sotsialisticheskii vestnik,* published in Paris. This seemingly well-informed periodical, like Trotsky's *Biulleten',* was widely read by émigré Russians, as well as by Soviet communists. Barmine reports that such periodicals were widely if covertly read in Soviet embassies by high-ranking personnel in the mid-1930s.

Appearing in that journal was the well-known and influential "Letter of an Old Bolshevik." The "Letter" was represented as an edited transcript of a conversation between Bukharin and Boris Nicloaevsky in Paris in 1936. Bukharin supposedly spoke to Nicolaevsky on the internal situation in the Soviet Union, and his remarks were published as the text of an anonymous Old Bolshevik in 1936 in the *Sotsialisticheskii vestnik.*[12]

The "Letter" is the origin of many of the essentials of the traditional interpretation of the Great Purges. The contents of the Riutin platform, Stalin's advocacy of the death penalty for Riutin (and the opposition of Kirov and others to it), the general "moderation" of Kirov, and the debate in the Politburo about the course of action regarding Kirov's assassin (with Stalin favoring the death penalty) are discussed here for the first time and have been widely cited and repeated.[13]

Actually, the "Letter" does not say that Stalin conspired in Kirov's death, and there is more than a suggestion that Kaganovich and

Ezhov, in conspiracy with the Leningrad NKVD, were involved.[14] The "Letter" describes a situation in 1934 in which these two represented the opposite point of view from Kirov's liberalism. Supposedly, they argued for a "continuation of class struggle" policy in contradistinction to Kirov's "relaxation" line. According to the "Letter," these two tendencies *contended* for Stalin's support, while Stalin himself remained neutral.[15]

This intriguing scenario, spelled out in the "Letter," was unfortunately distorted by Boris Nicolaevsky, who argued that – from the time of the Riutin platform in 1932 – Stalin had sided with the Kaganovich-Ezhov position and against Kirov's "liberalism." Although Nicolaevsky introduces this assertion as coming from the "Letter," it is not found there. Nicolaevsky also said that the "Letter" suggested Stalin's involvement in the Kirov murder, which it did not.[16]

Notwithstanding the unfortunate uses to which the "Letter" has been put, "internal" problems and contradictions weaken the document. The first two sentences of (Bukharin's) "Letter" are, "Here in Russia, the Zinoviev–Kamenev–Smirnov Trial came upon us like a thunderbolt. Recent events and present occurrences almost beggar description." Bukharin was in Paris no later than the end of April 1936. He could not possibly have described the reaction to the August trial to Nicolaevsky in April.[17] The "Letter" also describes the debate in the Politburo over the fate of the "Riutinists" in 1932 and "remembers" Kirov's speech against the death penalty and the vote against Stalin. The only way for Bukharin to have found out about Politburo debates and votes (if, in fact, this part of the "Letter" comes from Bukharin) would have been for someone else to have told him.[18] The same holds true for the reports in the "Letter" on the Politburo discussions following Kirov's death.

The problems of the "Letter" and its credibility are even more serious. Nicolaevsky (through the "Letter") tagged Kirov as a "moderate," but at the very time that Bukharin was *ending* his visit to Paris, Nicolaevsky was publishing in *Sotsialisticheskii vestnik* an account of how Kirov and Kaganovich formed a "hard-line" bloc against the "liberalism" of Stalin, Molotov, Voroshilov, and others in the Politburo! There were other stories about how Kirov was "conservative."[19]

Clearly, the "Letter" is a spurious source, and one should be at least circumspect and dubious about its claims. It represents only Nicolaevsky's collection of contradictory and unattributed rumors floating around Europe in the 1930s.[20] They include Kirov as moderate, Kirov as conservative; Stalin killed him, Stalin did not; there were even published rumors that Stalin had taken up with a Caucasian princess in the Kremlin, and that Kirov was a womanizer and the assassin a jealous husband.[21] Each of the émigré and defector sources represents a variant on the vast pool of such rumors and stories, but clearly none of them was in a position to know anything about their veracity. The authors seemed to pick the stories that fit together into particular schemes, and subsequent historians followed suit.

Indeed, in the rush to support a particular scenario, scholars have been strangely selective in their use of émigré memoirs. They have accepted and used those that supported their preconceptions and ignored those that did not. Students have embraced the rumors and flawed stories of Orlov, Barmine, and Nicolaevsky while ignoring accounts that call Kirov a "conservative," describe underground oppositionist plots in the thirties, and argue for the existence of a planned military coup against Stalin.[22] The point is not that these unused memoirs are any more credible than the familiar ones, but that all memoir accounts should be subjected to intense critical attention that takes contradictions into account. All claims or hypotheses based solely on secondhand gossip or rumor should be rejected according to elementary rules of evidence.

One group of sources that fares better under critical scrutiny consists of the revelations and memoirs appearing in the Soviet Union during the Khrushchev era. Khrushchev launched his de-Stalinization campaign with his "Secret Speech" in 1956 to the Twentieth Party Congress.[23] More details were supplied at the Twenty-Second Congress in 1961, when Khrushchev needed to denounce the participation of Kaganovich, Molotov, Malenkov, and others in the crimes of the 1930s.[24] A large number of memoirs, biographies, articles in *Pravda,* and revised histories written in the 1956-64 period contributed to the official attack on Stalin's "cult of personality," as Khrushchev had called it.

According to Khrushchev, the cult of personality encouraged "willfulness," "arbitrary use of power," and "violations of socialist legality." Stalin's sickly, suspicious nature led to brutality and the repression of innocent people. Khrushchev said that accusations against people were fabricated, that torture was used by the NKVD to extract false confessions (and later retractions were ignored), and that people were expelled from the party and/or sentenced without trial in gross violation of their rights. Khrushchev accused Stalin of putting forth the false theory about the class struggle's becoming sharper as one approached socialism and using this theory as an excuse for widespread repression of innocent people. Had the party not been strong, it would have collapsed.[25]

Khrushchev claimed that a "special commission" of the Politburo had, since Stalin's death, been looking into the validity of accusations and charges of the 1930s. They had found lists containing the names of persons slated for arrest that had been drawn up by Ezhov and signed by Stalin.[26] The lists contained "thousands" of names, proving that Stalin had personally had a hand in the arrests. Other lists bore the approvals of Kaganovich, Molotov, and Malenkov.[27]

Khrushchev's revelations are interesting for a number of other reasons. First, like the other literary accounts, they are almost entirely self-serving. It is hard to avoid the impression that the revelations had political purposes in Khrushchev's struggle with Molotov, Malenkov, and Kaganovich. Khrushchev must have faced a sticky problem in damning "excesses" in which he had participated. He had headed the Moscow and Ukrainian party organizations at various times in the 1930s and was responsible for approving expulsions and arrests of those under him. As a young star, Khrushchev had led a mass demonstration in Moscow calling for the immediate execution of Marshal Tukhachevskii and his associates in 1937.[28]

Second, Khrushchev's focus was actually quite limited. Nowhere did he say that Stalin had a hand in Kirov's assassination. Although indicating that there was still a lot of "mystery" around the crime, and that the Leningrad NKVD had something to do with it, he never accused Stalin, although it would have been easy to do so. Further, he limited his critical remarks on "repression" to 1937–38. There was no discussion of the verification and exchange in 1935–36, and, although he said that Kirov's death was used as an excuse for stepping up repression, he did not really explain why the repression resulting from the assassination was delayed until 1937. Stalin's "crimes" were essentially confined to 1937–38 and to the illegal repression of loyal Stalinist party members. Khrushchev asserted that Stalin's assumption of total power at the expense of "democratic norms" in the party led to these "crude violations of socialist legality." Serious as these "mistakes" were, they failed to destroy the party and its traditions, which survived the interlude.[29] In the final analysis, Khrushchev officially blamed Stalin for the Great Purges. His remarks are important as official condemnation of Stalin's "willfulness" but are less than earthshaking from an analytical or scholarly point of view.

Most of the other Khrushchev-era memoirs, biographies, and historical works followed this general theoretical scheme, and all works dealing with the period carried at least obligatory paragraphs about the near-fatal effects of Stalin's "cult of personality" on the party.[30]

One such work, however, was never published in the Soviet Union – Roy Medvedev's *Let History Judge.* This biography of Stalin contains the most complete unofficial Soviet account of the period from a communist point of view. Unlike Khrushchev, Medvedev accused Stalin of Kirov's death, of planning the repression in advance, and of sadistically decimating the generation of Old Bolsheviks. It is a completely and uniformly bitter condemnation of Stalin by a former communist.[31]

Nearly all Medvedev's work is based on the post-1956 recollections of surviving party members. Many such reminiscences appeared in the press in 1956–64, usually in connection with obituaries or anniversaries, and Medvedev apparently collected such statements and interviews as the basis of his work. He made virtually no use of central or local press sources, published material, or contemporary documentation. However, his introduction shows that he was familiar with the vast corpus of Western scholarship about Stalin, and in some places where Old Bolshevik circumstantial testimony is lacking (Stalin's hand in Kirov's death, for example), he seems to rely on Western versions.[32]

This and subsequent work by Medvedev are parts of a pro-Bukharin polemic that may have originally been aimed at supporting the rehabilitation of Bukharin, which never took place.[33] Medvedev argues that Stalinism was a petit-bourgeois corruption of Leninism, that NEP and Bukharinism represented Lenin's *real* thinking, that Bukharin (if not Trotsky) was innocent of any wrongdoing, and that he and his policies should be rehabilitated.[34]

Medvedev's is probably the most useful account of the fates of various people. He compiled lists based on the recollections of his reporters, and his book is a mine of informative details. Like the previously cited works, however, its problem is the distance between his sources and central events. Like all the above sources, none of Medvedev's often anonymous informants was close enough to the center of power to tell *why* things were happening or indeed exactly what was happening. Medvedev is able to catalog events better than other writers, but he is not able to chronicle or analyze Moscow's decisions or attitudes with first-hand evidence. All his informants were on the "outside," and their firsthand experience extended only to themselves and their associates. Their speculations about why this happened or about Stalin's position are little better than ours.

A work that deserves passing mention because of its current popularity is the *Gulag Archipelago* by Alexander Solzhenitsyn. Solzhenitsyn's work, according to its subtitle, is an "experiment in literary investigation," and it also consists of various memoirs and testimonials from unnamed persons on their experiences in camps and prisons from 1917 through the 1950s.[35] Unlike Medvedev's book, the *Gulag* is a literary, rather than empirical, masterpiece. Solzhenitsyn makes no attempt to be analytical or to explain *why* events happen. He artfully weaves thousands of personal horror stories into a captivating piece of subjective literature that brilliantly portrays the personal, psychological effects of being repressed. Yet the work is of limited value to the serious student of the 1930s for it provides no important new information or original analytical framework.

In fact, Solzhenitsyn's political point of view is not new. He traces the crimes of Stalin to a Leninist heritage – stressing the Leninist seeds of repression. But he does not stop with a standard anti-Bolshevik stance and often attributes the problem to Peter the Great and Western rationalism, which had corrupted the profoundly spiritual and compassionate Russian people. This anti-Westernism makes Solzhenitsyn the leading current spokesman for classical nineteenth-century Slavophilism and paternal Muscovite monarchy. Methodologically, Solzhenitsyn very much resembles other émigré accounts, and his book is thus the most brilliant example of a genre based on rumor, hearsay, and personal impression.

Solzhenitsyn's political and moralistic point of view tends to blur analytical categories. It makes no essential distinctions between trials of political opponents, the suppression of armed uprisings, the removal of derelict and criminal party administrators, attempts to impose literary norms, and murder by the police. All these are undifferentiated manifestations of repression or terror "from above," despite the fact that they took place decades apart and for different reasons. Solzhenitsyn's "waves" of repression all come from the same source, move in the same direction, and inexorably sweep over the victims (and the reader). Almost by definition, from the vantage point of the opponent or victim, however innocent, one sees only undifferentiated terror.

Many of the linchpins of the Western interpretation are based almost solely on an uncritical acceptance of rumors from persons not in a position to know. This is not to say that these works are worthless lies bearing no relation to the truth. They are quite valuable descriptions of personal experiences and should be taken as such. But they are not primary sources that cast light on central decision making, or even on events on a national scale. Because many of these writers were victims or opponents, they may have known less about high policy than we do.

One need only scan the footnotes of any standard account of the Great Purges to see how much of the basic material of this view comes from the speculations of these contradictory and self-serving sources, who were in no position to report anything but gossip. Most Western accounts were written during the post–World War II period, and their authors relied on émigré and defector accounts for the vital underpinnings of their view.[36] The inaccessibility of Soviet archives on these events compounded this tendency. Yet if one applies strict rules of evidence and of source criticism to these works, accepting only that which the informant can report firsthand, several aspects of the Western interpretation collapse.

Although the main weakness of the sources is their removal from the events they so freely judge, the question of political bias is also worth considering, as it is in other areas of historical inquiry. Orlov, Trotsky, the Mensheviks, and Khrushchev were all self-interested political actors and had little incentive to produce an objective view. Obviously, the other great source of bias is the Stalinist side. The explanatory works produced during the Stalin era (primarily the trial transcripts and brief mentions in outline histories) are not particularly valuable either.

The monstrosity of Stalin's crimes and a generation of Cold War attitudes have contributed to what would be considered sloppy and methodologically bankrupt scholarship in any other area of inquiry. Historians of modern Europe would not try to study the politics of World War I by relying on the memoirs of soldiers from the trenches without exhausting the available press, documentary, and archival materials.

A historiography characterized by Stalinist, Trotskyist, Bukharinist, dissident, and monarchist polemics does no service to modern scholarship. Fortunately, the historiography of the Stalin period – like that on the French or Russian revolutions – is beginning to outgrow its partisan, Great Man stage of development. It is time to use all the sources in studying the political history of Stalinism.

Notes

Introduction: the Great Purges as history

1 See the *History of the CPSU (b), Short Course,* Moscow, 1938, for example. M. Sayers and A. Kahan, *The Great Conspiracy: The Secret War Against the Soviet Union,* Boston, 1946, also follows this line.

2 Major interpretive works are Robert Conquest, *The Great Terror,* New York, 1968; Zbigniew Brzezinski, *The Permanent Purge,* Cambridge, Mass., 1956; John A. Armstrong, *The Politics of Totalitarianism,* New York, 1961; Isaac Deutscher, *Stalin: A Political Biography,* London, 1949, and *The Prophet* (3 vols.), New York, 1963; Merle Fainsod, *How Russia Is Ruled,* Cambridge, Mass., 1953, 1963, and *Smolensk Under Soviet Rule,* Cambridge, Mass., 1958; and Roy Medvedev, *Let History Judge,* New York, 1972. Also notable are Adam Ulam, *Stalin: The Man and His Era,* New York, 1973; Robert C. Tucker, *Stalin as Revolutionary, 1879–1929,* New York, 1973; and Alexander Dallin and George Breslauer, *Political Terror in Communist Systems,* Stanford, Calif., 1970.

3 "The consolidation of personal rule in a totalitarian system depends on the constant elimination of all actual or potential competitors for supreme power." Fainsod, *How Russia Is Ruled,* 441.

4 Deutscher, *Stalin,* 376–77.

5 Fainsod, *How Russia Is Ruled,* 441.

6 See Hannah Arendt, *The Origins of Totalitarianism,* New York, 1960.

7 Brzezinski, *Permanent Purge,* ch. 2. Brzezinski argued that terror (and thus purges) were inherent parts of developed totalitarian systems and that violence was inevitable in any leadership change.

8 Medvedev, *History,* stresses Stalin's psychological problems and cites "revenge" as the main reason for the "Great Purge" of the Old Bolsheviks (p. 191). Robert Tucker has also emphasized this point in *Stalin as Revolutionary.*

9 On the one hand, it was useful to Stalin and others in the Moscow government to give the impression of a disciplined and dedicated membership solidly united under democratic centralism. Stalin (and Lenin before him) described the party the way they wanted it to be. On the other, it was in

the interest of his political enemies to portray the bureaucracy as a uniform, servile, monolithic machine. The totalitarian view was convenient both for Stalinists and anti-Stalinists.

10 See the Bibliographic Essay for a detailed treatment of the memoir sources on the period.

11 Louis Gottschalk, Clude Kluckholn, Robert Angell, *The Use of Personal Documents in History, Anthropology, and Sociology,* Bulletin of the Social Sciences Research Council, no. 53, New York, 1945, 21. Paul Fussell, *The Great War in Modern Memory,* Oxford, 1975, 310. For a reconsideration of the uses of autobiography, see Kenneth D. Barkin, "Autobiography and History," *Societas,* Vol. 6, no. 2, Spring 1976, 83–103.

12 Conquest, *Terror,* 754. Such statements would be astonishing in any other field of history. Of course, historians do not accept hearsay and rumor as evidence. Conquest goes on to say that the best way to check rumors is to compare them with one another. This procedure would be sound only if rumors were not repeated and if memoirists did not read each other's works.

13 H. G. Skilling and Franklyn Griffiths, eds., *Interest Groups in Soviet Politics,* Princeton, N.J., 1971; and David Joravsky, *Soviet Marxism and Natural Science,* New York, 1961, and *The Lysenko Affair,* Cambridge, Mass., 1970. Jerry Hough (in Jerry Hough and Merle Fainsod, *How the Soviet Union Is Governed,* Cambridge, Mass., 1979) describes a "very recognizable political process" in which institutions and points of view are represented and function within an "institutional pluralism." (see pp. 536, 543–8).

14 See Sheila Fitzpatrick, *Education and Social Mobility in the Soviet Union, 1921–1934,* New York, 1979; Kendall Bailes, *Technology and Society Under Lenin and Stalin,* Princeton, N.J., 1978; Nicholas Lampert, *The Technical Intelligentsia and the Soviet State,* New York, 1979.

15 R. W. Davies, *The Socialist Offensive: The Collectivization of Soviet Agriculture, 1929–1930,* Cambridge, Mass., 1980, and *The Soviet Collective Farm,* Cambridge, Mass., 1980; Eugene Zaleski, *Stalinist Planning for Economic Growth, 1933–1952,* Chapel Hill, N.C., 1980.

16 See William O. McCagg, *Stalin Embattled, 1943–1948,* Detroit, 1978; Werner Hahn, *Postwar Soviet Politics: The Fall of Zhdanov and the Defeat of Moderation, 1946–1953,* Ithaca, N.Y., 1982; Timothy Dunmore, *The Stalinist Command Economy: The Soviet State Apparatus and Economic Policy 1945–1953,* New York, 1980; even the older Robert Conquest, *Power and Policy in the USSR,* New York, 1961, uses a conflict approach.

17 "Stalin's direct subordinates and their proteges...had considerable leeway to pursue their activities and intrigues and to push their own interests." Hahn, *Postwar Soviet Politics,* 183.

18 Martin Broszat has written that "Hitler practiced no direct and systematic leadership but from time to time jolted the government or the Party into action, supported one or the other initiative of Party functionaries or department heads and thwarted others, ignored them or left them to carry on without a decision." See his *The Hitler State,* New York, 1981, xi. See also Edward N. Peterson, *The Limits of Hitler's Power,* Princeton, N.J., 1969; Karl A. Schleunes *(The Twisted Road to Auschwitz,* London, 1972)

discusses the incremental and uncertain nature of Nazi policy formation.

19 The best recent assessments are found in the following sequence of articles: S. Rosenfielde, "An Assessment of the Sources and Uses of Forced Labor, 1929–1956," *Soviet Studies,* no. 1, Jan. 1981, 51–87; Stephen Wheatcroft, "On Assessing the Size of Forced Concentration Camp Labour in the Soviet Union, 1931–1956," *Soviet Studies,* no. 2, April 1981, 265–95; Robert Conquest, "Forced Labour Statistics: Some Comments," *Soviet Studies,* no. 3, July 1982, 434–9; and Stephen Wheatcroft, "Towards a Thorough Analysis of Soviet Forced Labor Statistics," *Soviet Studies,* no. 2, April 1983, 223–37.

20 See Fainsod, *Smolensk,* for a full description of the Archive. These files were captured by the Germans in 1941, and by the United States from Germany in 1945. We do not know the principles, if any, by which the Germans selected files. We do not know how many of the region's files we have and how many we lack, although we do have what appear to be fairly complete "runs" of several years for certain party organizations. In addition to problems of completeness, we should be aware that the use of provincial records that document a struggle with the center are bound to reflect local perspectives and values. In other words, although the center–periphery struggle was a vital concern in the provinces, one cannot know its relative importance to the Moscow authorities who were occupied with additional matters. Only access to central archives will allow us to assign relative importance to various political struggles. Ultimately, though, the Smolensk files are the only party archival sources we have, and despite their limitations they represent an extremely valuable and rich lode.

21 Fainsod was concerned with a great many topics and was able to devote only one chapter and small parts of a few others to the Great Purges. Students who have used the files know that his coverage of them was uneven, and some documents cited in the present study naturally escaped his attention. The few subsequent works based on the Smolensk Archive are not about the Great Purges. See Daniel Brower, "Collectivized Agriculture in Smolensk: The Party, the Peasantry, and the Crisis of 1932," *Russian Review,* vol. 36, no. 2, April 1977, 151–66; and William Rosenberg, "Smolensk in the 1920s: Party–Worker Relations and the 'Vanguard' Problem," *Russian Review,* 125–50.

22 Robert H. McNeal, "The Decisions of the CPSU and the Great Purge," *Soviet Studies,* vol. 23, no. 2, Oct. 1971, 177–85. McNeal's *Resolutions and Decisions of the CPSU,* Toronto, 1974, and his *Guide to the Decisions of the Communist Party of the Soviet Union 1917–1967,* Toronto, 1972, are basic research tools.

23 Traditionally, émigré memoirs have been the source bases for works on the Great Purges. For methodological reasons, however, memoir accounts will be considered primary and valid only for events the author(s) experienced firsthand. Second- and third-hand accounts are disqualified. These issues are treated in the Bibliographic Essay in this volume.

24 It is surprising that Fainsod never did this, because he pioneered the study of center–periphery relations and elucidated the relationship between local (lower) and central (upper) organizations. See Fainsod, *Smolensk,* ch. 3.

1. The Communist Party in the thirties

1 Moshe Lewin, *Russian Peasants and Soviet Power: A Study of Collectivization,* London, 1968; Davies, *Socialist Offensive.*
2 Fitzpatrick, *Education and Social Mobility in the Soviet Union;* Bailes, *Technology and Society;* Nicholas Lampert, *The Technical Intelligentsia and the Soviet State,* New York, 1979.
3 Conquest, *Terror,* ch. 6.
4 Roy Medvedev, *Let History Judge: The Origins and Consequences of Stalinism,* New York, 1971, 156; For an alternative view that questions the source bases and plausibility of the story, see Hough and Fainsod, *How the Soviet Union Is Governed,* 160–1; and Ulam, *Stalin,* 374.
5 See Sheila Fitzpatrick, *Cultural Revolution in Russia, 1928–1931,* Bloomington, Ind., 1978; and Bailes, *Technology and Society.*
6 For Stalin and the "revolutionary-heroic" tradition, see Stephen Cohen, *Bukharin and the Bolshevik Revolution, 1888–1938,* New York, 1973; Bailes, *Technology and Society,* 274; and Jerry Hough, "The Cultural Revolution and Western Understanding" in Fitzpatrick, *Cultural Revolution,* 241–53. In his speech "The Tasks of Business Executives" (Feb. 4, 1931), Stalin said, "To slacken the tempo would mean falling behind. And those who fall behind get beaten. We are 50 or 100 years behind the advanced countries. We must make good this distance or we shall be crushed." *Pravda,* Feb. 5, 1931.
7 The "cultural revolutionaries" and activists helped to defeat Bukharin and the Right Opposition in 1929. A. Avtorkhanov, *Stalin and the Soviet Communist Party,* New York, 1959, 11–107, describes the 1929 political battle from the vantage point of a young Bukharinist. Nikita Khrushchev, *Khrushchev Remembers,* Boston, 1970, 36–56, tells the same story from the vantage point of one of the young radicals who "stood with the general line of the party" and defeated Bukharin. According to Khrushchev, the Bukharinists controlled the leading positions of the Moscow Committee. Stalin and his partisans then turned to the lower, *raion* organizations where activist and radical sentiments were strong and unleashed the enthusiasts against the rightist leadership under the slogan of "self-criticism." This political battle, which had national implications, was fought out in the Moscow Party Committee, control of which was a crucial political position.
8 See Bailes, *Technology and Society,* 302, passim.
9 Valentin Kataev, *Time Forward!,* trans. Charles Malamuth, Bloomington, Ind., 1970. Speaking of the characters in the book, Kataev says, "Of course, it is not necessary to reveal the pseudonyms to you. You have guessed them long ago, and it is all the same to the reader." See pp. 25, 237, 231, 235.
10 Molotov replaced Uglanov as head of the Moscow Committee and was a perpetual opponent of the rightists. Jerry Hough ("Cultural Revolution in Western Understanding") identifies him as a radical. Kuibyshev headed the Supreme Economic Council during the first Plan and after 1928 was a confirmed enthusiast. See Bailes, *Technology and Society,* 124–7, 271. Much more research needs to be done to positively identify various

party leaders as adherents of one or another view. For Krzhizhanovskii's role see Bailes, *Technology and Society,* 184–5, 274.

11 See Stalin's articles "Dizzy With Success," *Pravda,* March 2, 1930, and "Reply to Kolkhoz Comrades," *Pravda,* April 3, 1930. To explain Stalin's siding against the use of violence in these speeches, some scholars have maintained that he was forced by the Central Committee to write these articles, although there is little evidence. See Medvedev, *History,* 87, for example.

12 Karl Bauman was the radical head of the Rural Department of the Moscow Committee and seems to have been responsible for the extremist policy toward the kulaks in 1929–30 that resulted in so much violence. In 1931, he was demoted and became the head of the Central Asian Department of the Central Committee and in 1934 was head of the Science Department. See Avtorkhanov, *Stalin and the Soviet Communist Party,* 125, 163. Stalin's "New Conditions – New Tasks" speech is in *Pravda,* July 5, 1931.

13 Stalin did both in the same speech. See his address to the January 1933 plenum of the Central Committee. *Pravda,* Jan. 10, 1933.

14 This account follows Eugene Zaleski, *Stalinist Planning for Economic Growth, 1933–1953,* Chapel Hill, N.C., 1980, 115–29.

15 This may have been an exaggeration, because some of the targets were not reached.

16 *Pravda,* Jan. 10, 1933.

17 *XVII s''ezd Vsesoiuznoi Kommunisticheskoi Partii (b) 27 ianvaria – 10 fevralia 1934g.: stenograficheskii otchet* [Seventeenth congress of the all-union Communist Party (Bolsheviks) January 27–February 10, 1934: stenographic report], Moscow, 1934, 354.

18 Ibid., 435–6.

19 Ibid., 436, 648–50.

20 Bailes, *Technology and Society,* discusses the shortage of qualified proletarian applicants and the incompetence of some of the *praktiki* who had been accepted to fill the quotas. See p. 178, for example.

21 There seems to have been a shift of personnel in and around 1932 that may represent the transfer of radicals from positions where they could harass moderates. Karl Bauman's demotion has already been noted. N. I. Ezhov was removed from the Agricultural and Industrial departments of the Central Committee in 1932 and given personnel responsibilities; D. A. Bulatov was moved from his position as head of the Organization-Instruction Department of the Central Committee to the NKVD. At about the same time, the moderate Krzhizhanovskii was placed in charge of a revamped educational system that discarded the proletarian quotas.

22 Hough believes that Stalin "went out of his way" to associate himself with moderate policies. "Cultural Revolution in Western Understanding," 249.

23 Stakhanovism will be discussed in Chapter 5.

24 See Robert V. Daniels, *The Conscience of the Revolution,* New York, 1969.

25 The standard work is Cohen, *Bukharin.*

26 For examples of these recantations, see *Pravda,* July 13 and Oct. 27, 1929. For a detailed treatment of Trotskyism in the Soviet Union based on archival sources, see Pierre Broue, "Les trotskystes en union sovietique" (The

Trotskyists in the Soviet Union), *Cahiers Leon Trotsky,* no. 6, 1980, 5–65.

27 See Conquest, *Terror,* 51–7.

28 Leonard Schapiro finds their punishment mild. See his *The Communist Party of the Soviet Union,* New York, 1971, 394–6.

29 The "Letter of an Old Bolshevik" suggests that both hard and soft factions competed for Stalin's support. See Boris Nicolaevsky, *Power and the Soviet Elite: "The Letter of an Old Bolshevik" and Other Essays,* New York, 1965, 43, 48–50, 60–2; Nicolaevsky also reports other rumors that Stalin favored a hard line and was thus opposed by Kirov. Ibid., 77–8.

30 The following oppositionists addressed the Seventeenth Congress: Lominadze, Bukharin, Rykov, Tomskii, Preobrazhenskii (in the discussion of Stalin's speech), Piatakov, Zinoviev, Kamenev, and Radek. Articles by Zinoviev appeared in *Pravda* on May 31, July 11, and Aug. 1, 1934, and an article by Kamenev was published on Nov. 6, 1934. Stalin's remarks are in *XVII s"ezd,* 28, 35.

31 Even a cursory scan of the Smolensk Archive shows the preoccupation of party secretaries with economic concerns in the early 1930s. See also Fainsod, parts 2 and 3.

32 *XVII s"ezd,* 551–2.

33 Ibid., 553.

34 Ibid., 288.

35 Ibid., 555.

36 Ibid., 251–9.

37 Ibid., 28, 35.

38 This shift in emphasis on party functions probably parallels the transfers of radicals to "party work" between the First and Second Five Year Plans.

39 The three began to collaborate on an overhaul of history textbooks in 1934. See *Pravda,* Jan. 25, 26, 1936.

40 *XVII s"ezd,* 34–5.

41 Ibid., 23, 33.

42 Ibid., 33–5. Apparently the old Rabkrin (workers' and peasants' inspection) and Tsentral'naia Kontrol'naia Komissiia (TsKK; Central Control Commission) had been lax in investigating instances of "non-fulfillment" of decisions by bureaucrats. Stalin announced the formation of two new agencies (the Soviet Control Commission and Party Control Commission) that were to conduct continuing "investigations" rather than occasional "raids" on bureaucrats. Formation of the two new commissions shows the determination of the Moscow authorities to control regional bureaucracies.

43 The system of committees derived from the prerevolutionary tradition of underground organizations in the Social Democratic Party.

44 Adurakhman Avtorkhanov (pseud. A. Uralov), *The Communist Party Apparatus,* Chicago, 1966, 161.

45 Orders often appeared "in the Central Committee" on dates when the Central Committee as a whole was not in session. See any issue of *Partiinoe stroitel'stvo* (Party construction) for an example. Often beginning "the Central Committee orders," these directives could only have come from the permanent offices (literally, "in the Central Committee" building)

and staff. These permanent offices were the Secretariat. See Fainsod, *How Russia Is Ruled*, 220, and especially Robert McNeal, *Guide to the Decisions of the Communist Party of the Soviet Union*, Toronto, 1972, Introduction.

46 Fainsod called the first secretary of the Western Region, Rumiantsev, a "little lord" and "the Great Man of Smolensk." *Smolensk*, 74. Elsewhere, he used the word "viceroy." *How Russia Is Ruled*, 225.

47 See Fainsod, *Smolensk*, ch. 1, for more on the history of Smolensk.

48 Ibid., 17. See also *Partiinoe stroitel'stvo*, nos. 19–20, Nov. 1935, 56 (hereafter *PS*). This was the official journal of the Cadres Department of the Central Committee and dealt with organizational matters.

49 Fainsod, *Smolensk*, 55.

50 Smolensk Archive file RS 924 contains protocols (nonverbatim summaries) of meetings of the Western Obkom Buro for 1936. Each protocol begins with the names and positions of those attending the meeting. Smolensk Archive files are identified by three types of codes. The majority are numbered with the prefix "WKP," derived from the German initials for Vsesoiuznaia Kommunisticheskaia Partiia (All-Union Communist Party, in Russian); thus WKP 324. Other files have other prefixes, such as RS 924. Still others are identified with only numbers (116/154e, for example). In the notes below, these will be preceded by "file"; thus, file 116/154e. The pages within each file are numbered in most cases.

51 Born in 1886, Rumiantsev was an industrial modeler involved in trade-union work before and during the revolutions of 1917. He commanded a punitive detachment and served on a revolutionary tribunal during the Civil War. He later held various territorial-party posts in the Caucasus and Urals in the early twenties. Rumiantsev and his associates were the leaders of the *oblast'* party during collectivization and the First Five Year Plan. See *Who Was Who in the USSR*, Metuchen, N.J., 1972, 485. For the Smolensk scandal, see Fainsod, *Smolensk*, ch. 2.

52 The Tsentral'nyi Isopolitel'nyi Komitet (TsIK; central executive committee of soviets) was the official government structure which paralleled (but was subordinate to) the party.

53 The special department within any party committee had unspecified functions. Its apparent subordination to the first secretary had led to speculation that it was the liaison between party and police (Fainsod, *How Russia Is Ruled*, 194). The Smolensk Archive suggests that the special department also had clerical functions. The head of the special department (who held the rank of assistant secretary) functioned as personal secretary to the first secretary, handling his personal correspondence, the sending and receiving of mail, etc. The head of the Special Department of the Central Committee was Alexander Poskrebyshev, who was Stalin's personal secretary. All orders of the Central Committee were sent over the signature of Poskrebyshev acting as the personal secretary and "at the request of Comrade Stalin." See WKP 225, p. 22, for an example. Kulakov served the same function for Rumiantsev in Smolensk.

54 The Party Control Commission's representatives sat on most party committees to check on malfeasance in the party apparat.

55 The ORPO was the personnel department of the Central Committee, re-

sponsible for assigning party cadres to leading positions and registering party membership. It replaced the old Cadres Department of the Central Committee in 1934.

56 Uborevich was one of the most important military commanders of the Red Army. He was a member of the Western Obkom by virtue of his military assignment, although he rarely attended *buro* meetings. See file RS 924, passim.

57 Scholars have implicitly accepted Smolensk as typical, for much of our understanding of local party affairs derives from Fainsod's Smolensk study.

58 Fainsod, *Smolensk,* 263, 278.

59 WKP 313, pp. 130–1; WKP 385, pp. 352–68. Belyi District is particularly well documented in the Smolensk Archive.

60 M. Savinov, "Likvidatsiia posledstvii trotskistskogo-bukharinskogo vreditel'stva" (Liquidating the consequences of Trotskyist-Burkharinist wrecking), *PS,* no. 14, July 15, 1938, 23. *Vlast' sovetov,* (Soviet power) No. 7, 1938, 34; Fainsod, *Smolensk,* 284, 288; M. A. Vyltsan, *Zavershaiushchii etap sozdaniia kolkhoznogo stroia* (The final stage in the creation of the collective farm system), Moscow, 1978, 119.

61 *Istoriia KPSS,* tom. 5, chast' 1, Moscow, 1970, 49; V. M. Selunskaia, *Izmeneniia v strukture sovetskogo obshchestva, 1921 – seredina 30-kh godov* (Changes in the structure of Soviet society, 1921 to the mid-1930s), Moscow, 1979, 230. WKP 101, passim.; WKP 323, p. 156; WKP 324, pp. 1–2. The average nationally today is around 10–12%.

62 WKP 321, pp. 139–140.

63 See Fainsod, *Smolensk,* ch. 10, for examples.

64 WKP 203, pp. 126–31; WKP 322, pp. 84–5, 372–4.

65 See *XVII s''ezd,* p. 103; WKP 362, p. 12. My thanks to Roberta T. Manning for information on Belyi.

66 WKP 362, pp. 231–2.

67 File 116/154e, pp. 45–54, 79–84; WKP 89, pp. 63–4; WKP 85, pp. 185–6; WKP 385, pp. 185–8.

68 WKP 362, pp. 82–97.

69 See Chapter 3.

70 File 116/154e, p. 45.

71 P. N. Pospelov et al, eds., *Istoriia Kommunisticheskoi Partii Sovetskogo Soiuza* (History of the Communist Party of the Soviet Union), vol. 4, part 2, Moscow, 1971, 284–5 (hereafter *Istoriia KPSS*).

72 A. Shil'man, "Tekushchie voprosy partiinoi raboty" (Current questions of party work), *PS,* nos. 19–20, Nov. 1935, 50–51. Information on those expelled in the city of Smolensk is in WKP 384, pp. 215–17.

73 File 116/154e, p. 45.

74 For examples, see WKP 361.

75 Students have been eager to accept this view, although the evidence suggests that the Stalinist Secretariat was not very efficient. Jerry Hough has recently questioned the primacy of patronage in explaining Stalin's rise to power. Hough and Fainsod, *How the Soviet Union Is Governed,* 145–6.

76 See Fainsod, *Smolensk,* 134–7, for an example of a personnel dispute between a lower and higher party body. Fainsod implies that local committees often proposed their own leaders, who were subject only to

confirmation (rather than selection) by the Central Committee; Ibid., 87–9. See also Shil'man's letter to Belyi in WKP 40, p. 3.

77 File 116/154e, p. 88.

78 Party committees were not ordered to send regular reports (protocols) on their work to superior party bodies until a Central Committee order of October 15, 1936. See "Ob otchestnosti partiinykh organov" (On the responsibility of party organs), *PS*, no. 20, 1936, 37.

79 WKP 109 contains examples of reports written on squared paper. *Pravda* often complained about the paper shortage.

80 Some of these are very interesting. For example, WKP 478–81 contains samples of antifascist propaganda from the thirties. WKP 461 consists solely of blank membership cards for the League of Militant Atheists. Most of the files, however, are simply disordered and confusing, and even clerical procedures were on a very low level.

2. What was a purge?

1 These ideas are also described in Lenin's "One Step Forward, Two Steps Back (The Crisis in Our Party)", *Polnoe Sobranie Sochinenii* (Complete works), 5th ed., Moscow, 1958–65, vol 8, 185–414, in "Two Tactics of Social Democracy in the Democratic Revolution," ibid., vol. 11, 1–131, and in many of his other writings before 1905. The best summary of the Bolshevik–Menshevik dispute is still Leopold Haimson's *The Russian Marxists and the Origins of Bolshevism*, Boston, 1966.

2 See F. A. Pukhov, "Deiatel'nost' kontrol'nykh komissii VKP(b) po ukrepleniiu partii v periode ee general'noi chistki v 1929–1930gg" (Activity of the control commissions of the VKP(b) in strengthening the party in the period of the general purge in 1929–1930), *Izvestiia Voronezhskogo Gosudarstvennogo Pedagogicheskogo Instituta (Proceedings of the Vornoezh State pedagogical institute), tom. 80, Voronezh, 1968*, 76.

3 *"KPSS v tsifrakh"* (KPSS in figures), *Partiinaia zhizn'*, (Party life), no. 19, Oct. 1967, 8–10. Questions of party membership and sources are treated in T. H. Rigby's authoritative *Communist Party Membership in the USSR, 1917–1967*, Princeton, N.J., 1968, ch. 1.

4 *Pravda*, Oct. 19, Nov. 4, 1918. The Central Committee had discussed the membership question as early as May. See *Pravda*, May 19, 1918, and the discussion in Rigby, *Membership*, 70.

5 *Vos'moi s"ezd RKP(b): Protokoly*, (Eighth Congress of the RKP(b): protocols), Moscow, 1959, 423. Rigby, *Membership*, 76.

6 For examples of these usages see *KPSS v rezoliutsiiakh i resheniiakh s"ezdov, konferentsii i plenumov TsK, 1898-1970 gg.* (The Communist Party of the Soviet Union in resolutions and decisions of congresses, conferences and plenums of the Central Committee, 1898–1970), 8 vols., 8th ed., Moscow, 1970– , vol. V, 98–103.

7 Ibid., 98.

8 Pukhov, "Deiatel'nost'," 75.

9 E. M. Iaroslavskii, ed., *Kak provodit' chistku partii* (How to conduct a purge of the party), Moscow and Leningrad, 1929, 5.

10　Iaroslavskii, *Kak provodit*, 7–8.

11　Victor Kravchenko provides a firsthand account of such a proceeding in *I Chose Freedom*, New York, 1946, ch. 10.

12　Iaroslavskii heard appeals fairly frequently. Kravchenko had an interview with him (ibid., 250–1), as did Eugenia Ginzburg when she was expelled from the party in 1937. See her *Into the Whirlwind*, New York, 1967. ch. 7.

13　"O chistke i proverke chlenov i kandidatov VKP(b)" (On the purge and verification of members and candidates of the All-Russian Communist Party (b)), *KPSS v rezoliutsiakh*, vol. 4, 238.

14　A. Sol'ts, "K chistke" (Toward the purge), in *Kak provodit, 31.*

15　A. Mitrofanov, "Uchastie bespartiinykh v chistke partii" (Participation of non-party [persons] in the purge of the party), in *ibid.*, 36–40.

16　Ibid., 8–14.

17　Ibid., 21.

18　Ibid., 26.

19　Ibid., 6–7.

20　This assumes, of course, that Iaroslavskii's statements were true.

21　Fainsod, *Smolensk,* 216–20.

22　See Pukhov, "Deiatel'nost'," 84, passim. Appeals were sustained (thus reversing the lower decision to expel) when the only charge was simple passivity or political illiteracy. See WKP 296, p. 115.

23　The announcement simply mentioned the forthcoming operation. *KPSS v rezoliutsiakh*, vol. 5, 98–103.

24　*Pravda,* April 28, 1933.

25　Also, no communist was to be purged for "excessive firmness" in carrying out party policy.

26　*Pravda,* April 28, 1933.

27　*KPSS v rezoliutsiakh*, vol. 5, 98.

28　This was the first time an ad hoc body had been created to carry out a purge.

29　Ian Rudzutak (1887–1938) was an Old Bolshevik from Latvia who had served 10 years (1907–1917) in tsarist prisons at hard labor. From trade-union work in the twenties he became peoples' commissar of communications (1924–30) and was on the Politburo after 1926. He headed the control commission after 1931, and in 1933 he chaired the central purge commission

30　L. M. Kaganovich (1893–1969) had done organizational work for the Central Committee since 1923, was a Central Committee secretary in 1924, and was first secretary of the Ukraine during the twenties. He headed the Moscow party organization from 1930–5, after which he took charge of the chaotic railroad system. He was an industrial troubleshooter in the thirties, becoming commissar of heavy industry in 1938. He was a Politburo member after 1930. An Old Bolshevik, he joined the party in 1911.

31　S. M. Kirov (1886–1934) was an Old Bolshevik who had organized the Bolshevik revolution in Siberia in 1917. He fought in the South in the Civil War (with Stalin) and was also active in the Caucasus. He headed the Leningrad party organization from 1927 to 1934 and was an active campaigner against the opposition. Elected to the Politburo and Secretariat in 1934, he was one of the country's most influential leaders. He was assassinated in December 1934.

32 N. I. Ezhov (1895–1940?) was head of the Central Committee's personnel, or "cadres," department. Joining the party in 1917 in Petrograd, he took part in the October Revolution and served in regional party posts until he went to work for the Central Committee in 1927. From 1930–4, he was head of the Cadres Department of the Central Committe, and in 1935 he took over the Control Commission. In 1936, he became head of the NKVD and in this capacity lent his name to the famous Ezhovshchina. He was a Central Committee secretary from 1935 and a candidate member of the Politburo in 1937. He disappeared in early 1939. His career will be treated in detail in Chapter 5.

33 Matvei F. Shkiriatov (1883–1954), a tailor by trade, joined the party in 1906. After an active role in the October Revolution and Civil War, he joined the Control Commission in 1922 and was its representative to the Politburo from 1926. His entire career until his death was involved in Control Commission work.

34 The eight are I. I. Korotkov, K. G. Sidorov, A. S. Slavinskii, A. A. Sol'ts, E. D. Stasova, M. F. Shkiriatov, E. M. Iaroslavskii, and R. S. Zemliachka.

35 *PS,* no. 11, June 1933, 1–11.

36 Iaroslavskii, *Za Bolshevistskuiu,* 43.

37 *Pravda,* April 28, 1933.

38 *Pravda,* April 28, 1933.

39 WKP 176, p. 75.

40 *XVII s" ezd,* 285–6.

41 See "Itogi proverki partiinykh dokumentov" (Summary of the verification of party documents), in *KPSS v rezoliutsiakh,* vol. 5, p. 252.

42 *XVII s"ezd,* 286.

43 These are incomplete figures given by Iaroslavskii in his speech to the Seventeenth Congress in early 1934. *XVII s"ezd,* 287, 298.

44 *Istoriia KPSS,* 283. Different figures (17 percent expelled, 12 percent demoted) were given in *Partiinaia zhizn',* no. 20, Oct. 1947, 79.

45 WKP 384, p. 231. Fainsod could not discover why the purge rate in Smolensk was so low. Neither could the present research.

46 *PS,* no. 1, Jan. 1934, 22. The figures for Leningrad, which use slightly different categories, were as follows: class alien, 13 percent; double dealers, 5 percent; degenerates, 11 percent; violators of discipline, 17 percent; corrupt careerists, 26 percent; passives, 27 percent.

47 *XVII s"ezd,* 287.

48 Ibid., 299.

49 Ibid., 287.

50 *Partiinaia zhizn',* no. 20, Oct. 1974, 79.

51 L. M. Kaganovich, *Report on Organizational Problems of Party and State Construction,* Moscow, *1934, 106.*

52 *Istoriia KPSS,* 283.

53 WKP 226, p. 3.

54 WKP 384, p. 231, suggests that in the city of Smolensk 909 persons had
    left the party before the *chistka* for reasons not connected with the purge:
    nine times the number actually expelled in the operation.
55 Rigby, *Membership,* 204.
56 *Spravochnik partiinogo rabotnika,* vol. 8, 306 (hereafter *SPR*).
57 Ibid., 307. Also in *PS,* no, 21, Nov. 1933, 47.
58 WKP 176, p. 7. This file also contains a reference to the October 11 deci-
    sions discussed above: WKP 176, p. 81. The Nov. 13 decision has never
    appeared in print, nor has any reference to it.
59 *XVII s"ezd,* 285–6.
60 For Trotsky, the 1933 *chistka* was not a matter of ideology. In March 1933
    he supported "the process of purging the party of the raw material, the
    ballast." Writing about the party, he agreed that "there is no reason for it
    to have two million people in it." *Writings of Leon Trotsky [1932–33],* New
    York, 1972, 167.
61 See "Ob obratnom perevode v chleni i kandidati partii perevedennykh po
    chistke v 1933g v kandidati partii i sochuvstvuiushchie" (On the restora-
    tion to member and candidate party member of those transferred to candi-
    date and sympathizer in the purge of 1933), in *PS,* no. 1, January 1935,
    79. The point continually stressed here was that an individual approach to
    readmissions and careful verification would prevent problems from aris-
    ing again.

3. The Verification of Party Documents of 1935: a case study in bureaucratic ineptitude

1 Although no decision was published in Oct. 1934, the date is given in A.
   P. Pavlov, *Kommunisticheskaia partiia v borbe za zavershenie sotsialistischeskoi re-
   konstruktsii narodnogo khoziaistva. Pobeda sotsializma v SSSR (1933–1937g.)*
   (The Communist Party in the struggle to complete the socialist reconstruction of the national economy. The victory of socialism in the USSR
   [1933–1937]), Moscow, 1959, 51. See also B. N. Ponomarev, ed., *History
   of the Communist Party of the Soviet Union,* Moscow, 1960, 492. Fainsod believed that the *proverka* was designed to increase terror in the wake of the
   Kirov assassination and that the *uchet* issue was a "guise" for a new purge.
   Fainsod, *Smolensk,* 223. Clearly, the verification was a bureaucratic procedure planned before the Kirov assassination. In addition, see "Ob uchete
   kommunistov v partorganizatsiiakh Tikhoretskogo parovozoremontnogo
   zavoda i Krasnodarskogo parovoznogo depo Severokavkazskoi Zh.d."
   (On the registration of communists in the party organizations of the
   Tikhoretskii locomotive repair plant and the Krasnodarsk locomotive de-
   pot of the Northern Caucasus Railroad), *PS,* no. 22, Nov. 1934, 48. "O
   narusheniiakh poriadka vydachi partbiletov i uchetnikh kartochek v
   Tashkentskoi partorganizatsii kommunisticheskoi partii (b)" (On violations of order in the disbursement of party cards and file records in the
   Tashkent organizations of the Communist Party), *PS,* no. 21, Oct. 1934,
   61; "O rezul'tatakh proverki Vostochno-Kazakhstanskoi partorganizatsii," (On the results of the verification of the Eastern Kazakhstan party organizations), *PS,* no. 21, Nov. 1934, 63.

2 *PS,* nos. 1–2, Jan. 1935, 37–9. Although the Central Committee decision of Dec. 13 is mentioned, it was never published in full or in part.
3 The ORPO was both an accounting and assignment department. Within it, there were various sectors that dealt with specific areas, such as the Accounting Sector. See Fainsod, *How Russia Is Ruled,* 194–6. The abolition and reestablishment of cadres departments in 1934 is another example of improvisation and pragmatism in party leadership. The ORPO would be again reorganized in Sept. 1935. See "Struktura otdela rukhovodiashchikh part-organov TsK partii" (Structure of the Department of Leading Party Organs of the TsK of the party), *PS,* no. 17, Oct. 15, 1935, 73–8.
4 Ezhov's connections with the KPK will be discussed more fully in subsequent chapters. Documents over his signature connected with the *proverka* were mostly from the ORPO, although there is at least one from the Orgburo. See file 116/154e, pp. 38, 46, 88, for examples.
5 The practice of sending trusted emissaries from the center to investigate local conditions was common. For an earlier example, see Iakovlev's investigation of the "Smolensk scandal" in 1929 in Fainsod, *Smolensk,* 48–50, and in WKP 33.
6 WKP 384, p. 64–5. Vladimirov was chief of the city ORPO.
7 Ibid., 63. An "Informational Summary" on the progress of the local verification with examples of chaos and errors in party documents was published on May 22 by the city party committee. Although the summary was ostensibly based on the city committee decision of April 8, it was published after receipt of the Central Committee's May 13 letter. The way in which details of *uchet* chaos were listed suggests that it may have been a popularization of the May 13 letter. See WKP 384, pp. 66–7.
8 *Istoriia KPSS,* 284.
9 See articles in *PS,* no. 4, Feb. 1935, 32–5, 35–6, for examples.
10 See *Pravda,* April 5, 1935, for the first appearance of "Party Life" and May 16, 1935, for "Party Accounting." The latter was linked to the May 13 letter announcing the *proverka.*
11 The letter is in WKP 499, pp. 308–9. Although it was signed "Central Committee of the VKP(b)," it was probably written by Ezhov inasmuch as it contained similar language to a speech he later gave on the *proverka* in December 1935. (*Pravda,* Dec. 26, 1935).
12 A large number of examples of the theft and misuse of party cards was listed in various reports and circulars. See file 116/154e, pp. 79–84. These reports were based on local information on accounting chaos that had been forwarded to the center. See WKP 384, pp. 146–151, for such local examples in the city of Smolensk.
13 The ORPO directed the *proverka.* The reports went to its Accounting Sector and *PS* published the results. Ezhov was therefore the main *uchet* specialist.
14 These reports were prescribed in Orgburo instructions "on how to draw up statements on the *proverka* of party documents," which exhorted local secretaries to make careful note of all problems and mistakes encountered in the operation. See "Extract of Protocol 30" of the Orgburo meeting of June 2, 1935, in file 116/154e, p. 38.
15 WKP 499, p. 309. This is an example of the attempt made by the Central

Committee to fix personal responsibility for "fulfillment of decisions."

16 The verification of members individually and in person was an important aspect of the *proverka* and would later be cited as one of the few good points of the campaign.

17 WKP 384, pp. 142–3, is an example of such a form. The two-page blank contained spaces for detailed statistical information on those expelled: "How many expelled for not having party cards?," "How many of these had been expelled earlier but retained their cards illegally?," etc.

18 It could be argued that the categories set out in the *proverka* report forms constituted predetermined categories for expulsion. They were: alien persons working in the apparat and using their position to secure party documents; spies and those connected with them; White Guards and kulaks; Trotskyists and Zinovievists; swindlers and cheats. However, categories were specified to obtain concrete examples for national publication in "supplemental enclosures" for propaganda purposes. The vast majority of those expelled in the *proverka* were not in these categories.

19 Ezhov's remarks appeared in his final report on the *proverka* (*Pravda*, Dec. 26, 1935). Zhdanov's comments were part of his speech to the Saratov Kraikom, discussed in the following chapter. See *Pravda*, July 12, 1935.

20 *Pravda*, Jan. 18, 1936 (Zhdanov), and May 18, 1936 (Ezhov).

21 See J. Arch Getty, "Party and Purge in Smolensk: 1933–1937," *Slavic Review*, vol. 42, no. 1, Spring 1983, 60–79; Nils Erik Rosenfeldt, "Problems of Evidence," ibid., 87; and J. Arch Getty, "Reply," ibid., 93.

22 *Pravda*, May 14, 16, 26 (editorial entitled "Again on Party Accounting"). On May 26, the pace-setting Moscow Committee highlighted the *uchet* issue in one of its resolutions. *Pravda*, May 27, 1935.

23 There is probably so little information in the Archive on the first *proverka* because it was as cursory as previous attempts had been. The dates on the first reports on the verification can be fixed from the July 1935 Central Committee report. See file 116/154e, pp. 46–9.

24 The decision, "On fulfilling the closed letter of the Central Committee, VKP(b) of May 13, 1935 in the party organizations of the Western *Oblast'*," was dated June 27; published in *PS*, no. 13, July 1935, 46; and first mentioned in *Pravda* on July 7, 1935.

25 Fainsod believed that the Central Committee rebuked Smolensk for being reluctant to purge more members. *Smolensk*, 223.

26 Similar things happened in Saratov Krai. An article in the same issue of *PS* called "On the political mistakes of the Saratov *Kraikom*" made many of the same points and would be the subject of a major Zhdanov speech in the coming weeks.

27 File 116/154e, p. 44. The cover letter was typical party secretarial style, beginning "sending you the first communication on fulfilling the May 13 letter" over Stalin's signature. Stalin's signature, plus the rejoinder to "give special attention" to the report may have been part of the attempt to impress local secretaries with the seriousness of the matter. The report itself was addressed to "Secretary of the Central Committee Comrade Stalin" and was signed by Ezhov (as Central Committee secretary) and Malenkov (as deputy chief of the ORPO). Thus, according to the arrangement of the documents, Ezhov and his assistant Malenkov were re-

porting on the progress of the *proverka* to Stalin, who, as Central Committee secretary, was forwarding the report to local leaders.

28 Ibid. Underlined by hand on printed copy from Moscow. The same hand addressed this particular copy of the report "to Kovalev," who at this time was first secretary in Belyi Raion.

29 Ibid., p. 85.

30 I. P. Rumiantsev, "Vtoraia proverka partdokumentov" (The second verification of party documents), *PS,* no. 17, Oct. 1935, 19.

31 File 116/154e, pp. 46–9.

32 Although the decision was not published until the first week in July, it was conveyed to Smolensk immediately, for meetings to consider it were held as early as June 29. Whether the Smolensk authorities received a written copy and if that copy was identical to the subsequent printed resolution is unknown. No copy of the letter is available.

33 WKP 384, p. 23.

34 WKP 384, p. 70 (emphasis added). This document is especially interesting. On the one hand, if specific instructions accompanied the transmission of the June 27 Central Committee censure, they may have included this warning against hysterical denunciation. On the other hand, if the Central Committee sent no such instructions, then the Oblast' and city leaders took it upon themselves to "tone down" the operation in such a way. In the latter case, self-preservation may have been a motive.

35 Meeting of party committee in Factory No. 35, Aug. 7, 1935, in WKP 89, pp. 63–4.

36 The slips assigned to Arkhipov, a secretary of the city party committee, are in WKP 384, pp. 39–50.

37 This was necessary because of the extreme mobility and poor registration of communists. Of all those finally expelled in the *proverka* in Smolensk, only one-fifth had joined the party there. The rest had transferred from other party organizations, the Red Army, or (for 8%) from "no place at all." See ibid., pp. 215–17.

38 There are hundreds of such requests for information and *kharakteristiki* on members in the Archive. For examples, see WKP 90, WKP 239, WKP 355, WKP 356, and WKP 385.

39 WKP 384, p. 71.

40 Ibid., 73. The rate was similar in Belyi Raion (WKP 385, p. 154). In the Western Oblast' as a whole two-thirds of the statements were supported according to a Central Committee report in file 116/154e, p. 87.

41 For a selection of these cases, see WKP 89, pp. 63–4; WKP 384, pp. 32–7; and WKP 93, pp. 71–4.

42 WKP 384, pp. 72–3.

43 The final report on the *proverka* in Belyi, for example, did not even mention the alien-enemy theme as a result of the verification. WKP 385, pp. 152–5.

44 WKP 93, pp. 41–2.

45 WKP 384, p. 53.

46 WKP 89, p. 38.

47 WKP 384, p. 51.

48 Ibid., p. 54; WKP 89, p. 38.

49 For example, "Organize Mass Criticism From Below," a speech by Stalin to the Komsomol in May 1928, stressed these points and linked criticism to the fight against bureaucratism. He used the Smolensk scandal of 1928 as an example of bureaucratism. He returned to this theme in "The Right Danger in the CPSU(b)" in April 1929, and "mass criticism from below" seems to have been a frequent slogan against the Right Opposition. See I.V. Stalin, *Problems of Leninism*, Moscow, 1947, 285, 295–7.

50 See his "Cadres Decide Everything" speech discussed above. Arkhipov, Smolensk city party secretary, told the meeting in Factory No. 35 in August 1935 that "speaking against a comrade does not mean undermining him... it means teaching and educating him, but many of us do not understand this." (WKP 89, p. 62). It should be remembered that *kritika/ samokritika* was also applicable to the rank and file. Part of good cadres policy included the criticism of average members by one another in such matters as style of work, political literacy, passivity, etc. Theoretically, such mutual criticism was always to be constructive.

51 WKP 384, p. 54; WKP 89, p. 42.

52 WKP 89 comprises the files of the party group in Factory No. 35 in Smolensk for 1935. The July 7 meeting is on pp. 35–7, and the related resolution is on pp. 38–9.

53 WKP 384, p. 56.

54 The Smolensk city party activists had noted that criticism was particularly weak in the city organizations and its development there was "especially important." Ibid., p. 69.

55 WKP 89, pp. 41–57. This was an extraordinary "closed meeting" of the entire factory committee, which comprised 119 members.

56 Ianishevskii was apparently an unpopular factory director. He was also accused of being a former member of the Socialist Revolutionary Party and protector of class enemies. Ibid., pp. 44, 48. Nothing happened to him as a result of these accusations.

57 Ibid., pp. 42, 46, 50–1.

58 Ibid., p. 53.

59 Ibid., p. 47.

60 Ibid., p. 53. Monchinskii's position in the factory committee before this meeting is unclear. After it, however, he was on the presidium of every committee meeting. Rappoport, on the other hand, apparently had to beat a hasty retreat, as his place as emissary from the city committee was taken over by the other city party secretary, Arkhipov.

61 A resolution of the city committee during the *proverka* noted that "already in the process of conducting this work on the *proverka*, it is clear that not only workers in the City Committee, but also leaders of party cells do not know many of the communists [working under them]." WKP 384, p. 69.

62 Ibid., pp. 57–8.

63 Ibid., pp. 28, 46, 54.

64 For examples, see ibid., p. 261; WKP 93, p. 69.; and WKP 322, p. 81.

65 It was based on reports submitted to the Central Committee during the second two weeks in July. The August report is in file 116/154e, pp. 85–8. Like the first, this report was to Stalin from Ezhov and Malenkov, and

contained the same subdivisions (i.e., local leadership, quantitative facts, further results, etc.).

66 The second secretaries of the *oblast'* committees were responsible for submitting the *akti* to the Central Committee; ibid., p. 85.

67 In the list of organizational purge rates, the Western Oblast' was first: twenty-three percent of the cards checked were being held back. Ibid., p. 85. But, later in the report, the Western Oblast' was discussed in more detail, and it was revealed that only 7.4 percent of the members were being expelled, while the remaining 15.6 percent were simply being investigated.

68 Also in *Pravda,* July 7, 1935, in the "party life" section.

69 File 116/154e, p. 88.

70 The figure was given by Rumiantsev in *PS,* no. 17, Oct. 1935, 21. The article was published on October 15, but the information was undated–perhaps the end of September would be close. *Proverka* meetings took place every week or two during August and September: Factory No. 35 met on July 21, August 14, and August 28 in connection with the *proverka.* (WKP 89). Often expulsions of up to four members took place at each meeting after reports on background information. All expulsions were by majority vote of the meeting, and often the vote went for censure or reprimand, rather than expulsion. See ibid., pp. 71–4, for an example with voting results.

71 *Pravda,* Oct. 13, 1935.

72 Pravda, Oct. 20, 1935; and *PS,* no. 18, Oct. 1935.

73 WKP 385, pp. 152–6; WKP 93, p. 69; Shil' man in *PS,* nos. 19–20, 1935, 49–57.

74 WKP 384, p. 120, shows the division of responsibility among the members of the city committee *buro.*

75 WKP 385, p. 153.

76 Kovalev's report, unlike many others, was neat, clear, and well written. In 1937, he would be hired by the *oblast'* committee, probably as an instructor.

77 WKP 384, p. 251; WKP 385, p. 153; WKP 89, p. 151.

78 WKP 385, p. 154. *Kritika/samokritika* was the "chief weakness" of party work in Factory No. 35 (WKP 89, p. 148) and at the local Institute of Marxism-Leninism (WKP 93, p. 69). The report of the city committee made a point of saying that 1,000 of the 4,000 members at the meetings spoke up (WKP 384, p. 258), as did other organizations: Of 18 at the Council of Trade Unions, 15 spoke (WKP 384, p. 191). Some reports even had a separate section entitled "increased activity of many communists." In Brick Factory No. 1, Comrade Bogdanov had never before spoken at meetings because "in the factory, they don't like criticism." Now, supposedly, he would be an active participant. There were many other such examples.

79 Shil'man, "Tekushchie...."; *PS,* nos. 19–20, Nov. 1935, 52.

80 Ezhov's report is in *Pravda,* Dec. 26, 1935. The 81% completion rate is based on 93% of the members and 53% of the candidates.

81 I. P. Rumiantsev, "Vtoraia proverka partdokumentov" (The second veri-

fication of party documents) *PS,* no. 17, Oct. 1935, 19–21, gives the Smolensk figure. The national rate was given in a progress report in the same *PS* issue.

82 Shil'man in *PS,* nos. 19–20, Nov. 1935, 49; and "Zadachi proverki partdokumentov" (Tasks of the verification of party documents), in *PS,* no. 17, Oct. 1935, 2–3.

83 WKP 384, pp. 251–5.

84 File 116/154e contains several copies of such supplements: 46–9, for example.

85 WKP 385, pp. 185–8.

86 WKP 89, pp. 63–4.

87 Later, when Stalin and others commented on the *proverka,* they denounced such grounds for expulsion.

88 Shil'man in *PS,* nos. 19–20, Nov. 1935, 51.

89 WKP 384, pp. 59, 151; WKP 385, pp. 185–6.

90 See Shil'man, "Tekushchie...," 50.

91 Fainsod, *Smolensk,* p. 231; WKP 384, p. 257.

92 WKP 385, p. 155.

93 Shil'man, "Tekushchie...," 54.

94 WKP 384, pp. 241–5.

95 A. Gavrilov, *Vnutripartiinaia demokratiia v bol'shevistskoi partii* (Inner party democracy in the Bolshevik Party), Moscow, 1951, 99.

96 *WKP 384, pp. 241–5.*

97 *Pravda,* Dec. 26, 1935; and *KPSS v rezoliutsiakh...,* vol. 5, 231–52.

98 This probably referred to those party secretaries responsible for bungling the first *proverka* and thus "failing in party work."

99 B. Ponomarev *et al.,* eds., *History of the Communist Party of the Soviet Union,* Moscow, 1973, 487; A. P. Pavlov, *Kommunisticheskaia partiia v borbe...,* 50–1. There had been an abortive 1934 attempt to exchange party cards before the Kirov assassination. See "O poriadke obmena partbiletov obraztsa 1926g. na partbilety obraztsa 1934g" (On the procedure for exchanging 1926-form party cards for 1934-form party cards), *PS,* nos. 19–20, Oct. 1934, 45. (decision dated Aug. 20, 1934), and "O srokakh obmena partiinikh biletov" (On the dates of the exchange of party cards), *PS,* no. 22, Nov. 1934, 48. No "1934 form" cards were ever produced, and no exchange took place until 1936, when 1926 cards were exchanged.

100 "Instruktsiia o poriadke i tekhnike obmena partiinykh biletov i drugikh partiinikh dokumentov" (Instruction on the procedure and technique of the exchange of party cards and other party documents) (confirmed by Central Committee 1/14/36), WKP 54, p. 203.

101 Ibid., 203–5.

102 Ibid., 205–8.

103 A separate set of instructions described in detail the possible entries and prescribed wording for each line on the new party cards. Often, several paragraphs were devoted to the correct responses for a single line. Ibid., 277–81.

104 Ibid., 203.

105 The new section "party accounting" first appeared in *Pravda* on Jan. 15,

1936. See also *Pravda,* Jan. 25, 28, and "On the Eve of the Exchange" on Feb. 6, 1936. An article on February 29 by Leningrad party secretaries stressed fewer mistakes and "holding firmly to the rules."

106.*Pravda,* March 14, and editorial on March 16, 1935.

107 WKP 384, p. 270. Apparently, it took three months to organize and begin a typical *uchet* operation.

108 *Pravda,* May 24, 1936. The actual order is dated May 23.

109 See "Ob itogakh obmena partdokumentov v . . ." (On the summaries of the exchange of party documents in . . .), *PS,* no. 22, Nov. 1936, 48–52.

110 See *PS,* no. 23–24, Dec. 1936, 77–80; *PS,* no. 1, Jan. 1937, 53–57; and "O partiinikh biletakh obraztsa 1926g" (On 1926-form party cards), *PS,* no. 2, Jan. 1937, 64.

111 WKP 384, p. 272.

112 WKP 385, pp. 292–3, 335.

113 *PS,* no. 9, May 1936, 36; also see Rigby, *Membership,* 209, n. 26.

114 WKP 385, pp. 292–3.

115 Fainsod, *Smolensk,* 232–3.

4. Radicalism and party revival

1 "Party revival" was used by William O. McCagg, Jr., to describe a phenomenon of the 1940s. The Stalin–Zhdanov party reforms of the 1930s, with their emphasis on propaganda, ideology, mass campaigns, and non-economic party functions, were similar to the revival that McCagg associates with Zhdanov in the 1940s. See McCagg's *Stalin Embattled: 1943–1948,* Detroit, 1978, 104, passim.

2 The assassination is discussed here because it has traditionally been regarded as an integral part of the crescendo of terror in which scholars have included virtually all events of the thirties. Paradoxically, it is necessary to treat it here to show its irrelevance to the problems within the apparatus.

3 Boris I. Nicolaevsky, *Power and the Soviet Elite: "The Letter of an Old Bolshevik" and Other Essays,* New York, 1965, 33, 89, 95. Ch. 1 provides details on the "Letter."

4 Ibid., 98–102.

5 See the appendix for a discussion of the Kirov assassination.

6 Francesco Benvenuti, "Kirov in Soviet Politics, 1933–1934," discussion paper no. 8, Soviet Industrialisation Project Series, University of Birmingham Centre for Russian and East European Studies, 1977, 29–30. Quoted by permission of the author. Recent works, some of them supposedly based on closed Soviet materials, have revealed few new details. See, for example, the disappointing Anton Antonov-Ovseyenko, *The Time of Stalin,* New York, 1981, 84–103, an apocryphal work replete with fictional dialog. Jerry Hough, in a recent survey of the evidence, has also concluded that the evidential base for an anti-Stalin (or pro-Kirov) faction is quite weak. See Hough and Fainsod, *How the Soviet Union is Governed,* 159–160.

7 Leon Trotsky, *The Revolution Betrayed,* New York, 1937, 286; Grigori To-

kaev, *Betrayal of an Ideal,* Bloomington, Ind., 1955, 241; and *Sotsialisticheskii vestnik* (Socialist Herald), no. 8, April 1934, 19. This is why Trotsky could not directly charge Stalin with the crime–Kirov's adherence to Stalin's line eliminated a possible motive. NKVD complicity, however, made sense to Trotsky, just as the possible involvement of Ezhov and Kaganovich made sense to the Old Bolshevik.

8 *XVII s"ezd,* 252–3, 259.

9 Hough and Fainsod, *How the Soviet Union Is Governed,* 161–3. At the Seventeenth Congress, Stalin had said, "There is nothing to prove and, it seems, no one to fight."

10 WKP 178, pp. 134–5. A similar instruction from the TsKK and the Commissariat of Workers' and Peasants' Inspection dated May 25, 1933, is found on pp. 137–8 of the same file.

11 Nicolaevsky, *Power,* 90; and S. Kucherov, *The Origins of Soviet Administration of Justice,* Leiden, 1970, 72–6. See also Louis Fischer, *Men and Politics,* New York, 1941, 225–9, for these events. Given the harrowing events of 1937, this limitation on police powers turned out to be more apparent than real. Stalin's plans for the police in 1934 are not known, but this reform was in principle an institutional check on the police.

12 The decisions abolishing are in *KPSS v rezoliutsiakh,* vol. 3, pp. 256, 260. See also *Pravda,* Feb. 11, 16, 1935, for the celebration of the new *kolkhoz* rules.

13 See Sheila Fitzpatrick, "Cultural Revolution in Russia, 1928–1932," *Journal of Contemporary History,* vol. 9, no. 1, 1974, 33–52; and especially S. Fitzpatrick, "Culture and Politics Under Stalin: A Reappraisal," *Slavic Review,* vol. 35, no. 2, June 1976, 211–31.

14 See S. Krasnikov, *Sergei Kirov,* Moscow, 1964, 194–5, for example.

15 S. V. Krasnikov, *S. M. Kirov v Leningrade* (S. M. Kirov in Leningrad), Leningrad, 1966, 187–8.

16 *Pravda,* Jan. 25, 26, 1936.

17 WKP 186, pp. 66–9. The letter is printed rather than typed and is signed by Rumiantsev, the *oblast'* first secretary.

18 See Fainsod, *Smolensk,* ch. 10, for examples of financial corruption in the Western *Oblast'.* John Scott, *Behind the Urals,* Bloomington, Ind., 1941, also contains graphic examples, as does John Littlepage, *In Search of Soviet Gold,* New York, 1937.

19 WKP 186, p. 69. Also contributing to the problems was "completely insufficient revolutionary vigilance."

20 *Pravda,* Jan. 26, 1935.

21 *Pravda,* March 1, 1935. Ezhov replaced L. M. Kaganovich at KPK. Kaganovich then assumed general responsibility for railroad transport. His activities in the railroads were frequently discussed in the national press. See *Pravda,* April, 24, 1935, for an example of full-page coverage of party work on the railroads under his leadership. Ezhov's name appears on documents from the center on this question during 1935 (See, for example, file 116/154e, pp. 49, 84, 88), and he gave the report on the conclusion of these activities in Dec. 1935 to the Central Committee plenum (*Pravda,* Dec. 26, 1935).

22 Ezhov's radicalism and subsequent activities are discussed in Chapter 5.

23 *Pravda,* Jan. 25 and 26, 1936, mentions the three together as the organizers of this effort.

24 These opposition movements had also called for populist participation and party elections.

25 An editorial on party education (which appeared the same day that Zhdanov took over all agitprop and press departments of the Central Committee) suggested that political education deprived the opposition of supporters. *Pravda,* Nov. 22, 1938.

26 Yet it would be facile to argue that Stalin decided to destroy the Trotskyist opposition and then to adopt their policies in the mid-thirties. First, the following analysis will show that the decision to liquidate Trotskyists was not taken until mid-1936, when the democracy campaign was two years old. Second, Zhdanov's reforms had other, more direct motives. Agitation and pressure from rank-and-file activists were to provide "control from below," which Stalin would defend as a means of reforming and checking on the work of party secretaries. "Control from below" complemented and reinforced control from above.

27 This decision is known only indirectly. Apparently it was never published. It is mentioned in a work on party democracy: A. Gavrilov, *Vnutripartiinaia demokratiia, 98–9.*

28 Of course, one should be skeptical of calls to allow rank-and-file members to decide "important questions." Yet the encouragement of the activists against the local secretaries would become a key theme in the future.

29 *PS,* no. 8, April 1935, 7–15.

30 *PS,* nos. 1–2, Jan. 1935, 19–29, 30–3, 48–52, 69–70. This combined issue of the journal was almost entirely devoted to this subject.

31 The Kiev plenum had been held on Feb. 22, 1935. This was one of a number of regional plenums in February that passed resolutions of this kind. One was held in Smolensk. (*Pravda,* March 5, 1936).

32 *Pravda,* March 6, 11, 28 (education); March 7, 28 (party history); March 11, 26, 29 (youth work). *Pravda,* on March 28, 29 devoted a large amount of space to these party work matters. See also *PS,* no. 5, March 1935, 39–41, for example.

33 *Pravda,* March 15, 1935.

34 "O zadachakh partiino-organizatsionnoi i politiko-vospitatel'noi raboty" (On the tasks of party-organizational and political-educational work), *PS,* no. 8, April 1935, 7–16.

35 Ibid., p. 7.

36 Ibid., p. 9. This probably referred to the hesitancy of local officials to "boldly promote" members of the new technical intelligentsia into responsible positions and to support them.

37 The histories of the various oppositional movements were singled out as appropriate topics for political education.

38 Ibid., p. 16.

39 See front-page editorials in *Pravda,* on April 3, 7, 12, 17, and important analyses and articles on April 2, 4, 6, 8, 19. Ponomarev wrote on party history in *Pravda,* April 10, 1935.

40 This is from the files of the Tumanovo Raion committee. WKP 322, p 81.

41 WKP 89, p. 3. The factory committee then noted that its own record in such things as political education and preparation of meetings was not particularly good.

42 WKP 93, pp. 1–10.

43 Ibid., pp. 11, 29–30. The lack of self-criticism by the two former leaders was especially denounced.

44 WKP 94, p. 27.

45 *Pravda*, May 6, 1935. It was also published in Stalin's *Problems of Leninism*, pp. 657–62.

46 WKP 322, p. 81. This was one of four orders received by the *raion* committee in June 1935 from the *obkom buro*. One concerned being vigilant against corruption (as shown by the recent demotion of A. Enukidze), one concerned Stalin's "Cadres Decide Everything" speech; one was on the lessons of the Leningrad Gorkom Resolution. The records of these *obkom* orders are contained in a file dealing largely with 1937 and are sandwiched between materials dealing with events of the Ezhovshchina and democracy campaign of that year.

47 *Pravda*, May 27 and 29, 1935.

48 For example, there is the KPK reprimand given to Kovalev, first secretary in Belyi Raion by the KPK Buro. Dated July 22, 1935, it was for violations of established *kolkhoz* rules connected with choosing personnel. It seems that Kovalev selected personnel purely administratively. See WKP 237, p. 178.

49 In 1966–7, Mao Zedong initiated the slogan "Bombard the Headquarters" for the Chinese Communist Party and unleashed the Red Guards against the party apparatus. He criticized the party machine for being bureaucratic and economic-minded to the exclusion of politics ("Put Politics in Command") and for repressing the "political spirit" of the masses. In the "Great Proletarian Cultural Revolution" that followed, the party and government bureaucracy was almost totally removed by action from above and below. Although this movement was not as violent as the events in the USSR in the 1930s, the parallels are very strong. In both cases, the center (for its own purposes) unleashed the rank and file against the established bureaucracy in the name of political purity, democracy, and the rights of the party rank and file.

50 The speech was published a week later in *Pravda*, July 12, 1935. A Central Committee decision based on Zhdanov's report was published in *PS*, no. 13, July, 1935, 44–5, and the speech itself appeared in *PS*, no. 13, Aug. 1935, 6–22. It was considered important enough to be published separately as A. A. Zhdanov, *Uroki politicheskikh oshibok Saratovskogo kraikoma* (Lessons of the political mistakes of the Saratov Kraikom), Partizdat TsK, VKP(b), Moscow, 1935.

51 *PS*, no. 13, Aug. 1935, 18.

52 *Pravda*, March 16, 24, May 7, 1936.

53 *Pravda*, March 17, 1936.

54 *Pravda*, March 17, 1936; *PS*, no. 7, April 1936, 5.

55 WKP 186, p. 157, is a letter from Secretary Shil'man to all *raion* party committees telling them not to automatically fire expellees, especially

skilled ones, from their jobs. It is dated Oct. 21, 1935. The Central Committee finally issued an order to this effect on Nov. 21, 1936. See *PS*, no. 23, Dec. 1936, 77.
56 *Pravda,* May 24, 1936.
57 *Pravda,* May 28, 31, 1936.
58 *History of the CPSU,* Moscow, 1973, 488.
59 *Pravda,* June 5, 1936.
60 *Pravda,* June 7, 1936. An article on "working with passives" (as opposed to expelling them) appeared in *Pravda,* June 3 and 4 – before the plenum.
61 *Pravda,* June 9, 1936.
62 *Pravda,* June 10, 1936.
63 *Pravda,* June 8, 1936.
64 *Pravda,* June 19, 1938.
65 *Pravda,* June 26, 1936.
66 See *PS*, no. 11, June 1936, 42; *PS*, no. 17, Sept. 1936, 21.
67 *Pravda,* July 10, 1936.
68 WKP 384, pp. 277–8.
69 See Robert H. McNeal, "The Decisions of the CPSU and the Great Purge," *Soviet Studies,* vol. 23, no. 2, Oct. 1971, 177–85.
70 *Pravda,* May 18, 1936.
71 *Istoriia KPSS,* 285.
72 *Pravda,* July 8, 1935, June 5, 1936. *Pravda,* Nov. 23 – Dec. 1, 1936, gives much coverage to the constitution.
73 Stalin explained this justification in his speech on the new constitution. *Pravda,* Nov. 26, Dec. 6, 1936.

5. Radicalism and enemies of the people

1 See the appendix on the Kirov assassination.
2 This letter was mentioned by Stalin in a speech on March 3, 1937 (*Pravda,* March 27, 1937), and in a number of places in the Smolensk Archive, although its text is not available. See WKP 316, p. 1, for example.
3 *Pravda,* March 29,.1937. The letter also called for increased political education as a means to prevent future terrorist acts against the party. "One must never forget that knowledge and understanding of the history of our party is an important means furthering revolutionary vigilance of party members." *Pravda,* Nov. 22, 1938.
4 For example, meetings took place at the Smolensk Institute of Marxism-Leninism (WKP 93, pp. 36–39, 41–49, 71–74), in city party and Komsomol cells (WKP 316, pp. 1–8, 16, 64–93), on collective and state farms (WKP 353, p. 6), and in *raion* committees (WKP 237, p. 48, and WKP 87, pp. 1–35).
5 Fainsod, *Smolensk,* 222–3.
6 WKP 237, pp. 12–14.
7 WKP 316, pp. 97–8. The size of the city party committee is given in WKP 384, p. 231. In the Nevel District, only six persons were expelled. WKP 237, pp. 8–9.
8 The only person expelled in Dec., G. B. Ladokha, was expelled for active

membership in a Trotskyist organization. The five expulsions the following month, also for alleged "active participation" in such cells, resulted
from the Jan. 1935 letter.

9 WKP 237, pp. 55–6. We do not know whether all those arrested were convicted and sentenced.

10 Stalin later complained that local party secretaries had minimized the Jan.
1935 letter (*Pravda*, March 27, 1937), but he had not pressed the matter in
1935. For a discussion of the official confusion after the assassination, see
the appendix.

11 See WKP 499, pp. 322–8. There is good reason to believe that Ezhov was
the author of the July letter. Several of the final paragraphs began with the
phrase "Only the absence of Bolshevik vigilance can explain the fact
that. . . ." This formulation had appeared in Ezhov's report and in the
resolution based on it at the Dec. 1935 Central Committee plenum. In the
first two such paragraphs in the July 1936 letter, the absence of Bolshevik
vigilance had allowed Trotskyist agents and formerly expelled Trotskyist
and Zinovievist enemies to penetrate the party apparatus. (Two such lax
organizations penetrated by enemies were the Gorky *kraikom* and the Vy-
borg *raikom* of the Leningrad committee, past and present Zhdanov
strongholds.)

12 *Pravda*, Sept. 26, 1936, provides the only official biographical information
on Ezhov.

13 It was rumored that Ezhov, an orphan, was raised by Aleksandr Shliapni-
kov, a radical Saint Petersburg metalworker and Bolshevik. Roy A.
Medvedev, *On Stalin and Stalinism*, Oxford, 1979, 99–100. According to
Medvedev, those who knew Ezhov found him "pleasant, considerate, and
devoid of bureaucratic arrogance."

14 *Pravda*, March 17 and 20, 1932. This account of Ezhov's 1932 position follows Bailes, *Technology*, 181–4. For other examples of Ezhov's radicalism,
see his "Kondrat'evshchina v bor'be za kadry" (The time of Kondrat'ev
in the struggle for cadres), *Sotsialisticheskaia rekonstruktsiia sel'skogo khoziaistva*
(Socialist reconstruction of the rural economy), no. 9–10, Sept.–Oct.
1930, 1–9; and "Gorod–na pomoshch' derevne" (The city to the aid of
the countryside), *Sputnik agitatora (dlia derevni)* (Agitator's companion [for
the countryside]), March 1930, 4–7. My thanks to Lynne Viola for these
references.

15 *Pravda*, May 29, Aug. 28, Oct. 16, 1935, discussed the activities of the
KPK and gave the names of many of those expelled for various crimes.
Corruption was also covered in *PS*, nos. 6 & 15, May and Aug. 1935, in
sections entitled "Activities and Decisions of the Party Collegium on
Party Delinquencies." See also *Pravda*, March 17, 1936, and *PS*, no. 7,
April 1936, 42–5, 3–49, passim.

16 *Pravda*, July 18, 1937. Although it made a formidable symbolic impression, the original purpose of the shaved head during the Civil War was
prevention of head lice. Isaak Babel', author of the *Red Cavalry* stories of
elemental class violence during the Civil War, seems to have been fascinated by Ezhov in 1937–8. Ilya Ehrenburg, *Memoirs 1921–1941*, New
York, 1963, 427.

17 Trotsky's 1929–40 correspondence comprises the "Exile Correspondence" section of the Trotsky Papers at the Houghton Library of Harvard University. Opened first in Jan. 1980, these papers carry the prefix bMS Rus 13.1, but will be designated below as Trotsky Papers II, to distinguish them from the long-available earlier sections of the Trotsky Papers. For Sedov's role, see the many documents cataloged under his name in the Trotsky Papers II, as well as Jean van Heijenoort, *With Trotsky in Exile*, London, 1978.

18 Trotsky Papers II, 4782.

19 The Dewey Commission, *The Case of Leon Trotsky*, New York, 1937, 91, 264, 273. See also *Biulleten' oppozitsii*, no. 52–3, Oct. 1936, 38–41.

20 Trotsky Papers II, 15821. The letters are dated from April 1932 to December 1932. Those to Sokolnikov and Preobrazhenskii were sent to London, that to Radek in Geneva. Other letters were sent to Kollontai and Litvinov. Copies of these letters have been removed from Trotsky's papers, but whoever removed them failed to retrieve the certified-mail receipts signed by Trotsky's secretaries.

21 *Biulleten' oppozitsii*, no. 31, Nov. 1932, 18–20. The memorandum is signed "KO," an abbreviation of "Kolokolnikov," which was the code name of longtime Trotsky loyalist Ivan N. Smirnov.

22 Trotsky Papers II, 13095.

23 Ibid. Quoted by permission of the Houghton Library.

24 Trotsky Papers II, 4782. Quoted by permission of the Houghton Library. Pierre Broue has examined some of these documents from a different angle. See his "Trotsky et le bloc des oppositions de 1932" (Trotsky and the oppositional bloc of 1932), in his *Cahiers Leon Trotsky*, no. 5, 5–37.

25 Trotsky Papers II, 8114. Quoted by permission of the Houghton Library.

26 *Case of Leon Trotsky*, 271. See also Robert H. McNeal, "Trotskyist Interpretations of Stalinism," in Robert C. Tucker, ed., *Stalinism: Essays in Historical Perspective*, New York, 1978, 30–52.

27 Van Heijenoort (*With Trotsky*, 93–102), who was one of Trotsky's secretaries, is convinced that Zborowski was a Stalinist agent. NKVD defector Alexander Orlov, in testimony before a U.S. Senate hearing, also denounced Zborowski and provided detailed information. See U.S. Senate, Subcommittee to Investigate the Administration of the Internal Security Act, *Testimony of Alexander Orlov*, Washington, D.C., 1962.

28 See Iagoda's and Bulanov's testimony at the 1938 show trial (*Report of Court Proceedings in the Case of the Anti-Soviet Bloc of Rights and Trotskyites*, Moscow, 1938, 552–83) for a discussion of Ezhov's participation from early 1936. Ezhov was probably working full time on the investigation of the opposition by March 1936, because the last edition of *Partiinoe stroitel'stvo* with his name on the masthead is no. 5, March 10, 1936. By the March 25 issue, Malenkov had replaced him as editor. Ezhov's new interest in the opposition came at precisely the time that his *proverka* and *obmen* were coming under fire (see Chapter 4).

29 Iagoda's sympathy for defeated oppositionists was documented by Serdiuk to the Twenty-Second Congress in 1961: *Pravda*, Oct. 31, 1961. Iagoda's investigators sometimes helped their victims by carefully

circumscribing and limiting their confessions. See Tokaev, *Betrayal,* 249; and the Bukharin trial transcript (*Report of Court Proceedings*), 553.

30 WKP 499, pp. 322–8.

31 Gabor Rittersporn sees conflict between those Moscow leaders who preferred a hunt for enemies in the party apparatus and the instigators of the August trial who tried to limit condemnation to former oppositionists. See his *Phenomenes et realites Staliniens – Tensions sociales et conflits politiques en URSS, 1933–1953* (Stalinist phenomena and realities – social tensions and political conflicts in the USSR, 1933–1953), Paris (forthcoming), 1985, ch. 2. In his view, Stalin favored a hunt for enemies within the apparatus from the beginning but was outvoted by others.

32 See *Report of Court Proceedings: The Case of the Trotskyite–Zinovievite Terrorist Centre,* Moscow, 1936, 68, for Kamenev's mention of Bukharin. Vyshinskii, the prosecutor, announced that he was beginning an investigation into the activities of Piatakov, Bukharin, Rykov, Tomskii, and others. Ibid., 115. *Pravda,* Sept. 10, contains the procurator's announcement that the investigation of the rightists was being dropped. That the incrimination of Bukharin and company may have been Ezhov's doing is supported by the fact that it was he who delivered the report against Bukharin at the February plenum in 1937. See also note 55 below.

33 See front-page editorials in *Pravda,* Aug. 7 ("Umet' raspoznavat' vraga" [How to recognize the enemy]) and Aug. 9 ("Bol'shevistskaia bditel'nost' na liubom uchastke" [Bolshevik vigilance in every place]), 1936.

34 *Ibid.* See also *Pravda,* Aug. 26, 1936, "Prislushivat'sia k golosu mass, k ikh signalam" (To listen to the voice of the masses, to their signals). These articles denounced "rotten liberalism" toward the opposition.

35 WKP 99, pp 106–8; WKP 106, pp. 33–4; WKP 319, pp. 40–2; WKP 239, pp. 195–214.

36 *Pravda* editorial of Aug. 24, 1936; File RS 924, Protocol of Meeting of Obkom Buro of Aug. 25, 1936.

37 Khrushchev claimed that Stalin and Zhdanov (who were apparently on holiday together) sent a telegram to the Politburo proposing the removal of Iagoda for being "four years behind" in the unmasking of enemies. (Khrushchev, *Secret Speech,* 35–6.) It is often thought that "four years behind" referred to the Riutin Platform of 1932. (Conquest, *Terror,* 218, for example). Yet the targets of the recent Zinoviev trial and of Stalin's telegram were Trotskyists, not the rightist authors of the Riutin document. From the vantage point of fall, 1936, the important event of four years before was the 1932 bloc, not the Riutin Platform. It had been exactly four years since the formation of the Trotsky–Zinoviev bloc. Although Khrushchev's version cannot be accepted without question, the particular signatures of Stalin (de facto first secretary) and Zhdanov (a critic of Ezhov's *uchet* operations) would lend authority to the proposal. The appointment while Stalin and Zhdanov were on holiday suggests the ad hoc or reactive nature of the decision.

38 Both main NKVD defector accounts agree that Ezhov brought with him 200–300 of "his people" from the party Secretariat to the NKVD. See Walter Krivitsky, *In Stalin's Secret Service,* 146; Orlov, *Secret History,* 213–14.

This may be something that they can report first hand. There is oblique confirmation in a reference to Ezhov's "rebuilding" the staff of the NKVD. *20 let VchK-OGPU-NKVD* (Twenty Years of the VchK-OGPU-NKVD), Moscow, 1938, and in *Pravda*, Dec. 20, 1937.

39 Conquest, *Terror*, ch. 4, for example.

40 The next two show trials in Nov. 1936 (Novosibirsk) and Jan. 1937 (Moscow) accused Trotskyists. Bukharin and the rightists were not denounced until after the beginning of 1937. Additionally, Procurator Vyshinskii's press statement of Sept. 10 exonerated the leading rightists, but not Trotskyists like Piatakov who had been mentioned at the same time.

41 The "Letter of an Old Bolshevik" suggests that Stalin did not choose "hard" over "soft" policies toward the opposition until sometime after the June 1936 death of Maksim Gorky, who supposedly had influenced Stalin toward a "soft" attitude: "It is certain that Gorky's death finally untied the hands of those in Stalin's immediate entourage [Ezhov and Kaganovich] who demanded haste" in the persecution of the opposition. "Letter," 60–2.

42 Bailes (Technology, chs. 6, 7, 9) describes Ordzhonikidze as an economic moderate in opposition to Stalin. This view minimizes the importance of Stalin's moderate statements, such as those at the January 1933 Central Committee plenum and at the Seventeenth Party Congress in 1934.

43 Ordzhonikidze and Stalin had been friends since pre–World War I days in the Caucasus.

44 See G. K. Ordzhonikidze, *O zadachakh tiazheloi promyshlennosti i Stakhanovskom dvizhenii* (On the tasks of heavy industry and the Stakhanovite movement), Moscow, 1936, and *Stat'i i Rechi* (Articles and speeches), Moscow, 1957.

45 See I. Dubinskii-Mukhadze, *Ordzhonikidze*, Moscow, 1967, 6–7. Ordzhonikidze protected Victor Kravchenko on several occasions. See his *I Chose Freedom*, New York, 1946, 195–7, 237.

46 *Pravda*, Feb. 5, 1936.

47 "V Ts.K., VKP(b)," *Pravda*, Sept. 1, 1936.

48 See Zaleski, *Stalinist Planning*, ch. 8.

49 See the "Khronika" section of *Pravda*: June 17, June 24 (Forests), July 15 (State Bank), Aug. 9 (Forests), Sept. 3 (Agriculture), Sept. 30 (Communications), Oct. 2 (Forests), Oct. 20 (RSFSR commissariats). For the characterization of Molotov, see speeches in *Pravda* by Kirilenko (Oct. 26, 1961), Shvernik (ibid.), and Satiukov (Oct. 27, 1961). At about the same time, L. M. Kaganovich advocated the theory of "counterrevolutionary limit-setting on output" in order to destroy moderates in transport. See Beshchev's speech in *Pravda*, Oct. 28, 1961.

50 Molotov's speech to the February 1937 plenum of the Central Committee: *Bol'shevik*, no. 8, April 15, 1937, 29–31.

51 See Davies, *Mission to Moscow*, 182–3; and Bailes, *Technology*, 302–3. For opposition of local managers to the Stakhanov movement in the Donbas, see *Pravda*, May 1, 11, 15, 1937.

52 "Speech to the First All-Union Conference of Stakhanovites," given on Nov. 17, 1935. *Pravda*, Nov. 18, 1935.

53 Piatakov last appeared in public on June 25 (*Pravda*, June 26, 1936). He signed a note to *Pravda* on Aug. 21, 1936, condemning Zinoviev. The date of his arrest is unknown.

54 Conquest, *Terror*, 221. Officially, Molotov made an oblique reference to Ordzhonikidze's attempts to save Piatakov. See his speech in *Pravda*, Feb. 21, 1937.

55 Apparently, one of the defendants at the August Zinoviev trial had denounced Piatakov, because Vyshinskii's statement to the court mentioned that he was beginning an investigation of him. (*Report of Court Proceedings . . . Trotskyite–Zinovievite Terrorist Centre*, 115). Yet nowhere in the published testimony is Piatakov mentioned. That this important testimony was censored from the published edition shows that Piatakov's fate was still undecided.

56 *Pravda*, Oct. 28, 1936.

57 *Pravda*, Nov. 23, 1936.

58 *Pravda*, Nov. 20–6, 1936.

59 *Pravda*, Nov. 26, 1936.

60 *Report of Court Proceedings in the Case of the Anti-Soviet Trotskyite Centre*, Moscow, 1937. John Littlepage, who accompanied Piatakov on his purchasing trips to Berlin, believes that Piatakov may indeed have been guilty of funneling Soviet government funds to the opposition through Sedov. See his *In Search of Soviet Gold*, New York, 1938, ch. 9.

61 Khrushchev spoke on Ordzhonikidze's suicide in his report to the Twenty-second Congress (*Pravda*, Oct. 29, 1961); see also Zinadia Ordzhonikidze, *Put' bol'shevika* (Path of a Bolshevik), Moscow, 1938; Medvedev, *History*, 194–7; Dubinskii-Mukhadze, *Ordzhonikidze*, 6–7; I. Paramonov, *Puti proidennye* (Paths traveled), Moscow, 1966, 207–8; Bailes (*Technology*, 282–8) believes that most of Ordzhonikidze's associates were arrested after his death. Granick (*Management*, 51) believes that the first plant managers (and all department heads in Heavy Industry) were arrested in the period following the February plenum. Because Ordzhonikidze's death and the plenum were only days apart, it is impossible to choose one over the other.

62 Actually, the breakup of Ordzhonikidze's empire began shortly before his death. The Commissariat of Defense Production was formed from Heavy Industry personnel in December 1936 (*Pravda*, Dec. 9, 1936). Three days later, Heavy Industry's Gold Trust was shaken up (*Pravda*, Dec. 12, 1936). In Aug. 1937, much of the central Heavy Industry bureaucracy (including Heavy Industry Commissar Mezhlauk) was detached to form the Commissariat of Machine Building (*Pravda*, Aug. 23, 1937). Altogether, the Commissariat of Heavy Industry was broken up into about a dozen smaller entities after Ordzhonikidze's death. See Bailes, *Technology*, 288.

63 *Pravda*, Feb. 21, 1937.

64 Ezhov seems to have given a speech with the same title at the same meeting. See Khrushchev, *Secret Speech*, 36.

65 Jerry Hough has noted that "Stalin . . . attempted to institutionalize a varied flow of information by organizing his subordinates into competing party and administrative hierarchies" and that "a large part of Stalin's motivation seems to have been a desire not to orchestrate policy in accord-

ance with some personal vision, but to avoid the need to make major policy choices at all." Hough and Fainsod, *How the Soviet Union Is Governed,* 167, 183.

66 Ordzhonikidze was never denounced or criticized. His anniversaries continued to be observed, and he remained in good odor throughout Stalin's lifetime.

67 See front-page articles in *Pravda,* Feb. 6, Feb. 8 ("Bol'shevistskaia samokritika..." [Bolshevik self-criticism...]), Feb. 14 ("O zaznaistve..." [On conceit...]), 1937.

68 See *Pravda,* Nov. 21 ("Zasedatel'skaia suetnia" [Speechifying]), 1936. Also note the account of the meeting of the Rostov *gorkom* reported on Dec. 11, 1936 ("Na plenume Rostovskogo gorkoma" [At the plenum of the Rostov Gorkom]).

69 For the various final confirmations of the exchange of party documents in various regions, see *PS,* nos. 23–4, Dec. 1936, 73–9, and no. 1, Jan. 1937, 53–7. Although some of the confirmations were less than enthusiastic, the Secretariat did finally admit the generally satisfactory completion of the operation.

6. The crisis matures: 1937

1 *Pravda,* March 6, 1937.

2 McNeal, *Resolutions and Decisions,* 181.

3 *Pravda,* March 6, 1937.

4 *Pravda,* March 29, April 1, 1937: both on second page. The rambling nature of his speeches (particularly the concluding one), the delay in publication, and the lack of any mention in the plenum's press release that Stalin had even addressed the meeting suggest that his remarks were not originally intended for publication. They therefore take on greater political and interpretive significance than his more olympian public pronouncements.

5 Khrushchev, *Secret Speech,* 36. Note the similarity to the title of Molotov's speech to the same meeting discussed in the previous chapter. Khrushchev may have confused the titles of speeches by political allies Ezhov and Molotov. *Izvestiia,* March 17, 1937, reported that Bukharin and Rykov attended the plenum and defended themselves against the charges. See also Roy A. Medvedev, *Nikolai Bukharin: The Last Years,* New York, 1980, ch. 10. Bukharin was probably arrested on or about Jan. 16, 1937 – the last day his name appeared on the masthead of *Izvestiia.* This is also about the time that Radek finally agreed to implicate Bukharin and the rightists in his pretrial interrogation.

6 *Pravda,* March 29, 1937.

7 Ibid. Stalin avoided any direct reference to Bukharin and the rightists. Medvedev (*History,* 174) takes note of Stalin's neutrality at the meeting, saying that Molotov and Kaganovich took the lead in the attack on the rightists.

8 *Pravda,* March 29, 1937.

9 He noted later that embittered rank-and-file members who had been ex-

pelled by "heartless bureaucrats" could be used as "reserves" by enemies.

10 Adam Ulam believes that when Stalin asked the secretaries to train officials to take their place, he was serving notice that he intended to replace
(destroy) them. Of course, the context of Stalin's remarks clearly shows
that Stalin was talking about temporary replacements and cadres for
newly formed party committees. Ulam, *Stalin,* 430–1.

11 "The preparation of party organizations for elections to the USSR supreme soviet under the new electoral system and the corresponding reorganization of party political work," *Pravda,* March 6, 1937.

12 Gavrilov, *Vnutripartiinaia demokratiia,* 7–46.

13 *Pravda,* March 6, 1937.

14 Ibid.

15 *Pravda,* April 1, 1937. This was published four days after the first speech.

16 See Jonathan Harris, "The Origins of the Conflict Between Malenkov
and Zhdanov, 1939–1941," *Slavic Review,* vol. 35, no. 2, June 1976, 287–
303. Harris's important work describes a 1940s-era Zhdanov with distinc-
tive ideas about the role of the party. Harris's Zhdanov believed that the
party should retire from direct control of the economy and trust such administration to a new, loyal, Soviet apparatus. The party should concentrate on political education and the ideological preparation of "politically
steeled" cadres. Zhdanov favored an organization of the Central Committee Secretariat to facilitate education and propaganda rather than industrial administration. Such views brought Zhdanov into conflict with
Malenkov. The present research suggests that Zhdanov may have earlier
clashed with Malenkov's predecessor in ORPO, Ezhov.

17 *Pravda,* March 1, 1937.

18 *Pravda,* May 30, 1937 ("13th Congress of the KPU(b)"), elaborated on
the celebrated Nikolaenko affair. Comrade Nikolaenko, a "little person,"
had complained about first secretary P. P. Postyshev's regime in the
Ukrainian Communist Party. "Everything began and ended with Postyshev....There was too much applause," Nikolaenko said. She complained to Politburo member S. V. Kosior, who forwarded the matter back
to Postyshev. Postyshev quickly branded Nikolaenko a "counterrevolutionary" and expelled her from the party. Stalin intervened and restored
Nikolaenko's party membership. The story was a morality play for 1937,
complete with persecuted little person, evil party secretary, and benevo-
lent leader. As political theater, it dramatized the relationships of the time.
Postyshev's so-called opposition at the plenum (Khrushchev, *Secret Speech,*
38) was self-defense against the Nikolaenko charges as well as an attempt
to intercede for and save "his people."

19 These final remarks were in direct line with the Central Committee letter
of June 1936 on the expulsion of too many passives and the slow consideration of appeals. The Central Committee (and Stalin) would make the
same charges again at the Jan. 1938 Central Committee plenum. He was
clearly not referring to the Ezhovshchina – one could hardly stop an operation that had not yet begun. He was talking, as usual, about the formal-
bureaucratic conduct of local party officials.

20 Quoted in *Pravda*, April 21, 1937.
21 Quoted in *Pravda*, Jan. 19, 1938.
22 One might speculate that if, in March of 1937, Stalin had planned to annihilate the regional party secretaries, it is unlikely that he would have exposed himself by conducting the Feb. plenum as he did. First, it would have been pointless and needlessly dangerous to call a meeting of the powerful targets of a planned coup in order to debate a threatening extension of police powers. Stalin did not need their permission (or to tip his hand) if he planned to destroy them. Indeed he would not have needed a Feb. plenum at all. Second, Stalin's educational and organizational reform proposals were parts of a real sequence of attempts to reform, tame, and control the provincial apparatus short of destroying it.
23 See *Pravda*, Jan. 4, 21, and 24, Feb. 9, and 10, on vigilance; and Jan. 4 and 7, Feb. 4, 6, 13 (editorial), 23, 25, and 27, on democracy and party work. Most of the articles in *PS* at this time were on democracy and political education. See articles by A. Stetskii and N. Krupskaia (Lenin's widow) in nos. 1 (pp. 10–23) and 2 (pp. 22–5), Jan. 1937. Krupskaia's article is entitled "Lenin and Stalin on the struggle with bureaucratism." *PS*, no. 2, Feb. 1937, 22–5, carried articles on the Piatakov trial and vigilance alongside pieces on the new constitution and the selection of cadres.
24 *Pravda*, March 10, 17, 1937.
25 Of course, some of the statements at the local meetings were simply routine repetitions of the themes of the plenum. Similarly, some party committees seemed oblivious to and untouched by the incendiary events of the February plenum. See, for example, the protocols of the cell at the Medgorodok construction project in WKP 109, pp. 52–3.
26 The meeting is summarized in WKP 110, pp. 221–4, 387–409.
27 Ibid., 375–6, 381.
28 Ibid., 222.
29 WKP 103, pp. 59–60. The report covered the previous two years of the organization's work. The party committee had been in office that long without reporting to its membership.
30 Ibid., 78–83.
31 Ibid., 83.
32 WKP 111, pp. 2–66.
33 Ibid., passim.
34 Ibid., p. 22.
35 Ibid., p. 38, for example.
36 WKP 321, p. 96. NKVD chief Vinogradov was described as Kovalev's right-hand man and was expelled from the party shortly after Kovalev. See WKP 111, pp. 27, 91–4, 96, 110. The regional party committee was unhappy with Vinogradov's expulsion and tried to reinstate him, but the rank-and-file membership of his party organization made the expulsion stick. See WKP 111, pp. 99–101, 110.
37 WKP 321, pp. 87–8; WKP 111, pp. 2–6.
38 WKP 111, pp. 58–61.
39 WKP 111, pp. 2–6, 7.
40 Fainsod, *Smolensk,* 132–3.

41 A. S. Shil'man, "Training Cadres on the Basis of their Mistakes," *PS*, no. 8, April 20, 1937, 38–43.

42 See *Pravda*, March 6, 1937 (editorial), 11, 17, 19 for examples.

43 *Pravda*, March 21, 1937. The order was also published in *PS*, no. 6, March 20, 1937, 3–30, along with three editorials and several explanatory articles.

44 See *PS*, no. 7, April 1937, for articles by Zh. Meerson (pp. 29–33) and D. Protopopov (pp. 39–43) among others. *Pravda*, March 30, 31, April 4, 5, 10, 13, 14, 18. The article on April 14 on "Inner-party democracy and Bolshevik discipline" was written by the party's future ideologist, B. Ponomarev.

45 *Pravda*, March 29, April 1, 1937.

46 *Pravda*, April 2 ("Besprimernyi zazhim samokritiki [Unparalleled suppression of self-criticism]); April 5 ("Kak v Stalingrade dopolnili pis'mo Ts.K." [How in Stalingrad they supplemented the letter of TsK]); April 7 ("Ne rukovodiat vyborami" [They are not leading by means of elections]); April 9 ("O tainom golosovanii i teknike vyborov" [On the secret ballot and the technique of elections], and "Narushili printsip tainogo golosovaniia" [They violated the principle of the secret ballot]).

47 E. M. Iaroslavskii, "Ob otvetstvennosti rukovoditelei pered massami" (On the answerability of leaders before the masses), *Bolshevik*, no. 7, April 1937, 31–45.

48 Ibid., p. 41.

49 Although it is possible that the 1937 elections were simply a cynical attempt to soften up the *obkom* secretaries prior to liquidating them, it is hard to see why Stalin would need such a campaign. The elections would seem superfluous to a simple murder plot, but if the plan was to revolutionize power relationships throughout the apparatus, they would serve a useful purpose.

50 There was quite a campaign in the press before these elections. Party leaders were ordered to take responsibility for the organization of the elections, the free nomination of candidates, and the careful observance of procedural rules. The party slogan was "Elections do not run themselves." See *Pravda*, April 5, 10, 13, and especially 18, 1937. Joseph Davies, the U.S. Ambassador to Moscow, was struck by the electoral campaign. See his *Mission to Moscow*, 196.

51 WKP 110, pp. 245–6. The meeting lasted three days. See also the summary of complaints on pp. 261–2. There were similar proceedings of the party cell in the Tumanovo Raion NKVD in WKP 322, pp. 52–7 (the list of grievances is on pp. 55–6), and in the Roslavl' Raikom, WKP 105, passim. Complaints were also published in the press. WKP 203 is one of several files in the Smolensk Archive consisting of letters to the editor complaining about local conditions. See Fainsod, *Smolensk*, ch. 20, for his digest of such letters.

52 WKP 110, p. 252.

53 Apparently, Friedlander still commanded enough support to be included on the committee and to be reelected in the elections.

54 WKP 110, p. 261–2.

55 Cited in Gavrilov, *Vnutripartiinaia demokratiia,* 108.

56 WKP 110, pp. 258–9, 262–79.

57 Other examples of electoral meetings are in WKP 322, pp. 52–7, and WKP 105, passim. In the latter file, the tallies and the secret ballots themselves were retained for the Archive. The file contains records of other elections in 1937–8 in the party cell.

58 WKP 110, pp. 258–9, 262–79.

59 Fainsod believed that the elections were phonies and that appointments were still invariably made from above. See *How Russia Is Ruled,* 160. Yet party organizations that as recently as 1935 had elected their leadership through prepared lists now were forced to go through careful procedures with secret ballots, in which members of the old committees often were not reelected. Compare the two elections (1935 and 1937) in the party cell of the Tumanovo Raion NKVD: WKP 106, p. 1, *vs.* WKP 322, pp. 57–8.

60 See the election results published in *PS,* no. 10, May 15, 1937, 22; *Pravda,* May 23, 1937; and *PS,* no. 11, June 1, 1937, 12–24, passim.

61 See the account in *Partiinyi organizator* (Party organizer), the journal of the Leningrad Oblast' and city committees, no. 9, May 1937, 50–1. (hereafter *PO*) At the famous Hammer and Sickle Plant in Moscow, a two-hour mass meeting was held, during which thirty-three persons spoke out against the plant director. He was accused of rudeness, putting on airs, and separating himself from the rank and file. As a result, he was removed from his position in the election. (*Za industrializatsiiu* [For industrialization], April 20, 1937, cited in Granick, *Management,* 214–5.)

62 *PO,* no. 9, May 1937, 51.

63 Ibid., no. 10, May 1937, 13–14.

64 In addition to "The party committee ignores party meetings!" there was "On trade union democracy" and "The *raikom* report – a serious political document" in *PO,* no. 4, Feb. 19–24, 28–34. *PO,* no. 9, May 1937, 59–62, contained "Verifying the work of the *raikom* from below," and no. 12, June 1937, 40–46, had "The collective method of leadership and work with party cadres."

65 These were major topics in *Pravda* during this period. See March 6, 11, 17, and major editorials on March 19, 21, 25, and on April 5, 10, 11, 13, 18. An article on April 6 amplified Stalin's warning at the Feb. plenum not to use expulsion so freely against party members – it was only to be a last resort. The antibureaucracy campaign continued into May with articles on May 14 and 15 and a major editorial on trade-union democracy on May 20, 1937.

66 *Pravda,* March 25, 1937. Paparde was officially attached to the Western Obkom Buro as KPK representative. When the leadership of the Western Oblast' fell later in the summer, he became acting obkom first secretary, temporarily replacing Rumiantsev.

67 See Kataev, *Time, Forward!,* passim., and especially Scott, *Behind the Urals,* chs. 6, 9, 11, for examples of this simmering hostility. For examples of letters of complains see WKP 195, WKP 197, WKP 203, WKP 355, and WKP 362.

68 Stalinist and Khrushchev-era party histories note the Feb. plenum for the

establishment of party democracy and the correction of bureaucratic abuses. See Gavrilov, *Vnutripartiinaia demokratiia,* 103–6; and D. Bakhshiev, *Tsentralizm i demokratizm bol'shevistskoi partii* (Centralism and democratism of the Bolshevik Party), Moscow, 1948, 23–4. For the Khrushchev view, see *History of the CPSU,* Moscow, 1960, 511; and especially Pavlov, *Kommunisticheskaia partiia v borbe,* 95–7.

69 *XVIII s"ezd,* 28, 147–9. Between 1935 and 1939, Moscow created 4 new union republics, 40 new regional (*oblast'*) and territorial (*krai*) organizations, and 1,256 district (*raion*) administrations. If the size of the apparatus in the Western Oblast' is any guide, the reorganization required something like 200,000 additional party positions. The Western Obkom included in its *nomenklatura* about 3,100 leading positions in various departments, and the *oblast'* government structure listed about 1,000. So, if the average *oblast'* required around 4,100 positions, an increase of 40 would require about 164,000 new positions. If, as Fainsod suggests, the average *raion* party committee employed about 20 full-time party workers (+ 10 for the *raispolkom*), the increase in *raions* would require about 26,500 cadres for party work. (See Fainsod, *Smolensk,* 62–6, 112.) If the average *gorkom* was about the size of a *raikom* (as was the case in Smolensk), another 4,000 were required, bringing the total number of new positions in *oblast',* *krai,* and *raion* party and government organizations to about 195,000. To this figure must be added required staffs for the new additional republics and peoples' commissariats, the sizes of which are unknown but considerable. Of course, these are rough calculations, and their validity is subject to such considerations as the uniformity of *obkom* and *raikom* size. Indeed, the estimates may be on the small side because the Western Oblast' was a rural region with weaker (and smaller) party organizations than more urbanized areas.

70 First secretaries seem to have been removed at the party conferences in the Far East Territory, Voronezh, Iaroslavl', and the Northern Territory. *Pravda,* June 4, 10, 14, 15, 1937.

71 *Pravda,* June 19, 1937.

72 See the running coverage of events in Armenia in *Pravda,* May 7, 17, 27, 28, and June 6, 1937.

73 *Pravda,* June 5, 1937.

74 Those regional committees with "correct" political lines and "satisfactory" work were Moscow, Leningrad, Saratov, Orenburg, and Uzbekistan. Those with "unsatisfactory" work were Armenia, Far East, Iaroslavl', and Piatigorsk. Those committing "serious mistakes" were Ukraine, Kalinin, Voronezh, Cheliabinsk, Kirghiz, Kuibyshev, Stalinabad, Engel's, and Western.

75 WKP 238, pp. 155–60 is the published resolution of the Oblast' Conference. Each of these claims would be attacked and denied after Rumiantsev's fall. Since 1937 was the first year the plan fell short, Rumiantsev's claims may well be exaggerated.

76 A list of grievances and demands is in ibid., pp. 157–60.

77 The resolution suggests that Rumiantsev and his staff were reelected by

the delegates to the conference, although there are no specifics on the voting.

78 As was Kovalev in Belyi. See WKP 111, pp. 2–66, and Shil'man's account in *PS*, no. 8, April 20, 1937, 38–43. See also Fainsod, *Smolensk*, 132-4.

79 WKP 238, pp. 87–8.

80 *Pravda*, June 11, 1937. Their execution was announced the following day and in *Izvestiia*, June 14, 1937. Gamarnik committed suicide before he could be arrested; *Pravda*, June 1, 1937.

81 Some Khrushchev-era sources place the arrest of the generals between May 26 and 31, 1937. See P. I. Iakir and Ia. A. Geller, *Komandarm Iakir* (Army Commander Iakir), Moscow, 1963, 227, and P. N. Aleksandrov et al., *Komandarm Uborevich* (Army Commander Uborevich), Moscow, 1964, 230.

82 Conquest writes that this was "more than likely." *Terror*, 283. For a discussion of the long-term conflicts between party and military, see Roman Kolkowicz, *The Soviet Military and the Communist Party*, Princeton, N.J., 1967.

83 See Conquest, *Terror*, 294–6, for these events.

84 For the theory that the Nazis framed Tukhachevskii, see Lev Nikulin, *Marshal Tukhachevskii*, Moscow, 1964, 189–94; John Erickson, *The Soviet High Command*, London, 1962, 433; Walter Schellenberg, *The Schellenberg Memoirs*, London, 1956; and Khrushchev's speech to the Twenty-second Congress, *Pravda*, Oct. 29, 1961. The documents were supposedly passed to Stalin via Eduard Benes in Czechoslovakia (Eduard Benes, *Memoirs of Dr. Eduard Benes*, London, 1954, 14–20, and n. 8, p. 47). According to other accounts, *Stalin* ordered the preparation of incriminating documents and had them passed to the Germans, then the Czechs, then the NKVD, then to him. See *Le nouvel observateur*, no. 109, Dec. 14–20, 1966, 17. One wonders why such a roundabout procedure would have been necessary if Stalin planned to destroy the military men. Krivitsky (*I Was Stalin's Agent*) believes that there really was a military plot to carry out a coup, and Deutscher (*Stalin*, 73) believes that this was not unlikely. An anonymous but apparently well-informed contemporary writer in *Foreign Affairs* suspects the same thing: "Balticus," "The Russian Mystery–Behind the Tukhachevsky Plot," *Foreign Affairs*, vol. 16, no. 1, Oct. 1937, 44–63. A. V. Likhachev, editor of the émigré journal *Posev*, was an officer in the Far Eastern Red Army in 1937–8. Writing under the pseudonym A. Svetlanin, he argued that there was in fact a far-flung military conspiracy to overthrow the Stalinist circle. See his *Dal'nevostochnyi zagovor* (Far-Eastern conspiracy), Frankfurt, 1953.

85 WKP 110, p. 228. The uncovering of the military "conspiracy" was specifically attributed to Ezhov – not to the party, the Central Committee, Stalin, or anyone else. This was a rather unusual specificity. The resolution ordered party members to "rally around" Stalin in the present crisis.

86 WKP 440, pp. 156–60.

87 Legally, the Central Committee had to give its sanction for the arrest of

party members, especially that of any Central Committee members.

88 The militia cell meeting is in WKP 324, pp. 69–70. Rumiantsev and Uborevich were also linked together in the Shamilovo account, WKP 440, p. 156, and in the meeting of the Peoples' Court (Obsud), WKP 103, p. 139.

89 WKP 103, p. 126.

90 The fullest account of Kaganovich's remarks is in WKP 440, pp. 156–7.

91 Ibid. The doubt about Rakitov stems from the fact that he was transferred elsewhere shortly before the fall of his former associates. Questions were raised about him in WKP 103, p. 143–4. At this particular meeting, speakers asked such questions as "Were Rumiantsev and co. part of the Piatakov group?," "When and where will they be tried?" Unfortunately, the answers given were not recorded in the minutes.

92 This according to Comrade Lepin in the Peoples' Court; ibid., p. 126.

93 Ibid., p. 131. Kovalev was also denounced in the Shamilovo meetings, WKP 440, p. 157. Shamilovo was in Kovalev's former *raion*, Belyi.

94 WKP 440, p. 156.

95 WKP 103, p. 136.

96 WKP 238: Rumiantsev was listed on June 14 and Paparde by June 26, 1937.

97 Korotchenkov was also known as Korotchenko, especially when he held posts in the Ukraine. Later, he would be a Khrushchev associate. Previous to his tenure, Korotchenkov (like many other new *oblast'* secretaries) had been a minor party secretary in the Moscow party committee, which may have functioned as a kind of training ground for party officials. Many up-and-coming party secretaries in the early Stalin era served time in the Moscow committee, and replacements for fallen *obkom* secretaries sometimes were drawn from this pool. Thus, V. Ia. Simochkin, first secretary of the Krasnopresnensk District in Moscow, was sent to take over the Ivanov party organization in August 1937 following the fall of I. P. Nosov. (S. S. Deev et al., *Ocherki istorii Ivanovskoi organizatsii KPSS, Chast' vtoraia: 1917–1967* (Essays on the history of the Ivanov organization of the KPSS, second part: 1917–67), Iaroslavl', 1967, 296–7.

7. Epilogue: the Ezhovshchina

1 See speeches to the Twenty-second Party Congress by Beshchev (*Pravda*, Oct. 28, 1961), Shvernik (ibid., Oct. 26, 1961), and Serdiuk (ibid., Oct. 31, 1961). For the Molotov–Litvinov struggle, see Paul Raymond, "Conflict and Consensus in Soviet Foreign Policy, 1933–1939," Ph.D. dissertation, Pennsylvania State University, 1979. For a firsthand account of Molotov's decimation of the Commissariat of Foreign Affairs, see Evgenii Gnedin, *Katastrofa i vtoroe rozhdenie* (Catastrophe and rebirth), Amsterdam, 1977, chs. 1–3, 103–27.

2 John Littlepage reports that Serebrovskii, head of the Gold Trust, was able to have recalcitrant officials arrested (*In Search of Soviet Gold*, 94–8). Serebrovskii himself was soon arrested.

3 Ginzburg, *Whirlwind*, 75. See also F. Beck and W. Godin, *Russian Purge and the Extraction of Confession*, London, 1951, 192–200, for the theory that the excessive arrests of the Ezhovshchina were deliberately prophylactic.

4 See Davies, *Mission to Moscow*, 167–204. A cursory examination of the biographies of a few hundred party officials suggests tremendous turnover in the second half of 1937, followed by a lesser wave in mid to late 1938. These two waves may represent the rise and fall of radical officials.

5 *Biulleten' oppozitsii*, no. 70, 1938, 11. Some provincial secretaries (Beria, Khrushchev, Zhdanov) survived. However, their careers and sentiments in the 1930s were distinctly center- and Moscow-oriented.

6 These emissary activities were described by speakers at the Twenty-second Party Congress in 1961. The relevant speeches were by K. T. Mazurov (*Pravda*, Oct. 20, 1961), N. M. Shvernik (*Pravda*, Oct. 26, 1961), Satiukov and Shelepin (*Pravda*, Oct. 27, 1961), and Serdiuk and Dzhavakhishvili (*Pravda*, Oct. 1, 1961). Everywhere, the pattern resembled the Smolensk case.

7 Khrushchev, *Secret Speech*, 44, and the 1961 speeches by Mazurov, Shvernik, Satiukov, and Serdiuk cited in n. 6.

8 See J. Arch Getty and William Chase, "The Moscow Party Elite of 1917 in the Great Purges," *Russian History/Histoire Russe*, vol. 5, no. 1, 1978, 106–115. Victor Kravchenko was forced to produce purchase orders to prove to the NKVD that his material orders were not excessive and therefore criminal (*I Chose Freedom*, 215–37). See also John Scott, *Behind the Urals*, Bloomington, Ind., 1973.

9 Such as those in WKP 316 (unpaginated lists). The lists include the name, the charge(s), where and when they were made, and a reference to the relevant folio containing the documentation. Unfortunately, they do not give the final disposition of the cases.

10 WKP 103, pp. 126–209, contains most of the 1937 run for the Obsud. Page 56 provides the list of Buro members elected in Feb. 1937.

11 This tally was made available to me by Roberta T. Manning, based on her analysis of WKP 111 and WKP 321. The conclusions (and any errors) drawn from this information are mine.

12 See Barbara Katz, "A Quantitative Evaluation of the Economic Impact of the Great Purges on the Soviet Union," Ph.D. dissertation, University of Pennsylvania, 1974, 47–8, 59. Also see Raymond Bauer, "Arrest in the Soviet Union," Research Memo 30, Air Research and Development Command, Maxwell Air Force Base, Alabama, 1954, 1, 13–15.

13 All whose occupations were primarily connected with economics (domestic and foreign trade, economic planning, heavy industry, factory management, trade-union leadership) were arrested, whereas those in other occupations often survived (lawyers, doctors, scientists, etc.). Statistically, it seems that high position and economic occupation had more to do with one's fate than simple Old Bolshevik status. See Getty and Chase, "Moscow Party Elite," 113–14.

14 *XVII s"ezd*, 303.

15 *XVIII s"ezd*, 148.

16 Of course, expulsion from the party is a good barometer of the incidence

of the Ezhovshchina in the party, but it is less satisfactory as an indicator of its effects on society in general. Some persons who were not party members were arrested, as were some persons who had left the party previously. To fix the number of Ezhovshchina arrests, Conquest and others calculated an estimate for party arrests and then used various hypothetical "multipliers" (7:1 or 8:1) to arrive at a figure for the population as a whole. Yet nearly all authorities agree that most of the victims of the Ezhovshchina were officials or leaders in the party and government. Although Conquest used these multiplier ratios, he noted that ordinary citizens suffered much less than did party officials. Medvedev said that "numerically, the chief victims were hundreds of thousands of Party members" but on the same page asserted that "a still greater number of victims was claimed among non-Party people." Brzezinski believed that the "major effort of the purge was directed at the Communist Party," and Khrushchev in his 1956 and 1961 remarks gave the clear impression that the Ezhovshchina was mostly a matter of prominent leaders of the party and state. Lacking evidence, all estimates are equally worthless, and it is hard to disagree with Brzezinski's observation that it is impossible to make any estimates without erring in the hundreds of thousands or even millions. Brzezinski, *Permanent Purge*, 82, 91, 98-9; Conquest, *Terror*, 452, 699-713; Hough and Fainsod, *How the Soviet Union Is Governed*, 174-7; Kennan, *Soviet Foreign Policy, 1917-1941*, 89; Medvedev, *History*, 234, 239; Rigby, *Membership*, 212-13.

17 Rigby (*Membership*, 210-12) calculates that the total number of members expelled in 1937 "must have been under 100,000," or less than the *proverka* of 1935. Of course, more of those expelled in 1937 were liable to arrest than had been the case in 1935.

18 In addition, 11 members were expelled by lower bodies but reinstated by the *raikom*.

19 *XVIII s"ezd*, 521 (Zhdanov's speech).

20 See WKP 104, WKP 109 for examples. In both cases, the party secretaries remain the same throughout 1937. Most organizations, even if they spent time on the political events of the day, were still overwhelmingly concerned with economic and organizational matters. See WKP 112 and WKP 266 for the agendas of the party committees in Stalinsk Raikom and Bielsk, respectively.

21 Of course, a chaotic, disorganized, and confused terror is no different than efficient repression from the standpoint of the victim. The Ezhovshchina was no less brutal for its inefficiency and confusion.

22 Chubar' and Eikhe were promoted to the Politburo in 1935, only to fall in the Ezhovshchina. Pashukanis became RSFSR commissar of justice in 1936, only to fall the following year. V. I. Mezhlauk became commissar of heavy industry and deputy chairman of Sovnarkom in October 1937, but was arrested two months later.

23 *Biulleten' oppozitsii*, no. 62-3, 1938, 21-2. In the required Supreme Soviet candidate's speech to a meeting of Moscow voters, Stalin told his electors that good deputies should be determined, relentless, free from panic, wise, thorough, and should love the people. After rhetorically asking if all Soviet politicians were of this type, Stalin replied "I would say not." "Philistine

politicians" even existed among the Bolsheviks. Voters had an "obligation to keep deputies under control." Candidacy was no guarantee of merit, and candidates-cum-bureaucrats could well be Philistines and self-serving careerists. *Pravda*, Dec. 12, 1937.

24 Petro G. Grigorenko, *Memoirs*, New York, 1982, 75; Ginzburg, *Whirlwind*, 23–4. Ginzburg notes that "many people had saved themselves in just this way." Her grandmother advised her to leave town, but Eugenia refused. "Yes, Grandmother was right. My stupidity exceeded all bounds."

25 In October 1937, the Smolensk first secretary Korotchenkov, had to order district party committees not to appoint NKVD personnel to party posts without *obkom* approval. WKP 238, p. 178.

26 *Pravda*, May 11, 15, 1937.

27 *Pravda*, June 6, 1937 ("K novomu pod'emu vsei promyshlennosti" [Toward a new upsurge in all industries]), and the front-page editorial on June 24, 1937. ("Bol'shevistskaia samokritika i trudovaia distsiplina" [Bolshevik self-criticism and labor discipline]).

28 *Pravda*, Oct. 3, 1937. Publication in *Pravda* of Ts.I.K. (Tsentra'nyi Ispolitel'nyi Komitet; Central Executive Committee of Soviets) legal revisions was extremely rare and was meant to deal with immediate problems.

29 *Pravda*, Oct. 31, 1937.

30 *Pravda* announced the plenum on June 30, 1937. The "Polozhenie o vyborakh v Verkhovnyi Sovet SSSR" (Regulations on elections to the Supreme Soviet of the USSR) was published in *Pravda*, July 2, 1937, and in *PS*, no. 14, July 1937, 20–8.

31 *Pravda*, July 7, 8, 1937.

32 WKP 321, p. 97.

33 WKP 111, pp. 14, 33, 75.

34 WKP 321, p. 216.

35 Throughout September and October 1937, *Pravda* carried almost daily reports on the electoral preparations. The gist of these surveys was that local party organizations needed to work harder to prepare for the voting, and the implication was that local party leaders were dragging their feet. Some local activists were so fearful of open elections that they put forward separate "party candidates" rather than nonparty people (*Pravda*, Oct. 20, 1937, editorial). In reaction to local fears, *Pravda* continually stressed the close connection ("strong connection," "blood connection") between the party and nonparty masses. (*Pravda*, Oct. 13, 22, 1937, editorials). In Smolensk, First Secretary Korotchenkov had to threaten the *raion* newspapers to get them to pay attention to the elections. WKP 238, p. 181.

36 *Pravda*, Oct. 13, 1937. An editorial on the same day as the plenum announcement stressed once again the close connection between party and masses. The same plenum that restricted the scope of the elections voted Ezhov a candidate member of the Politburo.

37 WKP 111, p. 123.

38 *Pravda*, Dec. 7, 1937. The announcement was in the form of an "Address of the Central Committee" to the electors and filled the entire front page.

39 In 1937, party elections had been forums for rank-and-file criticism when stringent secret-ballot provisions had been followed. In 1938, though, the

rules were changed. Although elections to most party committees were still to be carried out by secret ballot, committee *buros* would now be elected at open meetings by open (voice) vote. *Pravda*, March 30, 1938.

40 WKP 321, pp. 281, 286.

41 One author has argued that Stalin suffered a political defeat in 1937–8, when his radical policies were defeated by a Politburo majority that favored an antipopulist "police purge." See Gabor T. Rittersporn, "Staline en 1938: apogee du verbe et defaite politique" (Stalin in 1938: apogee of the verb and political defeat), *Libre* (Free), no. 6, 1979, 99–164. On the other hand, it is not possible to demonstrate that he was forced to allow policies he opposed.

42 *Pravda*, July 3, 4, 13, 15, 18, 23, 24 for announcements of NKVD awards. On July 17, *Pravda* announced the renaming of Sulimov. Also see the remarkable poem "Narkom Ezhov" by Dzhambul, National Poet of Kazakhstan, in *Pravda*, Dec. 3, 1937.

43 *Pravda*, Oct. 13, 1937.

44 See *Pravda* for the speeches of Litvinov (Nov. 29), Khrushchev (Dec. 2), Chubar' (Dec. 8), Kaganovich (Dec. 10), Ezhov (Dec. 11), Dmitrov (Dec. 11), and Poskrebyshev (Dec. 11).

45 See *Pravda*, Dec. 8 (Voroshilov), Dec. 9 (Mikoian, Molotov), Dec. 11 (Zhdanov), and Dec. 12 (Stalin).

46 *Pravda*, Dec. 11, 1937.

47 *Pravda*, Dec. 20, 1937.

48 *20-let VChK-OGPU-NKVD* and *Pravda*, Dec. 20, 1937.

49 Ibid.

50 *Pravda*, July 27, 1937; also cited in *20-let VChK-OGPU-NKVD*.

51 Kendall Bailes (*Technology and Society*, 270) believes that one of the purposes of the Ezhovshchina was to assert the primacy of politics over economics in the planning process. Yet it is not entirely accurate to characterize the Ezhovshchina as the clear-cut destruction of moderates by radicals. Many radicals and former cultural revolutionaries perished in 1937–8: Karl Bauman, M. A. Savelev, A. I. Stetskii, and D. A. Bulatov were cultural revolutionaries who fell; Gleb Krzhizhanovskii, a leading moderate engineer, survived. One's position in 1937 was just as important as one's politics in predicting survival or arrest. Personal connections at the time (1936–7), which were often a function of one's radical or moderate views (or Old Bolshevik status), were also crucial.

52 For Mikoian's previous speech, see *Pravda*, Dec. 11, 1937. Mikoian's Dec. 20 speech was only summarized in the press, whereas the speeches of lesser lights such as Deputy NKVD Commissar Frinovskii and three others were published in full. Although Mikoian's text remains unknown, he made the curious and noncommittal remark that "Comrade Ezhov has given me materials" showing how common people loved and supported the NKVD. The summary of Mikoian's remarks was published in *Pravda*, Dec. 21, 1937.

53 For the photo see *20-let VChK-OGPU-NKVD*.

54 See the list in *Pravda*, Dec. 21, 1937. Those present were Kaganovich, Andreev, Dmitrov, Voroshilov, Zhdanov, Ezhov, Bratanovskii (a Moscow

party secretary), Molotov, Khrushchev, and Mikoian. Stalin's arrival for the concert was noted at the bottom of page one.

55 However, he never did condemn the police arrests, notwithstanding his remarks to the Eighteenth Party Congress in 1939.

56 M. I. Ryzhov, whom Ezhov had promoted to deputy commissar in August 1937, was transferred to Forests (*Pravda*, Dec. 30, 1937), M. D. Berman became commissar of communications (*Pravda*, Jan. 20, 1938). It should be noted that forests and communications were not implausible areas for former NKVD officials, for the police had considerable responsibility for timber cutting and canal construction. Nonetheless, Ezhov lost two deputies.

57 L. N. Belskii became first deputy commissar of means of communications (railroads). Additionally, P. V. Zhuravlev (former NKVD chief in Kuibyshev) was on the commissariat's collegium. Kaganovich was commissar of means of communications. *Pravda*, April 9, 1937.

58 *Pravda*, Feb. 20, 1938.

59 *Pravda*, April 9, 1938. Unlike his recently transferred deputies, Ezhov retained his post at NKVD. One suspects, though, that his leadership of the police was nominal or part-time, for he only surfaced publicly in connection with his duties at Water Transport. See *Pravda*, June 4, 24, and Oct. 28, 1938.

60 Fainsod, *How Russia Is Ruled*, 261, 442.

61 *Pravda*, Jan. 4, 1938 ("On The Heartless Consideration of Appeals"), Jan. 10 ("On False Vigilance"), Jan. 18 ("For What Were They Expelled in Stalingrad").

62 *Pravda*, Jan. 19, 1938; *KPSS v rezoliutsiakh*, vol. 5, 303–12. An English version is in McNeal, *Resolutions and Decisions*, 188–95. The decision was entitled "On Errors of Party Organizations in Expelling Communists from the Party, on Formal bureaucratic Attitudes Toward the Appeals of those Expelled from the VKP(b), and on Measures to Eliminate these Shortcomings." The first two phrases paraphrased the June 1936 Central Committee letter.

63 In the examples given, the KPK reversed about half the expulsions they considered.

64 *Pravda*, Jan. 19, 1938.

65 The January 1938 resolution, then, did not "signal" the end of the Great Purges. It was not a signal because it was at least the fifth in a series of public criticisms on the subject during the preceding three years. It did not mean the end of the Ezhovshchina because that operation would continue for several months and was not even the subject of the resolution. The resolution was about abuses by the party bureaucracy and represented another attempt to correct mistakes arising from the *uchet* campaign, which was now moving into its sixth year. The misinterpretation of the January 1938 resolution derives from the confusion of *chistka* with Ezhovshchina.

66 See front-page editorials in *Pravda*, Jan. 19, 22, 1938.

67 See Robert C. Tucker and Stephen F. Cohen, eds., *The Great Purge Trial*, and Conquest, *Terror*, ch. 11.

68 See *Report of Court Proceedings. . . Bloc of Rights and Trotskyites*, p. 1.

69 *Pravda*, Dec. 8, 1938.

70 *Pravda*, Dec. 12, 1938.

71 Students of the Chinese Cultural Revolution are familiar with campaigns to "reverse incorrect verdicts" at times of major political change.

72 *Pravda*, Jan. 22, 1938. The fables surrounding Ezhov's fall were outlined in Conquest, *Terror*, 622–7. Medvedev has provided a new story to the effect that, when Ezhov was eased out of the NKVD and into the Commissariat of Water Transport, he passed the time at meetings of that organization throwing paper airplanes and retrieving them from under the table. According to this particular rumor, Ezhov was excluded from the Central Committee on Stalin's initiative at the 1939 meeting of the "council of elders." (See Roy Medvedev, *On Stalin and Stalinism*, New York, 1979, 108–11.) A number of prominent personalities fell along with Ezhov. A. V. Kosarev and his fellow chiefs of the Komsomol were expelled (*Pravda*, Nov. 23, 1938). Writers Mikhail Kol'tsov and Isaak Babel' also fell with Ezhov. According to Ilya Ehrenburg, Babel's friends warned him to stop going to Ezhov's house, where the latter's wife maintained a literary salon. Ilya Ehrenburg, *Memoirs 1921–1941*, New York, 1963, 427.

73 Nadezhda Mandelstam, *Hope Against Hope*, New York, 1970, 72, 78; Medvedev, "New Pages," in Tucker, *Stalinism*, 219; Beck and Godin, *Russian Purge*, 168–9; Weissberg, *The Accused*, 400–21; Ginzburg, *Whirlwind*, 254–6. See *Pravda*, Oct. 22, 1938, for such a prosecution in Omsk. Ezhov's NKVD interrogators began appearing in prisons as well. Eugenia Ginzburg (*Whirlwind*, 389) met her own interrogator in prison.

74 At the time of Ezhov's fall, Zhdanov was given full charge of all press, agitation, and educational departments of the Central Committee. *Pravda*, Nov. 22, 1938.

75 D. Bakhshiev, *Partiinoe stroitel'stvo v usloviiakh pobedy sotsializma v SSSR*, (Party construction under conditions of the victory of socialism in the USSR), Moscow, 1954, 65; Armstrong, *Totalitarianism*, 72.

76 For examples see *Pravda*, Jan. 4, 1938 ("On heartless consideration of appeals"), Jan. 7 ("Bureaucratic consideration of appeals"), Jan. 10 ("On false vigilance"), Feb. 1 ("Correct mistakes like bolsheviks").

77 See the front-page editorial in *Pravda*, Aug. 7, 1938 ("Bolshevik fulfillment of the order of the January plenum of the Ts.K., VKP(b)").

78 This has usually been translated "purges," and Stalin's remarks have been taken to refer to the Ezhovshchina. This was not the case.

79 *XVIII s"ezd*, 28. This was the first time that Kirov's assassination and the *proverka* were explicitly linked. Stalin's intimation that the former caused the latter is curious because the *proverka* had been planned before the assassination.

80 *XVIII s"ezd*, 28.

81 Ibid.

82 Ibid., 519.

83 *XVIII s"ezd*, 519.

84 These examples recall the celebrated case of "little person" Nikolaenko, whom the Mocow authorities saved from local repression. See Chapter 6 above.

85 Ibid., 520.
86 This happened in organizations in Tambov and Aktiubinskii regions, for example. Ibid., 520-1. If Zhdanov had been talking about the Ezhov-shchina, he would never have expressed such indignation at the unjust re-moval of more than half of a party organization, for that had been the fate of the Central Committee itself in the Ezhovshchina: A total of 70% of them had been removed in the preceding 18 months.
87 Stalin at the Feb. 1937 plenum had spoken against persecuting people "who happen once upon a time to go along a street where some Trotskyist or other had once passed."
88 *XVIII s"ezd*, 522-3.
89 Ibid.
90 Fainsod, *How Russia Is Ruled*, 443; Brzezinski, *Purge*, 128-9. Brzezinski says that this represents a reassertion of the party over the police. This makes little sense, for it was the party that was being criticized.
91 *History of the CPSU*, Moscow, 1960, 493.
92 *XVIII s"ezd*, 26.
93 Ibid., 519, 521.

Conclusion: some observations on politics in the thirties

1 Natalie Babel', ed., *You Must Know Everything: Stories 1915-1937*, trans. Max Hayward, New York, 1969, viii. The burning "went on for many days and nights."
2 Fainsod argued that the imperfections of totalitarianism made the system bearable. (Fainsod, *Smolensk*, 450). One wonders how much inefficiency totalitarianism can stand and still have explanatory power.
3 Dunmore, *Stalinist Command Economy*, 2.
4 Zhdanov's advocacy of rank-and-file criticism and control of the bureauc-racy did not necessarily mean that his own Leningrad party organization was a democratic operation. There is no reason to believe that the Lenin-grad machine was any less bureaucratic or hierarchical than other re-gional committees. It was one thing to denounce the heartless bureaucrats in other places but quite another for Zhdanov to risk control of his political base with democratic experiments. Even a populist politician needs a de-pendable machine.
5 See Fainsod, *How Russia Is Ruled*, 190-200, for the best discussion of these rearrangements.
6 See Fainsod, *Smolensk*, 55-8, 222-37; Rigby, *Membership*, 205-14.
7 J. Arch Getty, "Party and Purge in Smolensk: 1933-1937," *Slavic Review*, vol. 42, no. 1, Spring 1983, 77-9.
8 I. V. Stalin, "Pis'mo v Detizdat pri Ts.K., V.L.K.S.M." (Letter to Detiz-dat of the TsK of the VLKSM), in *Sochineniia*, vol. 1 (14), ed. Robert H. McNeal, Stanford, Calif., 1967, 274. Dated Feb. 16, 1938, the letter was not published until late 1953.
9 One exception was a curious 1938 article in *Pravda*. Written by L. Il'ichev, "On the Role of Personality in History" noted that Marxism teaches that socioeconomic forces are the main factors in history and that, therefore,

the Great Man theory of history is incorrect. Of course, great men such as Lenin and Stalin have a tremendous impact on history, but "it is necessary to decisively unmask any sort of vulgarization or simplification on this question. . . . In several old textbooks on the history of the VKP(b), the history of the Bolshevik party is built around a circle of historical personalities. . . . Holding the people in contempt, fascist monsters promote the barbarous cult of the '*fuhrer.*' The course of history from the fascist point of view revolves around the activities of the '*fuhrer.*'" It must have taken little mental acumen to make the analogy with Stalin's cult of personality. *Pravda*, Nov. 27, 1938. Il'ichev is a deputy foreign minister at this writing.

10 Trotsky, *Revolution Betrayed*, 277.

Appendix: the Kirov assassination

1 Trotsky had said that perhaps NKVD provocateurs might have tricked Nikolaev into making the attempt, believing that it would fail. According to him, it might have happened that way. See Dewey Commission, *Case of Leon Trotsky*, 495. Boris Nicolaevsky speculated in 1941 that Stalin profited from the killing (see his article in the *New Leader*, Aug. 23, 1941, 1–6), but he made no accusation.

2 Alexander Orlov, *The Secret History of Stalin's Crimes,* London, 1954. Orlov was in Spain during the Great Purges, and his book consists of corridor gossip he picked up during brief visits to Moscow. He defected to the West in 1938, but it took him fifteen years to remember that Stalin killed Kirov.

3 Actually, the "Letter" did not say that Stalin had a hand in the Kirov assassination. It implied that Stalin was undecided between "soft" (Kirov) policies and "hard" (Kaganovich, Ezhov) ones. After posing the rhetorical question; "Who had an interest in getting rid of Kirov?" the Old Bolshevik maintained that "directing this resistance [to Kirov's alleged liberalism] were Kaganovich and Ezhov." "While Kirov was alive [they] did not venture to come forward into the open. . . . After Kirov's death, which the pair found very convenient, they came out into the open" ("Letter," 43, 48–50). See the Bibliographic Essay in this volume.

4 Khrushchev, *"Secret Speech,"* 35.

5 See Trotsky, *Revolution Betrayed*, 286; Tokaev, *Betrayal of an Ideal.* Tokaev was an underground participant in an oppositional cell in Leningrad in 1934 led by an army officer. He refuses to discuss his activities the week of the Kirov assassination, although he does say that he was on a "mission" for his group.

6 G. Liushkov, "Sutarin e no kokaijo" (An open letter to Stalin), *Kaizo*, no. 4, 1939, 106–24. My thanks to Hiroaki Kuromiya for a translation.

7 Ulam, *Stalin;* 375–88.

8 Khrushchev, *Secret Speech*, 35; *Pravda*, Oct. 29, 1961. G. Liushkov, a high-ranking NKVD official who defected in 1938, claimed that Nikolaev acted alone and that Borisov died in a genuine accident (Liushkov, "Sutarin," 106–24).

9 See Conquest, 78–9; Medvedev, 161–2.
10 The memoir literature suggests that most victims were convicted under one or more sections of Article 58 of the criminal code rather than the "Law of December 1." For a discussion of such judicial matters, see Rittersporn, "Staline," 110–12.
11 *Report of the Court Proceedings in the Case of the Anti-Soviet Bloc of Rights and Trotskyites*, 376.
12 *Pravda*, Dec. 6, 8, 1934, Jan. 16, 1935.
13 *Leningradskaia pravda*, Dec. 18, 1934.
14 *Pravda*, Dec. 23, 1934.
15 *Pravda*, Jan. 16, 1935.
16 *Leningradskaia pravda*, Dec. 6, 8, 11, 12, 18, 1934.
17 *Leningradskaia pravda*, March 20, 1935. The categories were carefully specified: 41 princes, 76 barons, 35 "big industrialists," 19 "big merchants," and 142 tsarist officials. The total was 1,074.
18 G. Katkov, *The Trial of Bukharin*, New York, 1969, 92–3. Zinoviev was sentenced to ten years and Kamenev to five. In subsequent proceedings, Kamenev received another five years.
19 *Pravda*, Dec. 22, 27, 30, 1934, and Jan. 10, 16, 18, 1935.

Bibliographic essay

1 The basic works on the Great Purges are uniformly based on memoir sources. Conquest, *Terror;* Medvedev, *History*; and Alexander Solzhenitsyn, *The Gulag Archipelago: An Experiment in Literary Investigation*, 3 vols., New York, 1973; all rely almost exclusively on personal accounts.
2 Much of the documentation in Medvedev's and Solzhenitsyn's works is of this form, as is much of the *samizdat* material. Such documentation is methodologically unacceptable in other fields of history. One would be dubious about a footnote to the "unpublished memoir of the Duc de _____" in a work on the French revolutionary terror.
3 Alexander Orlov, *The Secret History of Stalin's Crimes*.
4 Walter Krivitsky, a Soviet intelligence operative in Western Europe, complained about Orlov's excessive executions. See Water Krivitsky, *I Was Stalin's Agent*, New York, 1939. For Orlov's subsequent McCarthy-era testimony (in which he denounced David Dallin for helping NKVD agent Mark Zborowsky immigrate to the U.S.), see U.S. Senate, Subcommittee to Investigate the Administration of the Internal Security Act, *Testimony of Alexander Orlov*, Washington, D.C., 1962. Even Medvedev calls some of Orlov's stories "clumsy fabrications." *History*, 316–18.
5 Krivitsky was not an NKVD agent, but worked for Red Army Military Intelligence – a rival agency. For criticisms of his accuracy, see Conquest, *Terror*, 755–6, and Medvedev, *History*, 216.
6 Alexander Barmine, *Memoirs of a Soviet Diplomat*, London, 1938, and *One Who Survived*, New York, 1945. The first version of his memoirs does not suggest that Stalin had a hand in the Kirov assassination. By 1945, though, Barmine was able to discuss Stalin's complicity in the rerelease of

his account. Barmine's second memoir illustrates the problem of "contamination" from other secondary sources, some of which he cites. (Thus *One Who Survived*, 253, quotes Nicolaevsky.) It is difficult to tell how much Barmine remembers firsthand and how much he includes from other sources.

7 Victor Kravchenko, *I Chose Freedom*, New York, 1946. Kravchenko gives the impression that he was terrorized, but in fact he received frequent promotions and was thus a beneficiary of the "Great Purges."

8 Examples of this oft-cited genre include F. Beck and W. Godin, *Russian Purge and the Extraction of Confession*, London, 1951; Anton Ciliga, *The Russian Enigma*, London 1940; Elizabeth Lermolo, *Face of a Victim*, New York, 1955. Roy Medvedev warns against the use of *"parashas*, that is, rumors often made up in the camps themselves....As the rumors...passed from mouth to mouth, however, they appear to have sprouted all manner of spurious details." See Roy Medvedev, *Nikolai Bukharin: The Last Years*, New York, 1980, 141–2.

9 See Robert H. McNeal, "Trotskyist Interpretations of Stalinism," in Robert Tucker, ed., *Stalinism: Essays in Historical Perspective*, New York, 1978.

10 Examples are Max Eastman, *Stalin's Russia and the Crisis of Socialism*, London, 1940; Max Shachtman, *The Bureaucratic Revolution: The Rise of the Stalinist State*, New York, 1962; and Victor Serge, *From Lenin to Stalin*, London, 1937, and *Memoirs of a Revolutionary, 1901–1941*, London, 1963.

11 The Mensheviks were not a small and insignificant grouping of defeated old men. They operated several presses, were the authors of influential works on the Soviet Union, and sent agents illegally into the Soviet Union to maintain contact with underground supporters there. R. Abramovich, *The Soviet Revolution*, London, 1962, 382–7. Medvedev also reports that anti-Bolshevik political parties continued to exist underground in Russia in the thirties. *History*, 218.

12 *Sotsialisticheskii vestnik*, no. 23–4, Dec. 22, 1936, 22–33; ibid., no. 1–2, Jan. 17, 1937, 17–24; the "Letter" was also published separately as *The Letter of an Old Bolshevik: A Key to the Moscow Trials*, London, 1938. The version cited in this book is in Boris I. Nicolaevsky, *Power and the Soviet Elite: "The Letter of an Old Bolshevik" and Other Essays*, New York, 1965 (hereafter "Letter").

13 Before the publication of the "Letter," there was no hint that Kirov was a moderate.

14 After posing the rhetorical question: "Who had an interest in getting rid of Kirov...?," the Old Bolshevik maintained that "Directing this resistance [to Kirov's alleged liberalism] were Kaganovich and Ezhov." "While Kirov was alive [they] did not venture to come forward into the open....After Kirov's death, which the pair found very convenient, they came out into the open." "Letter," 43, 48–50.

15 The "Letter" compares the assassination of Kirov to that of Stolypin in 1911. In that incident, reactionary members of the court entourage organized the killing of Stolypin to cement their own conservative control over the Tsar.

16 Nicolaevsky's deft use of the "Letter" can be seen in his *Power*, 77–8. Af-

ter a quote from the "Letter" describing Kirov's liberalism, Nicolaevsky gave an analysis contrary to that in the "Letter": "Stalin...was at this time particularly insistent on the inevitability of 'sharpening the class struggle at the new stage' and demanded the stepping up and wider application of the policy of terror."

17 Roy Medvedev has recently shown that the "Letter" is a spurious source. For him, the "Letter" is a "compilation of many different rumors and reports which had leaked out through various channels to the West." Its "foreign authorship" is apparent. It contains a "fair proportion of conjecture. Many conversations that took place...*about* Bukharin have now become conversations *with* Bukharin." See Medvedev, *Bukharin,* 116–17.

18 In such a case, the lineage of the story of the Politburo votes would have begun with an unknown source, passed presumably through Bukharin, and come to us via Nicolaevsky. It is therefore thirdhand information of unknown origin. Historians interested in source criticism and evaluation are hardly reassured by Stephen Cohen's observation that, "in one form or another," Bukharin was the source of the "Letter." *Bukharin and the Bolshevik Revolution,* 472.

19 *Sotsialisticheskii vestnik,* no. 8, 1934, 15. This was the issue for April 1934, and it must therefore have been written and sent to press while Bukharin was in Paris.

20 Nicolaevsky never indicated which parts of the "Letter" came from Bukharin, Charles Rappoport (a French Communist), other sources, or from Nicolaevsky. Nicolaevsky, *Power,* 3–10. Conquest (*Terror,* 754) and others nonetheless accept the "Letter" as a valid source.

21 These rumors were reported in various memoir accounts by foreigners and others. see Davies, *Mission;* Louis Fischer, *Men and Politics,* New York, 1941; William Reswick, *I Dreamt Revolution,* Chicago, 1952; for example. Of course, all this was pure gossip.

22 Tokaev, *Betrayal of an Ideal,* claims that Kirov was anything but a liberal and that real oppositional underground groups killed him. A. Svetlanin (pseudonym for *Posev* editor A. V. Likhachev) was in the Far Eastern Red Army in 1937–8 and describes a genuine military plot against the Stalinist leadership, which Stalin smashed in a countercoup: *Dal'nevostochnyi zagovor.*

23 The edition of the speech used here is N. S. Khrushchev, *The Secret Speech Delivered to the Closed Session of the 20th Congress of the CPSU,* with introduction by Zhores and Roy Medvedev, London, 1956. This version is based on the U.S. State Department text, which had never been disputed by the Soviets. Although never published in the USSR, the speech was read to all party leaders, all registered party members, and, by the end of 1956, to meetings in factories, institutions, universities, and even to school pupils above the age of 14. It was, therefore, hardly secret. *Secret Speech,* 10–11.

24 These former leaders had been removed by Khrushchev in 1957 and labeled the "Anti-party Group." The Twenty-second Congress ordered the removal of Stalin's body from the Lenin mausoleum, accused him of more crimes and repressions, but never associated him with the assassination of Kirov.

25 Thus, according to Khrushchev's point of view, the problem was with Stalin's personality and not with the system.

26 There were apparently 383 such lists. *Secret Speech,* 44; *Pravda,* Oct., 31, 1961. Khrushchev apparently did not sign any of them.

27 The special commission never reported.

28 *Pravda,* June 12, 1937. Other inconsistencies in Khrushchev's account include an apparent confusion of Ezhov for Beria. Although Ezhov's name is mentioned occasionally, Beria is charged with as many misdeeds and repressions; however, the latter was merely a regional secretary until 1938. Further, many reports note that the police terror began to subside when Beria took over from Ezhov in 1938. Could Khrushchev have conveniently substituted Beria for Ezhov in his account? What else might he have blurred? At any rate, Beria's recent execution by Khrushchev and the leadership made him a convenient scapegoat. Khrushchev's opportunistic use of Beria certainly casts suspicion on the exactitude of his other assertions.

29 Khrushchev had to portray Stalinism as an interlude between the positive periods of Leninist leadership and his own rule. Molotov and his partisans may have argued that Stalin was the real heir to Lenin and that Khrushchev was the usurper (as Maoists have done).

30 See, for example, the various editions of the official *History of the CPSU* under the editorship of Boris Ponomarev (Moscow, 1960, 1964, 1972). Nearly any historical or biographical work published after 1956 mentioned the deleterious effects of the cult of personality, noting that, had the party not been strong, the damage would have been worse.

31 In various places in Medvedev's book, Stalin is depicted as a paranoid, psychotic, former tsarist police informer who took a mistaken position on Lenin's April Theses in 1917, military policy during the Civil War, Comintern policy in the twenties NEP, the situation in the country in 1929, diplomacy in the thirties, World War II strategy, and postwar economy. Medvedev does not explain how such a blunderer could command a following within the party.

32 For example, see his story of the personal confrontation between Stalin and Bukharin at the Feb. 1937 plenum of the Central Committee. Medvedev, *History,* 174.

33 Stephen Cohen in *Bukharin* argues that Bukharin's rehabilitation would have meant the rehabilitation of Bukharinism – implying that the whole system of collectivized agriculture could be questioned. However, Bukharin and some of the other defendants have had their *citizenship* (but not party membership) restored posthumously, and P. Pospelov, a Politburo member, said, "Neither Bukharin nor Rykov, of course, were spies or terrorists." *Stenographic Report of the All-Union Conference to Improve the Preparation of Scientific-Pedagogical Cadres in the Historical Sciences,* Moscow, 1964, 298.

34 Medvedev stressed the importance of Lenin's last articles on NEP, such as "On Cooperation," as representing the "real" thinking of Lenin on socialism. This would make Bukharin's gradualism the true heir to Lenin's theory. Such a static view of Leninism ignores the radical Lenin of "State and Revolution" and of the War Communism period, which was much

closer to Stalin's view in 1929. It is also doubtful that any of Lenin's 1921 statements applied in 1929. At any rate, it has become popular among some current Soviet dissidents to regard Bukharin as standing closer to Lenin than did Stalin. See Medvedev, *History,* 45.

35 Solzhenitsyn, *Gulag Archipelago.*

36 In Conquest, *Terror,* half the notes in the chapters "Stalin Prepares" and "The Kirov Murder" are to émigré and defector raconteurs who were not close to the events they describe. Two-thirds of the references in the chapter "Architect of Terror" are to such secondhand accounts, which can in no way be trusted for an account of the "architect."

Index

SOVIET AND EAST EUROPEAN STUDIES

Books in the series